MR. MENZIES' GARDEN LEGACY

PLANT COLLECTING ON THE NORTHWEST COAST

CLIVE L. JUSTICE

CAVENDISH BOOKS

VANCOUVER

Published in 2000 by
Cavendish Books Inc.,
Unit 23, 1610 Derwent Way
Delta, BC   V3M 6W1

Editor: Derek Hayes
Design: Clive Justice and Derek Hayes
Cover Design: Derek Hayes

ISBN   1-55289-019-8   (hardcover)
ISBN   1-55289-020-1   (paperback)

Canadian Cataloguing in Publication data

Justice, Clive L., 1926-
    Mr. Menzies' Garden Legacy

Includes bibliographical references and index.
ISBN 1-55289-019-8 (bound) --
ISBN 1-55289-020-1 (pbk.)`

1. Menzies, Archibald, 1754-1842. 2. Botany--
Northwest Coast of North America. 3. Plants--
Collection and preservation--History. I. Title.

QK31.M44187 2000   580' .92   C00-910694-4

Dedicated to the late Dr. W. Kaye Lamb, librarian, archivist, editor, Vancouverite, Menzies' scholar and nephew of Joseph Kaye Henry, botanist and resident of New Westminster, who wrote the first *Flora of British Columbia and Vancouver Island*.

ABOUT THE COVER ILLUSTRATIONS

The cover painting is by John M. Horton, CSMA, FCA, entitled *In Reflection*. It depicts the ships' boats of *Discovery* and *Chatham* in Simoon Bay off Sutlej Channel, near where it meets Fife and Tribune Channels east of Broughton Island north of Johnstone Strait and Vancouver Island.   In his Journal beginning 30 July 1792, Menzies says of this place:

Here the Arm took a sudden turn around to the Westward and soon after ended in a small Basin...The country on each side was covered with Pines, steep, Mountainous & rocky...In the Gully I found a new species of Henchera [Heuchera] and another Polystricum [a fern] with plenty of the two Vacciniums which were here very productive with red & black berries... Mr. Johnstone made the Latitude of this place in 50 deg 30' 30" North with the artificial Horizon;the Vertical rise of the Tide was about ten feet, but the stream either way was scarcely perceptible.

Although Menzies also found his namesake *Menziesia ferruginea* in this location, the plant shown on the cover is the first botanical painting of one of Menzies other and more well known discoveries, *Gaultheria shallon*, Salal. It was drawn by William Hooker for an 1828 edition of *Curtis's Botanical Magazine*, from the first plant to grow from seed in England. Frederick Pursh, who classified the plant discoveries of Lewis and Clark at the request of President Jefferson in 1806, noted *A. Menzies... the first discoverer of this shrub*.   The salal genus was named for Dr Jean François Gaulthier (1708-1756), a physician from New France and one of Canada's first botanists. *Gaultheria shallon* was brought to England in 1827 by David Douglas.

CONTENTS

FOREWORD   5

FOR KING AND KEW   7

FROM THE GRAND BANKS TO BANKS ISLAND   25

FROM PINNACE AND CUTTER   35

IN A NATURAL PARK   45

IN A SUBLIME AND BEAUTIFUL LANDSCAPE   55

FROM MENZIES BAY TO MENZIES POINT   67

NOOTKA NATURALISTS, MENZIES MEETS MOZINO   79

MENZIESIA AND OTHER NAMESAKES   85

MENZIES' PLANTS FOR THE GARDEN   101

MENZIES MISCELLANY   115

Notes   127

APPENDIX A
A Chronology of Coastal & Botanical Events
in the Pacific Northwest   133

APPENDIX B
A list of Hawaiian Plants discovered by Archibald Menzies   134

Bibliography   135

Index of botanical names   139

General index   141

ACKNOWLEDGMENTS

My heros have always been plant explorers and those who introduce plants into gardens. When I first saw the beautiful yellow cedar replicas of *Discovery* and *Chatham*'s ships' boats that boat builder Greg Foster of Galiano Island in Georgia Strait was building for the 200 year re-enactments planned around Captain George Vancouver's 1792 charting of Puget Sound, Georgia Strait and other B.C. coastal areas, I found that practically no one knew that Vancouver had a surgeon–botanist with him. This was Archibald Menzies, who became the first European to catalogue and describe the coastal trees, shrubs, flowers, mosses, ferns and seaweeds native to islands and coasts of "these waters." Further many of the Pacific Northwest plants that Archibald Menzies found here became common garden plants in England and elsewhere. This is what this book is all about.

I was a CESO volunteer in Kuala Lumpur when I first started writing it and the first chapters, handwritten, were typed with carbon paper copies by Josephine Kher who ran a secretarial service in that Malaysian city. Josephine is now a very dear friend. I am fortunate to have the critical editing expertise in English of writer and wife Wanda as well as having the botanical expertise of son Douglas, who is Curator of Plant Collections at the UBC Botanical Garden. This book has many plant names in it. Taxonomists keep changing them so that many of the names Menzies gave to the plants he discovered over two hundred years ago have changed. Douglas' editing will ensure that all the plant names are correct and relate to the very latest in taxonomic tinkering. I am also fortunate to have on board J.E. (Ted) Roberts of Victoria. who is the authority on the charting and technical aspects of the Vancouver voyage. I am greatly indebted to Bruce MacDonald, the present Director of the UBC Botanical Garden for allowing me to use the fine drawings by Leslie Bohm of Menzies' plants that appeared in the journal *Davidsonia* over the twelve year tenure of Dr. Roy Taylor, then garden director and *Davidsonia* editor. These are indicated by the initials and journal name: LB/Davidsonia. Leslie Bohm's drawings are supplemented by the fine botanical drawings of Jeanne Russell Janis that illustrate the five volume and now classic reference work, *Vascular Plants of the Pacific Northwest*, first published in 1971 by the University of Washington Press. Her work is credited as JRJ/VPPNW. I was saddened to learn that she passed away recently at the age of 96. Over her long life she had produced 11,500 drawings for over 32 books.

A book about plants in British Columbia is not complete without including work of the botanical artists who drew the plants for the B.C. Museum Handbooks. These are: Patricia Druker-Brammwell, Betty C. Newton, Ann Hansen, Frank L. Beebe, and Mary Bryant. Illustrations note these artists with their initials.

My thanks also to Barbara G. Briggs, Senior Assistant Director (Scientific) of the Royal Botanic Gardens, Sidney, Australia, for permission to use the Jamie Plaza photo of the newly discovered living fossil tree *Wollemia nobilis*.

Clive Justice

THE AUTHOR

CLIVE L. JUSTICE, MSc., FCSLA

Retired landscape architect and urban forester

After a thirty year career as manager and owner of a practice in landscape architecture, park and display garden planning, and urban forestry, located in Vancouver, Clive now devotes part of his time to service as a volunteer advisor with the Canadian Executive Service Organization (CESO), the Regional Aboriginal Business Advisory and the National Overseas Advisory outside of Canada.

Recently a part of Clive's time has been spent on researching and writing a doctoral dissertation on Canadian west coast and prairie ornamental gardens over the last century, at Simon Fraser. As a gardening judge he regularly judges in the city of Richmond's annual landscape and garden contest as well as the Japanese Gardener's Association annual garden contest.

Clive was born on Saltspring Island and has been married to his wife Wanda for fifty-two years. He is a Past President and Fellow of the Canadian Society of Landscape Architects, (FCSLA). As a founding member of the British Columbia Society of Landscape Architects (BCSLA), he was awarded a life membership in 1992.

In 1981 with a grant from the B.C. Heritage Trust and with the help of landscape architecture students from the University of British Columbia, Clive compiled and produced the Vancouver Heritage Tree Inventory. As a member of the Vancouver South Rotary Club, and a Paul Harris Fellow, Clive initiated the Rotary Heritage Forest project that oversaw 2500 school children plant 7000 coastal native trees in 1992 along the Vancouver portion of the Trans-Canada Highway.

Each year since 1992, in the persona of Mr, Archibald Menzies the Surgeon-Botanist with Captain Vancouver, Clive identifies and gives a school-grounds tree into the yearly care and stewardship of each treekeeper in several Vancouver school grade 5 classes.

Clive has received a number of awards. An early award was the first Vancouver Heritage Award for the inventory of the heritage trees in Vancouver; twenty two neighbourhoods, Stanley Park and UBC. The International Society of Arboriculture's (ISA) Gold Leaf Award for urban forestry and landscape beautification was awarded to Clive in 1991. The Vancouver chapter of the American Rhododendron Society, now the Vancouver Rhododendron Society, awarded him a Bronze Medal. In 2000, Clive was awarded the American Rhododendron Society Gold Medal for his help in preserving the wild rhododendrons in Sikkim that are the parents and grandparents of our garden hybrids, and for his work as advisor and writer on the rhododendron as a garden plant in the Pacific Northwest.

Cover painting: John Horton
Cover botanical illustration by William Hooker, from
Curtis's Botanical Magazine, 1827, courtesy Eileen Pinkerton

FOREWORD

There have been too few accounts of the contribution of plant collectors along the British Columbia coast. Similarly there are no good accounts of the subsequent use of the plants collected for horticulture. This book by Clive L. Justice provides new information about the special contribution that Archibald Menzies, a pioneer collector of plants, made to our palette of plants. Many plants collected by Menzies are now commonly used as part of our garden landscapes throughout the world. The wealth of material found in this coastal region of the Pacific Northwest is still an untapped resource for future generations. More exploration to collect plants for selection and breeding programs would further enhance our palettes.

The information found in this history represents a life of interest in plants of the coastal region by the author. This interest undoubtedly relates to the author's roots on a Gulf Island in the Strait of Georgia. There is a special affinity with the sea and the land that is developed when one grows up on these islands. There is also great appreciation for the conservation and love of the land and its plants. This is evident in the details he gives of the plant explorations and the lore of the plants discovered. The text is full of examples of how the knowledge of plants and their habitats is essential to their utilization in our urban landscape. Clive is at ease discussing these plants. He provides many new insights into how these plants have become welcome additions to our home gardens. Clive shares his enjoyment of these plants from the aesthetic point-of-view of a skilled Landscape Architect and a plant lover. He also shares his enjoyment of their discovery by Archibald Menzies.

This book is a good read, with many new and interesting facts about the plants and their collector. Any reader interested in the history of botanical collecting and the plants of this region will be much enlightened.

It is a pleasure to provide a foreword to this book by a good friend. We have spent a good many evenings together talking about the plants of this region and how they can be incorporated into our own landscapes. Now this information can be enjoyed through the dedication of Clive to the story of the exploration, collection and utilization of this unique coastal flora.

Roy L. Taylor, Ph.D.
Emeritus Director
Rancho Santa Ana Botanic Garden
(California native plants)
Claremont, California

Salal, *Gaulteria shallon,* from *Curtis's Botanical Magazine,* 1828, with accompanying text. This plant was first found and described by Archibald Menzies. It is also illustrated on the front cover.

1. 2.

W. J. H. Del.ᵗ   Pub. by S. Curtis Walworth Aug.ᵗ 1.1828.

Discovered by ARCHIBALD MENZIES, Esq. on the North-west coast of America, growing in pine forests, under the shade of trees where scarcely any other plant would live. Its handsome and graceful flowers, with the large, glossy, evergreen leaves, render it most desirable for the American border : but it was not till last year that we had any prospect of cultivating so great a rarity, when seeds arrived, both for the Horticultural Society of London and for the Glasgow Botanic Garden, gathered at the Columbia by Dr. SCOULER and Mr. DOUGLAS. These soon vegetated, and from the first plant that blossomed in our Botanic Garden early in May, 1828, the accompanying figure was made. There is no doubt that the plant will succeed well in the open air, treated like other North American shrubs, and that it will then produce stronger stems, and more numerous flowers.

1

FOR KING AND KEW

Soho Square, 22ᵈ February 1791

Sir,

The Business on which you are employed being of an extensive Nature, as it includes an investigation of the whole of the Natural History of the Countries, you are to visit, as well as an inquiry into the present state and comparative degree of civilization of the Inhabitants you will meet with, the utmost degree of diligence & preserverence on Your part will be necessary, to enable you to do justice to your employers, and gain credit for yourself... As far as you are able, you are to enumerate all the Trees, Shrubs, Plants, Grasses, Ferns, and Mosses you shall meet with in each Country you Visit, by their scientific Names... all such as you shall judge worthy of being brought Home, particularly those of which you shall procure, either living plants or seeds, in order, that the Persons who are employed in examining the Plants you furnish to His Majesty's Gardens at Kew, may be assisted in ascertaining their Names and qualities...

I am, &ca.
Jos: BANKS.

The time is the last one hundred years of ocean discovery, the great age of sail, the last half of the eighteenth and first half of the nineteenth century. The place, the Pacific Northwest, and the stories here related are about coastlines, charting and discovery of islands. In particular they are about the plants that a small band of men who accompanied the discoverers and chartmakers found along these coastlines. These men served a double duty by helping to maintain the health of the ships' crews as well as undertaking botanical pursuits. They were the ships' doctors, called Surgeon–Botanists, and sometimes Surgeon–Naturalists, whose botanical quest consisted of collecting and bringing back plants suitable not for food or medicinal use, although they did find some of both, but mainly for the ornamental adornment of grounds and gardens at home in England.

One ocean's edge where a few of these men botanized and collected lies along the northwest-ern coastline of North America, now the American States of Washington, Oregon and Alaska, and the in-between thousand mile stretch of coast with its myriad islands of Canada's Pacific province, British Columbia. While not as botanically rich as many areas of the world, its unique cool wet temperate climate and the flora that grow so abundantly there, played an important role in providing plants for the English garden and landscape.

With the similar maritime climate of many areas of the United Kingdom, the trees, shrubs, bulbs and flowers from the Pacific Northwest made an easy transition and adaptation to the English garden. Many of the plants introduced from the Pacific Northwest were able to hold their place and were not easily supplanted when the flood of ornamental plant discoveries came into the garden from the raids on the great wild plant banks of China and Japan that began in earnest with Robert Fortune's plant collecting in China in 1850[1].

It was not until the mid 1700s that Sir Joseph Banks, who had the idea and the passion to build and plant the greatest garden ever, brought the study of plants (botany) and the collecting of them out of the alchemist's den and into the garden. Plants – trees, shrubs, vines and flowers – collected in the wild were introduced as ornaments or objects of visual interest and beauty for the enjoyment of the English aristocracy and gentry in the grounds and gardens around their stately homes.

In 1777 when Banks became the special advisor and Director of the Royal Gardens at Kew, (an appointment received from his friend George III), he had already been to Newfoundland ten years earlier where he picked up a recipe for a beer that would help save the lives of sailors on the long sea voyages in the wide expanses of the North Pacific. Banks had become famous along with Captain Cook, the greatest of the sea explorers, in the *Endeavour* on a voyage to Australia and New Zealand. Banks got the science of plants into the geography books and on maps by naming Botany Bay. His place in botanical science was enhanced by having a genus of bizarre Australian plants, *Banksia*, named for him[2].

In his capacity of King's Representative it was Banks' avowed intention to improve the Royal Gardens at Kew, just outside London, to become the centre for plants from all over the world.

Kew was to be the foremost "Zoo" or "Ark" for plants. To this end, in the period 1750 to 1820, he commissioned and sent out professional plant collectors to scour continents, coastlines and islands for new plants to stock the garden and the herbarium at Kew.

The first of these collectors was a Kew Gardener turned collector, Francis Masson. He collected in Africa, Spain, then in North America, Madeira, the Canarys, the Azores, and the West Indies. Carl Peter Thunberg, who was a pupil of Linnaeus, the inventor of the binomial system for naming and classifying plants, was the second collector that Banks commissioned. Thunberg accompanied Masson in Africa, travelled to Japan and came home

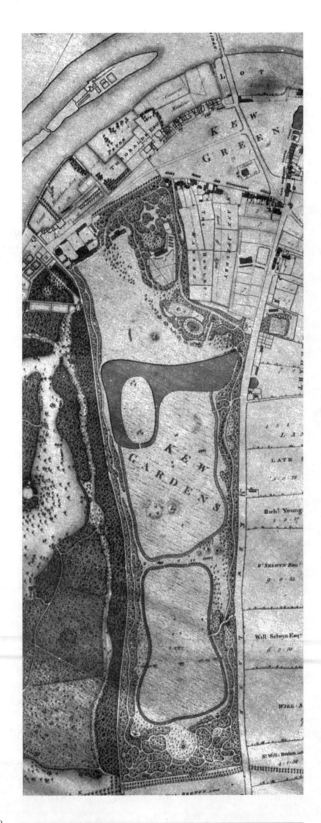

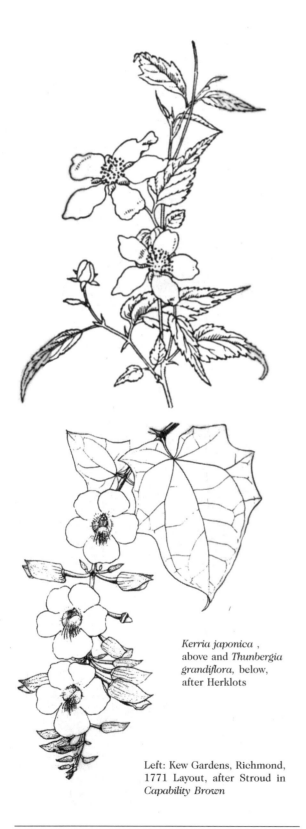

Kerria japonica , above and *Thunbergia grandiflora*, below, after Herklots

Left: Kew Gardens, Richmond, 1771 Layout, after Stroud in *Capability Brown*

to write his *Flora Japonica*, published in 1784.

There followed a series of plant collectors both amateur and professional: William Houstoun M.D., Archibald Menzies M.D., Sir George Staunton, William Kerr and Clarke Abel M.D. The latter two went to China.

Perhaps Masson, being just a gardener and not a partially or fully trained botanist, missed out having a genus (group of plant families) named after him. Thunberg and Staunton each received a genus of ornamental subtropical vines, *Stauntonia* and *Thunbergia*, the latter called the clock vines, in remembrance of their botanizing.

The now common garden shrubs: *Abelia, Kerria, Menziesia* and *Houstonia*, honour Abel, Kerr, Menzies and Houston for their botanical discovery efforts. The false azalea (*Menziesia*) and the tufted herb called the bluets (*Houstonia*) are less known than the tall bright yellow-flowered green-stemmed deciduous *Kerria* and the low pink-flowered, shiny dark green leaved evergreen shrub *Abelia*.

Then there were David Nelson and William Brown who raised the breadfruit trees *Artocarpus incisus* in Tahiti that subsequently triggered the mutiny on the *Bounty*.

Bounty was to take the breadfruit trees to Britain's Caribbean colonies, to islands such as Jamaica and Trinidad, there to be planted to provide cheap food for the slaves and indentured labourers on the sugar plantations. This was another one of Sir Joseph's great schemes. While it failed the first time with the mutiny, the breadfruit did make it to the Caribbean Islands some years later. Nelson was one of those of the eighteen crew who chose to go with Captain Bligh rather than with Fletcher Christian. William Brown, the other botanist with the *Bounty,* chose to stay with the mutineers and died on Pitcairn Island. Nelson made the epic *Bounty* longboat trip with Bligh and the others from Tahiti to Coupang in Dutch Timor only to die there of "inflammatory fever" on July 20 1789[3] .

Previous to the *Bounty* voyage David Nelson had sailed with Captain James Cook on his third voyage, botanizing and collecting on the outer Alaskan Islands, the coasts of the Bering Straits and in Tasmania. Botanizing on the latter island he found and collected foliage and flower buds with a peculiar "lid" (operculum) covering the flower buds of some unusual trees with peeling and shredding bark. This flower bud covering distinguishes the Eucalyptus from any other genus of trees. In 1788 L'Hertier gave the genus the name *Eucalyptus*. Except for a few species that occur in New Guinea and Indonesia, the genus is unique to Australia.[4] However, Nelson was never honoured by L'Hertier with a species epithet for any eucalyptus that he collected in Tasmania.

Almost none of the Eucalypts are suitable trees for gardens in the cool North temperate and wet climates of Northern Europe and the Pacific Northwest. However many of the 500 species of *Eucalyptus* are now used world-wide in reforestation and afforestation of drylands and deserts.

Although Banks laid the groundwork it was not until after he died in 1820 that the Hookers of Kew, first Sir William (appointmented by Banks), then his son Sir Joseph, continued as directors to finish building Kew into the greatest botanical gardens in the world. Kew today, after over two hundred years of development and redevelopment, is still the world's greatest botanical gardens with its arboretum, ornamental gardens, conservatories and herbariums. Beside being the repository and a bank for the largest collection of plants both living and dead, Kew is now the headquarters for the international registry of the world's endangered plants and animals.

In his youth Joseph Banks was a fishing companion and friend to the older Earl of Sandwich. When the Earl became the First Lord of the Admiralty, Banks was able to prevail on him for many favours, chief of which was to have Banks' own botanists on His Majesty's ships. These men were usually ship's surgeons who did double duty serving both as doctor for the ship and naturalist-collector for Sir Joseph. This is where the beer brewed from the needles of a tree comes into the picture.

Previously on voyages to the southern hemisphere, captains Cook and Bougainville[5] had learned how to reduce losses of their ship's crew to scurvy by ensuring a diet of green vegetables and

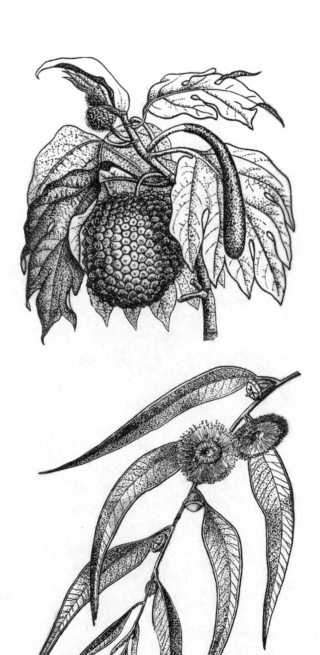

Breadfruit, *Arctocarpos incisa*, above, after Baillon and blue gum, *Eucalyptus globosus*, after Pflanzenfam.

Black spruce, *Picea mariana*,
after Sudworth in
Forest Trees of the Pacific Slope (FTPS)

tropical fruits, principally limes and lemons. While on voyages in the northern hemisphere to both the east and west coasts of North America the English ships' crews brewed and drank the concoction that Banks had discovered in Newfoundland, known as spruce beer. It was as effective as citrus fruit in mitigating the effects of lack of Vitamin C in the diet.

In April 1766 Joseph Banks, naturalist, made a voyage to the then British colony of Newfoundland in *Niger*, a fisheries' protection vessel, Sir Thomas Adams, Master. They reached the settlement of St. Johns on the east coast of Newfoundland's Avalon Peninsula a month later on May 12. Part of Bank's diary entry for that day reads as follows:

"the Country is coverd with wood Fir is the only tree which can be distinguished of which I observed 3 sorts Black Spruce [Picea mariana] of which they make a liquor calld Spruce Beer White Spruce [Picea glauca] & Weymouth Pine [Pinus strobus]."

Banks gives the recipe for spruce beer as part of his September 1st diary entry:

"When Chowder was mentioned Something was hinted about spruce beer the common liquor of the Country The receipt for making it
Take a Copper [kettle] that contains 12 Gallons fill it as full of the boughs of Black Spruce as will hold pressing them down pretty tight Fill it up with water Boil it till the Rind will strip off the Spruce boughs which will waste it about one third take them out & add to the water 1 gallon of Melasses Let the whole boil till the Melasses are dissolved Take a half hogshead, [A barrel holding 27 gallons] and put in 19 Gallons of water & fill it up with the Essence, work it with Barm [yeast] or Beer Grounds & in less than a week it is fit to Drink From this Liquor in itself very weak are made three kinds of Flip cald, [called], here Callibogus, Egg Calli & King Calli The first by simply adding Rum Brandy or Gin If you cannot get Either of the First as much as is agreable. The Second by heating the first with the addition of an Egg & some Sugar The third King

Calli by adding Spirit to the Contents of the Copper as soon as it is ready to put into the Cask & Drinking it Hot."[6]

Archibald Menzies was the third trained botanist Banks commissioned as a collector for the King's Gardens at Kew, first with Captain Colnett in the ship *Prince of Wales* to the Pacific Northwest Coast in 1788 and then with the Vancouver expedition in *Discovery* four years later. Although George Vancouver had been assigned a surgeon, Alexander Cranstoun, for the expedition to the northwest coast, and because of the great influence of Banks with the King and Admiralty through the First Lord, the Earl of Sandwich, was forced to accept the older Archibald Menzies as botanist. Banks was also able to ensure that his recipe for spruce beer was carried with the expedition. He gave it to both Menzies and Vancouver. Although Vancouver insisted he knew which 'pine needles' to use in brewing the beer, as he had been a midshipman with Cook on the latter's third voyage to the northwest coast in 1778, he agreed to have Menzies along to instruct the brewers and thus doubly ensure the health of the crew.

Menzies notes in several entries of his journal of the Vancouver voyage having to go ashore to tell the brewers what 'spruce' to use in making their brew. On July 31 1792 He was called ashore from *Discovery* at anchorage near Broughton Island, located just north of the east end of Johnstone Strait. As the brewers reported:

> *"None of that particular spruce on which they used to Brew [was] to be found near the landing place, on which I recommended another species, Pinus Canadensis, which answered equally well and made a Salubrious and palatable Beer."*[7]

Menzies' *Pinus Canadensis* was the early name for *Tsuga canadensis,* the Canada Hemlock of eastern North America. The needles and branches of the tree he suggested they use on this Pacific coastal brewing site were from a larger tree similar in appearance to the eastern Canada hemlock. It was the native western hemlock, *Tsuga heterophylla.*

Western hemlock, *Tsuga heterophylla,*
after Sudworth in FTPS, above,
with eastern arborvitae, *Thuja occidentalis,*
below, after Hosie in *Native Trees of Canada.*

Sitka spruce, *Picea sitchensis*,
after Sudworth in FTPS.

The brew concocted, using the method Banks called King Calli – by adding spirits, usually rum, just before putting the beer into the barrels – is probably the recipe used by the brewers in *Discovery* and *Chatham* on the Vancouver expedition. black spruce, *Picea mariana*, the conifer used in the Banks' Newfoundland recipe, was not present on any of the North Pacific coast brewing sites. The range of black spruce extends across northern Canada from Newfoundland only to the east side of the North Pacific coast mountains.

It can be assumed that Menzies as a trained botanist would chose a tree with needles and boughs that looked similar to the black spruce as he had known this tree from his earlier time on the Halifax Station. The tree that fitted the bill was the western hemlock, *Tsuga heterophylla*, which is common throughout Georgia Strait and the areas explored by *Discovery* and *Chatham*. Both black spruce and western hemlock have small cones and short needles. The spruce tree that is present all along much of the northwest coast is *Picea sitchensis*, the Sitka or tideland spruce. While it has the flat needles similar to hemlock, they are twice the length of the four sided needles of black spruce and the cones are four times as large.

Although it has never been put to the test, one suspects that needles from any single tree or a blend of trees of the Pacific Northwest coastal conifers would produce a palatable brew with the requisite amount of ascorbic acid to ward off the dreaded effects of scurvy.

Such was the effectiveness of spruce beer, that Vancouver with Menzies' help in choosing the right 'spruce' did not lose a single crewman to the dreaded scourge on either of the two expedition ships. This is even more impressive when you realize that the Vancouver expedition left England in 1791 and didn't land back in England until September 1795 some fifty-seven months later. The Vancouver expedition spent three summers on the Washington, British Columbia and Alaska coasts drinking spruce beer, and the winter of '92 - '93 in the then British Sandwich Islands, now Hawaii, eating limes, lemons and other fresh vegetables and fruits. Spruce beer is still bottled and sold in Quebec as a spring tonic; the ingredients and process are both a secret. It is safe to assume though, that an infusion of spruce boughs laced with rum and molasses might well figure in the modern recipe.

This story of saving lives by drinking a brew made from the needles of a conifer has a beginning well before Joseph Banks, George Vancouver and his Surgeon Botanist Archibald Menzies.

In the winter of 1534–35 a group of Jacques Cartier's men in New France survived the long cold eastern Canadian winter with the help of some Algonquin natives who showed the Europeans how to avoid the debilitating and deadly sickness brought on by lack of Vitamin C in the diet. They accomplished this by making and drinking daily an infusion or tea made from the needles of a local conifer. It is fairly certain that this tree was *Thuja occidentalis.* When Cartier returned to France and told the King of France, Francis I, of this tree that saved their lives, he named it arbor de vitae, the tree of life. Arborvitae remains today as the common name for this tree and the other thujas, usually and commonly also called cedars. This latter common name is usual when referring to the trees in a horticultural, ornamental landscaping or forestry context.

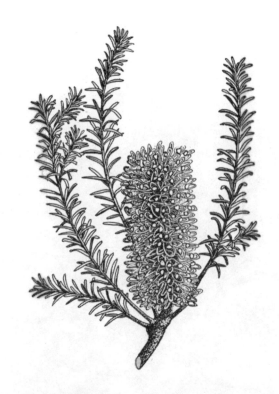

It appears that this remedy was forgotten for well over 150 years as ships crews and settlers to New France died of scurvy in great numbers on voyages and ironically in New France in settlements surrounded by forests peppered with this tree. Eastern arborvitae occurred from Nova Scotia, Acadia, New France, Upper and Lower Canada, northward to James Bay and westward to the Lake of the Woods. The European, mainly English, searchers from the Atlantic side for the Northwest Passage, sailing to areas in the north where this tree does not occur, refused to take up the Inuit diet of seal blubber that is high in vitamin C. This sealed their fates and provided stories of tragic ethnocentric heroism on which an empire was founded.

Along with this, according to one source, the French in New France failed to make the remedy because they tried without success to find this 'Tree of Life' with which to brew the tea, while all around them 'les Sauvage' lived out and survived the winters free of scurvy.

In order to get living plants home for his great garden at Kew, Sir Joseph Banks designed and had constructed on the quarter decks of several of His Majesty's ships a wooden box that became known as a Banks' garden hutch. Captain Vancouver raised great objection to the one built on the after-deck of his ship *Discovery*. It was a 7 x 13 foot 'box' that sat on the deck, which served as the floor of the structure. The 3 foot high sides consisted of a sill or curb with sliding, four-light windows, (the only glass in the structure), with alternating wood panel paired shutters. The top of the hutch had four removable wood grid gratings similar to a ship's hatch covers supported by and fitted onto two longitudinal beams. This gave about 75% shading. Inside there was a bench, which held rows of clay pots by the rims and several ten inch deep trays along with openings in the centre of the bench so that a person could stand in it and tend the plants.

While the appearance of this plant frame was appropriately shiplike it was never a very successful environment for transporting plants, keeping them alive, providing them with light and sunshine, keeping out deluges of water, protecting them from freezing temperatures or salt spray or from waves washing over the ship's deck. These garden hutches had their greatest success in reverse, by bringing out living English and European plants to the new convict colony in Australia founded on the shores of Banks' Botany Bay. It seems this too, the convict colonization of Australia, was also Banksian in origin.

In reference to the transfer of plants from England to Australia, Sir Joseph wrote from his residence in Soho Square to the Right Hon. Henry Dundas on the 30 April 1794:

Sir,

In the year 1789, I was employed at the desire of the then Secretary of State to contrive a plant cabbin for the conveying of living plants to the new colony at Sydney Cove, and to provide such trees and usefull plants of this country as the settlers there were not at the time possessed of, to be sent out in it. This cabbin was erected aboard the

Lowering the launches for a day of charting and botanizing.
Greg Foster reconstruction.

Left: Heathleaf banksia, *Banksia ericifolia*, after Baillon, and Joseph Banks, after a portrait by John Russell.

Guardian, Capt. Riou; and I have since learned from that gentleman that of near one hundred usefull fruit-trees and plants which it was fill' for the largest part were healthy and thriving after the ship was unfortunately wrecked on an island of ice almost at the termination of her voyage.

Since then no opportunity has happened convenient for renewing the attempt of sending out this useful supply. The few King's ships which have gone to that destination have been fitted out in distant ports, where it was impossible for me to attend myself to the business; I have therefore forebore until now to make any further application to the subject.

At present a very favourable opportunity offers itself. Captain Portlock, who, with Captain Bligh, succeeded in bringing the bread fruit from Otaheite [Tahiti] to the West Indies, is under orders for New South Wales, and is really desirous of carrying with him a cargo of usefull vegetables, the value of which to an infant colony knows how to appreciate, and the care of which he is particularly qualified for by his experience gained in the breadfruit voyage.

I therefore, sir, request that permission may be granted me to contrive a proper plant-cabbin, to be placed on the quarter deck of the Reliance, Captain Porlock's vessel, and that orders may be issued to the officers of the Deptford Yard to construct such a cabbin as I shall advise, provided the plan meets with Captain Potlock' approbation.

I shall also request that a sum not to exceed £125 may be issued to me for the purpose of providing useful fruit trees and esculent vegetables, the surplus, if any, to be accounted for by me, and the plants put on the Reliance in the plant-cabbin above mentioned; and to also engage a gardiner to take charge of said plants during their voyage, but to be under the direction of the Governor while he remains in New South Wales, and to return to England whenever the plant-cabbin is brought back, and to take charge of such plants as he shall have provided under the Governor's direction for his Majestie's Botanic Gardens at Kew. (signed) . . . Banks.

The Wardian Case as an ornamental terrarium in a Victorian parlour window, above, and the shipboard Wardian Case for transporting plants.

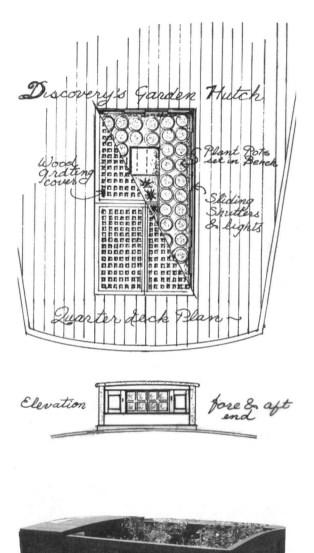

Banks' 'garden hutch' on *Discovery's* quarter deck.
Reconstruction from Royal Navy plans and a replica in
Vandusen Gardens, Vancouver

In 1842 Dr. N.B. Ward published a classic book entitled *The Growth of Plants in Closely Glazed Cases*. He considered that his cases had greater suitability for transporting and keeping plants alive and growing on the foredecks of ships. He wrote:

". . . prior to the introduction of the glazed cases, the large majority of plants perished from the variations of temperature to which they were exposed, from being too much or too little watered, from the spray of the sea, or when protected from this, from the exclusion of light. My late venerable friend Mr. Menzies informed me that, on his last voyage round the world with Vancouver, he lost the whole of his plants from the last cause."

On the last leg of *Discovery*'s voyage home in the south Atlantic Vancouver reassigned to other duties the seaman whose job it was to cover during rough weather and uncover during fair the Banks designed, open slatted-topped, glazed sided hutch that stood on the after-deck of *Discovery*. This reassignment led to a row between Vancouver and the surgeon–botanist and Menzies was charged with insubordination for objecting to the transfer. At a later hearing in London the charge was dropped. However all the plants Menzies had growing in the afterdeck cases were lost due to being deluged and flooded with heavy rain. It seems there were no scuppers so the hutch acted like a bathtub with no drain when the wooden gratings and tarpaulins that had been removed during the day were not replaced and secured at dusk after each sunny day. This effectively destroyed one aspect of botanizing contained in Sir Joseph's instructions to Menzies: *"Any curious or valuable plants that could not be propagated from seeds you are to dig up and plant in the glass frame, provided for the purpose."*

As to the other aspects of botanizing, Banks instructions to Menzies were all encompassing:

"You are to investigate the whole of the Natural History of the countries visited, paying attention to the nature of the soil, and in view of the prospect of sending out settlers from England, whether grains,

*fruits etc., cultivated in Europe are likely to thrive.
All trees, shrubs, plants, grasses, ferns, and mosses
are to be enumerated by their scientific names as
well as those* [names] *used in the language of the
natives,* [something Menzies did not do].

Banks continued: *"You are to dry specimens of all that are worthy of being brought home
and all that can be procured, either living plants or
seeds so that their names and qualities could be ascertained at His Majestie's gardens at Kew."*

Botanizing by boat along the sheltered
coastlines, islands and channels of British
Columbia's coastal areas gave Menzies access to a
great deal of vegetated shoreline and the land area
immediately behind the beaches and cliffs. This
pioneer method of botanizing enabled the early
naturalists to gain easy access to coastal flora of
an area without the hardships and difficulties of
having to traverse inaccessible, steep mountains,
heavily forested and trackless land areas and wild
rivers that confronted many later plant collectors
and botanists. The hardship and difficulty of overland and wild terrain travel and river crossing was
always a factor for those plant collectors that botanized in China, that "Mother of Gardens."[8]

Dead plants that are collected in the wild
end up in herbariums. These rooms or buildings
are essentially a library of paper folios on which
the pressed and dried plant specimens are
mounted, classified, described and stored on
shelves in rooms ranging from old wood open-
shelved cases in rooms with ventilation from open
windows, to the modern closed metal cabinets and
sophisticated ventilated and air conditioned rooms
such as those at the Museum of Natural History in
Chicago.

Much of Menzies' plant collections went
to Banks' own herbarium which ended up in the
British Museum after Sir Joseph's death, but many
went to the Kew Herbarium and the herbarium at
Edinburgh, Menzies' alma mater. Dr. Charles
Newcombe of Victoria B.C., who edited the British
Columbia part of Menzies' Journal of Vancouver's
Voyage lists eight botanists who examined, recorded
and corrected the classification mistakes of the
plants Menzies collected in the Pacific Northwest.
They were Sir J. E. Smith, founder and president of

Roy Forster, left, and the writer examining herbarium
sheets at the Academia Sinica, Chengdu, China, 1981.

Some herbarium sheets of ferns collected by J.D. Hooker in
Sikkim in 1848 at the Lloyd Botanic Gardens, Darjeeling,
West Bengal. *CLJ photo*

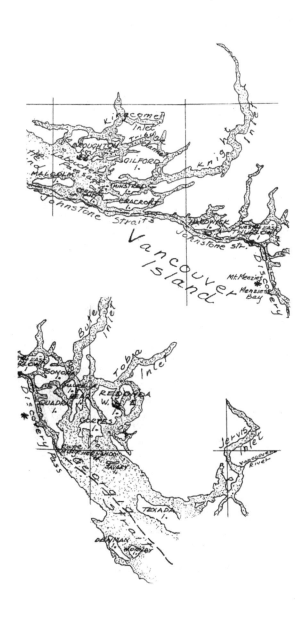

The east-west orientation of Mr. Johnstone's Straits, above, with the island-crowded north end of Georgia Strait.
Adapted from B.C. provincial maps. Dashed line indicates the navigable large ship channel.

the Linnean Society of London, from where comes that prestigious honour for botanists, *Fellow of the Linnean Society*, FLS. He was among the first to look at Menzies' pre-*Discovery* collections. After 1800 there were the botanists (we would call them taxonomists today), R.A. Salsbury, E.J.C. Esper, then Dawson Turner, Erik Acharius, Fredrick Pursh and Aylmer Burke Lambert. The taxonomic grandaddy of them all, Sir William Joseph Hooker, didn't get to look at Menzies' collections until 1830, recording them in his flora of North America, *Flora Boreali-Americana* completed ten years later.

Menzies records in his journal for 3 July 1792, after he had shown the brewers what 'pine' tree to use for their brew, that he returned to *Discovery* at anchor near Broughton Island and spent the rest of the day examining his collected plant specimens and writing descriptions of them. Presumably he had previously dried and mounted those he had collected earlier. Drying plants between papers in a plant press, arranging and mounting the collected specimens on sheets of elephant folio size (23 x 28 inch) hand-made paper along with examining and writing up a botanical description in Latin for each individual plant collected, were the major tasks of a field botanist's work. Many early botanical collectors did not have the convenience of a ship's cabin in which to undertake this plant preservation and recording. More often they did this work around a camp fire in the wilds or back in camp under canvas.

The ultimate in botanizing by boat was undertaken in 1940 by David Fairchild, head of the U.S. Bureau of Plant Introduction. He had a wealthy patron, Mrs. Anne Archibold, build him a junk-style boat with a specially fitted out laboratory for botanical work and provided a nephew as captain. The boat, named *Cheng Ho*, was fully equipped and motorized for a leisurely botanizing cruise around the South Sea islands of Indonesia, the Moluccas and the Philippines. The purpose of the voyage, during which they visited Luzon, Minandao, Java, Bali, Timor, Lesser Sundas, Halmahera and Sulawesi (Celebes) and other nearby islands in the Banda Sea, was to make collections of tropical fruits, trees and palms for the Fairchild Garden in Miami, Florida.[9] The voyage, from January to July 1940, was one month longer than Menzies' six months in 1792 on the Northwest Pacific coast.

Menzies' plant collections and discoveries of that spring and summer two hundred years ago and the botanical discoveries of the previous voyage in *Prince of Wales* and *Princess Royal* with Captain James Colnett to the northwest coast of America would have positioned Menzies as the premier field botanist and plant collector of the last decade of the eighteenth and first decade of the nineteenth centuries if events of the last part of the homeward leg of the Vancouver Expedition, and some subsequent ones, had not intervened.

On their arrival back in England in September 1795, George Vancouver considered that he had the right to Menzies' journals and plant collection, but when he asked for them, Menzies at first refused, until Sir Joseph Banks and the Admiralty had granted permission. This was in accordance with Banks' instructions to Menzies. This little hassle further alienated Menzies and Vancouver. The transfer to other duties of the rating who tended the afterdeck plant frame where Menzies had the living plants he had collected in the Pacific Northwest, California and Hawaii had led to the plants not surviving, and had also deepened the personal rift between Vancouver and Menzies. This was to be reflected in Menzies' waning enthusiasm in following up on his botanical discoveries. Since he was still in the Navy as a surgeon serving part of the time, after his return in *Discovery,* on station in the West Indies, he had no access to his journal or his botanical collections. Vancouver had the journal while Banks had the dead plants. Banks was concerned with other matters so he didn't assign a botanist to go over, classify, review or to publish any of Menzies' botanical findings. Sir Joseph had the discoveries of an earlier Surgeon-Botanist catalogued and published; these were the findings of William Houstoun who had botanized in the West Indies,[10] but the complete examination and classifying of all of Menzies plant collection did not occur until Sir William Hooker took it on thirty years later.

Menzies namesake, *Menziesia, ferruginea,* after Smith. From: *Menzies Journal of Vancouver's Voyage,* Archives of British Columbia Memoir V edited by Charles F Newcombe, 1923

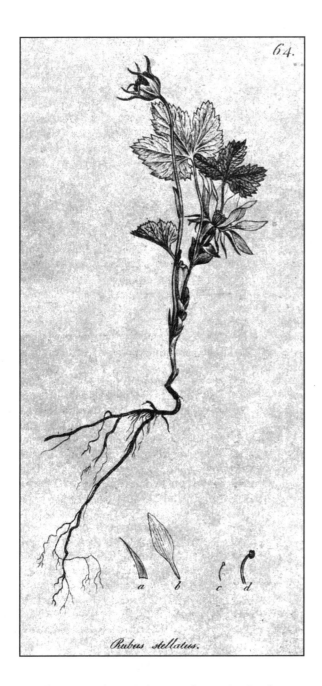

64.

Rubus stellatus.

Menzies raspberry, *Rubus parviflorus*, after Smith.
From: *Menzies Journal of Vancouver's Voyage*,
Archives of British Columbia Memoir V
edited by Charles F Newcombe, 1923

In 1802, seven years after his return from the Vancouver expedition, Menzies was invalided out of the Navy. He married and set up practice as a Surgeon in London. Busy with his practice he seems, even then, to have devoted little time to botany. He did, however, give advice and counsel to Botanist David Douglas, and Surgeon-Botanist John Scouler, before they came to the north Pacific in the mid 1820s. Douglas was to collect in interior British Columbia, Washington, Oregon, California and Hawaii for the Royal Horticultural Society; he was their first collector. Scouler was to botanize more casually from the Hudson's Bay Company's northwest coast supply vessels in which he served as surgeon. These ships provisioned and picked up the furs from the trading forts along the coast, from Fort Nisqually, near present day Olympia, north to Prince Rupert.

Menzies died in 1846 at age 88 without having a major work of botany to his credit. This and the loss of Banks' patronage after his return with the Vancouver voyage was a very serious and undeserved blow to Menzies' position as the first discoverer, describer and collector of most of the plants of the Pacific Northwest.

Many plants Menzies saw and collected in 1792–93 were claimed by later overland explorers and naturalists, such as Meriwether Lewis and William Clark, and Thomas Nuttall.

In 1804 US Army Captain William Clark was chosen by Captain Meriwether Lewis, who had been appointed by President Thomas Jefferson to undertake an expedition with him into the northwest territory. The expedition went up the Missouri River system, over into the Rocky Mountains, and into the headwaters of the Columbia River system. The forty-ninth parallel west of the Rockies was not yet the boundary between the US and Canada. Lewis and Clark descended the wild Snake River joining the main branch of the Columbia that came in from the north, reaching the Pacific Ocean in November 1805. Thirteen years earlier, in September 1792, Lieutenant Broughton in the *Chatham* had surveyed the Columbia from its mouth to the confluence of the Willamette. However, it was not botanized, as Archibald Menzies was in the *Discovery* with Vancouver on their way to San Francisco. *Discovery* was unable to navigate the sand bar at the mouth where the Columbia River meets the open Pacific, so continued south leaving Broughton and the crew of *Chatham* to chart but not to botanize the Columbia's shoreline.

Broughton named an island at the mouth of the Willamette, where it enters the Columbia, "Menzies Island". The name didn't stand like the others that Vancouver gave to features of Puget Sound and Georgia Straits; it was later changed to Hayden Island.

Archibald Menzies found the Pacific dogwood, the floral emblem of British Columbia, *Cornus nuttallii*, first in May 1792 at a location near present day Seattle but it bears the name of the English–American naturalist, botanist, ornithologist and eccentric, Thomas Nuttall, who was a collector for Dr. Benjamin Smith Barton, Professor of Botany at the University of Pennsylvania. One of the first illustrations of the Pacific dogwood was done by the great American ornithologist and friend of Thomas Nuttall, John James Audubon, for his ornithological classic on North American birds. He painted the band-tailed pigeon on a flowering branch of *Cornus nuttallii*.

It was Audubon who gave the Pacific dogwood the Nuttall epithet some forty years after Menzies' discovery of it on the shores of Puget Sound. Later Nuttall became an instructor in botany and curator of Harvard Botanical Gardens. In the second decade of the nineteenth century, Nuttall had travelled west botanizing with the Canadian voyageurs working for John Jacob Astor's fur company in the Missouri River Country when he found the dogwood in what is now Idaho.

Nuttall was the character "Old Curious" in Dana's classic book, *Two Years Before The Mast*. Dana, who was a student of Nuttall's at Harvard, met him in 1834 on the beach in San Diego, where he was collecting with Nathaniel Wyeth who was on his second expedition from Independence, Missouri to Fort Vancouver on the Columbia River.

Forty years before Dana and Nuttall's meeting on the San Diego beach, Archibald Menzies had visited San Diego, then a Spanish port and mission,

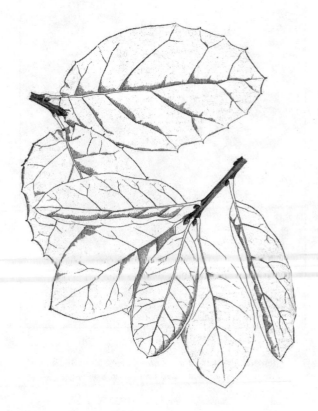

The California horse bean,
Parkinsonia aculeata, after
Sudworth in FTPS.

Left: California liveoak, *Quercus agrifolia*, acorns and
various leaf forms. After Sudworth in FTPS.

with the Vancouver expedition on its way across the Pacific to winter in the Sandwich Islands. They arrived in San Diego on 17 November 1792 having previously provisioned and made repairs in the Spanish ports of San Francisco, Monterey and Santa Barbara on their way down from Nootka. During their five day stay in Santa Barbara, Menzies had a chance to go ashore for some sightseeing and botanizing:

"Having previously obtained the Commandant's leave, I set out pretty early in the morning of the 12th [November 1792], & ascending the hills to the Eastward of the Presidio for the purpose of collecting Plants & examining the natural produce of the Country; the day was very favorable for my pursuits, but the season of the year & the arid state of the Country was much against it, for though I was surrounded by new and rare objects in almost every step of my journey, yet finding very few of them either in flower or seed I was able to receive but little pleasure or advantage from my excursion; I went through beautiful groves of the Ever green Oak [Quercus agrifolia], which were here pretty large trees, though at San Francisco, & Monterrey, the same plant seldom exceeded 15 feet high & grew in crabbed bushes, but here they had pretty large stems of nearly that height & no wise crouded, but scatterd, about to beautify the lawn and rich pastures with their shady and spreading branches, so that it was a delightful recreation to saunter through them." [11]

Three days prior to their departure from San Diego on 7 December Menzies recorded in his journal:

"Our friend the Father who visited us the other day & whose kind attention we were already much indebted for several articles . . . sent me on board the preceding evening a branch in bloom of Cassia [Parkinsonia aculeata], which I conceivd had been originally brought here from Mexico as I believe all of the genus are tropical plants. He sent me also a quantity of fruit [Simmondsia californica], in Kernels which he said were the natural produce of this Country, they were about the size of small kidney beans & their taste somewhat like bitter Almonds; . . . he sent along with them some of the

plants that produced them, which were immediately planted in the frame on the quarter deck & I have the pleasure to add were brought alive to England and placed in his Majesty's Royal Garden at Kew, & as there are many other Plants growing on shore near the landing which appeared new & ornamental, I employed two men this & the following day in digging them up & planting them in the frame, till all the vacant space was filled up with such plants as were likely to be a valuable acquisition to the same royal collection."[12]

Menzies had great expectations he would get his living plant collections home via Banks' hutch, so he engaged in some wishful and hopeful writing in his journal. Haven't we all done it! He was, however, denied the opportunity to edit his journal after his return home. Menzies journal was never edited and only parts of it were published in 1924 and 1925, some 132 years later. The British Columbia portion of his journal was published by the Archives of British Columbia, and the Spanish California visits were published in the *Quarterly of the California Historical Society.* The 1793 Alaska portion had to wait until 1993.[13]

Who was this Mr. Archibald Menzies Surgeon-Botanist whom Vancouver ranked as "always a gentleman", and what plants, in particular ornamental ones that he found and collected here over 200 years ago, would make their way into English, European and Pacific Northwest gardens and landscapes ?

Occurrence of *Arbutus menziesii,*
⬤ Dense stands, ✸ isolated groves and groups. Showing discovery dates for Pacific Madrone, *Arbutus menziesii,* by Archibald Menzies, near the northern limit of it's range and Fra Juan Crespsi at the southern limit in U.S. California.

2

FROM THE GRAND BANKS TO BANKS ISLAND

They first stopped off at Nootka on the west coast of Vancouver Island before proceeding to a group of mainland islands directly east across Hecate Strait from the Queen Charlotte Islands. Menzies named this group, Banks Islands, because as he wrote to Sir Joseph:

In a remote corner inland the natives had a short warlike weapon of solid brass, somewhat in the shape of the New Zealand pata-patos, about 15 inches long. It had a short handle with a round knob at the end; and the blade was of an oval form, thick in the middle but one becoming thinner toward the edges and embellished on one side with an escutcheon, inscribing Jos. Banks, Esq.. The natives put a high value on it; they would not part with it for considerable offers. The inscription and escutcheonal embellishments were nearly worn off by their great attentions in keeping it clean. . . . To commemorate this discovery I have given your name to a cluster of islands around where we were then at anchor.[1]

Archibald Menzies, naval surgeon, botanist, explorer and traveller was born at Stix, near Aberfeldy, Perthshire in Scotland and baptized in Weem Kirk on 15 March 1754. He came from a family of gardeners, having his father and four brothers all in the 'trade'. Archibald received his early botanical training on the grounds of Plean Castle (Castle Menzies) where his father was head gardener. At the age of fourteen, Archibald went on to the Royal Botanical Gardens at Edinburgh, where elder brother William was a gardener, there to continue his botanical studies and to study medicine under the watchful eye and tutelage of John Hope. As well as a student of Linnaeus, the "Father of Botany", John Hope was a physician who held the Regius Chair of Botany at the Royal Botanic Garden along with the chair of medicine at the University of Edinburgh. A contemporary of Archibald's at the medical school was the uncle of Charles Darwin, also named Charles, and J.E. Smith, Founder of the Linnean Society.[2]

After graduating Menzies entered the Royal Navy as Assistant Surgeon and by the early 1780s he was in Nova Scotia, posted to the Halifax naval station. While on the Halifax station he corresponded with and sent 'Acadian' plants to Sir Joseph Banks. One of these plants was the fern *Osmundia spectabilis*, that triggered his lifelong interest with the mosses of these non-flowering plants. This casual botanizing brought Menzies into a favourable position with Sir Joseph who took the young botanist under his wing.

In 1786 Banks saw to it, through his friendship with the First Lord of The Admiralty, that Menzies was appointed surgeon on the *Prince of Wales*, Captain James Colnett Master, for a two-year around the world private fur trading venture accompanied by the sloop *Princess Royal*. They arrived back in England in 1789 after having travelled around Africa's Cape Horn along the horse latitudes to Australia, across to New Zealand, north to Hawaii then across to the northwest coast of America. How the fifteen inch long pato-patos like weapon with the Joseph Banks inscription arrived on this north coast island has never been explained. No one since, including Banks himself (he expected things to be named for him), has ever mentioned where this trade item originated. Perhaps it was left on Cook's ship *Endeavour* after Banks' voyage with Cook and was later traded off. Anywhere on the northwest coast this knife would have been good for at least a dozen beaver or sea otter pelts.

In his famous book *British Columbia Coast Names*, Captain John Walbran recounts that Captain Charles Duncan of the *Princess Royal* is credited with the naming of Banks Island. Perhaps he took the suggestion for the name from Menzies whom as the expedition's surgeon was a ship's officer. Ships' captains keep logs and were the only ones traditionally authorized to bestow names on geographical features that they found; probably suggestions from other officers were welcomed.[3]

Today one of these islands between Hecate Strait and Grenville Channel retains the name Banks, while the largest of this group guarding the approaches to Douglas Channel and Kitimat was given the name of Princess Royal Island. The *Princess Royal* sailed with the *Prince of Wales* to Canton but did not accompany her back to England and returned to Nootka. Here she was seized by the Spanish, who considered the coast theirs, stripped her of guns and stores for the defence of Nootka, then sailed her to San Blas, the Spanish port on Mexico's Pacific coast. Renamed the *Princesa Real* she was subsequently returned to the British in Monterey as part of the settlement in which the Spanish gave up Nootka. This was in the arrangement made by Vancouver with Quadra in 1792.

It was on Banks Island that Menzies found and collected the plant that is in the genus of ericaceous plants honoured by the botanical taxonomists with his name. It is a deciduous azalea-like shrub, called not surprisingly false azalea with the scientific binomial *Menziesia ferruginea*. We shall return to the genus *Menziesia* later.

In 1788, after putting in at Canton, Menzies botanized on the way home to England. He visited Sumatra, Martinque, Cape of Good Hope and St. Helena, collecting seven ferns in Sumatra and eleven on the Cape. He also collected thirteen

Banks, Princess Royal and other mid- and north coast British Columbia Islands. The NNW bearing of the Inside Passage is a dashed line through Finlayson Channel, Graham Reach and Grenville Channel.

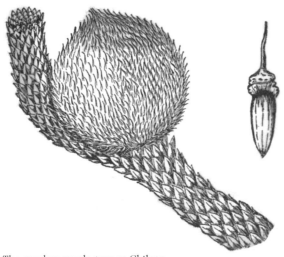

The monkey puzzle tree or Chilean pine, *Araucaria araucana*, large seed cone and winged seed, above with Chilean pine forest from a painting.

ferns from the Sandwich Islands, but as he visited these Hawaiian Islands at least five times it is hard to determine which ones he collected while visiting in *Prince of Wales*.

Menzies collected two trees from this exploratory fur trading voyage in *Prince of Wales* with visits to New Zealand and Santa Cruz on one of their returns from wintering in the Sandwich Islands. Menzies collected a third tree on his way home in 1795 with Vancouver when they visited Valpariaso on the southerly Chilean Pacific coast. These three Menzies' discoveries are evergreen conifers; the one from the California coast is the tallest growing tree in the world, the coast redwood; the tree from Chile is one of the most bizarre both in its physical features and its common name, the monkey puzzle tree; while the third tree that Menzies discovered from New Zealand is called the southern beech.

Menzies collected specimens of the redwood, this most magnificent of conifers at Santa Cruz in Spanish California, but did not collect any seeds. On this visit and on subsequent ones he always seemed to be in California at the wrong season for seed collecting. Santa Cruz is near the southern limit of the coast redwood's range. The major stands of this tree occur north of San Francisco and extend just into southern Oregon. These trees were logged so ruthlessly in the early part of this century it seemed they would be completely wiped out. But the "Save-The-Redwoods-League" was formed to buy up old growth groves of these three thousand to four thousand year old denizens, with heights of 275 to a high of 367 feet, in order to preserve them for posterity. The most famous of these groves is the one just across the Golden Gate Bridge from San Francisco on the slopes of Mt. Tamalpias in Marin County. It is named Muir Woods after John Muir, the great California naturalist and founder of the leading environmental group, the Sierra Club. This 47 acre stand of the magnificent coast redwood trees was declared a National Monument as early as 1907.

When botanist David Don finally looked at Menzies' plant collections after he had brought them back to England, he classified the Coast Redwood as *Taxodium sempervirens*, as the tree has some similarities to the deciduous southeastern North American Bald Cypress, *Taxodium distichum*. It was promptly forgotten, being of little interest as it was already growing in Kew Gardens. Then some sixty years later in 1847, an Austrian botanist, Stephan Endlicker, decided it was not a Bald Cypress at all and put it into a new genus that he called *Sequoia*! Armchair botanists are very inventive. This name honours an obscure Metis named Sequoyah who had published a syllabic Cherokee alphabet that enabled the Cherokees to become literate. So the trees became *Sequoia sempervirens*, with a little known linguist for the genus and a very ordinary specific epithet (evergreen) for the species. It seems Endlicker, who had never been to America, assumed the Cherokee were a Cal-ifornia tribe of indigenous peoples. Neither seems quite appropriate for this tallest of all trees.[6]

　　To add some further confusion, a tree named the "bigtree" is also native to California but in the mountains inland (Tulare, Fresno, Madera, Mariposa, Tuolumne and Calaveras Counties). It was also placed by the armchair botanists into the genus named *Sequoia*, being called *Sequoia gigantea*. The bigtree was introduced to England and Scotland by William Lobb and John D. Matthews in 1843, after a quick trip to California. They took back seed collected by others so they probably never saw the tree. Menzies never saw it either, but as a field botanist, if he had seen it he most certainly would not have classified it as a *Sequoia*. The tree has foliage or needles totally unlike the Coast Redwood; it looks very much like a Japanese genus of conifers, the *Cryptomeria*. It was the time of great coniferous taxonomic confusion and equally great patriotic fervour in England and the eastern United States when this difference between the two great trees, the tallest on the coast and the largest inland, was to be straightened out by the jingoist-botanists in both countries. They put forward respectively the names *Wellingtonia* and *Washingtonia* for the genus name. They did agree to keep the species epithet *gigantea*. Fortunately neither of these genus names were accepted as 'valid'. So Wellington, the hero of the Napoleonic wars was left with a New Zealand city, a boot and a meat pie, while Washington, hero of the

The coast redwood, *Sequoia sempervirens,* discovered by Menzies but mis-identified as a swamp cypress. After Sudworth in FTPS.

Right: The bigtree, (giant redwood, giant sequoia, Sierra redwood, wellingtonia etc.) *Sequoiadendron giganteum,* after Sudworth in FTPS.

American revolution got a capital city, a U.S. state and hundreds of streets in towns across the United States named after him. The bigtree today is still commonly known as *Wellingtonia* in some parts of England and in New Zealand.

A strange taxonomic compromise was finally made so that this biggest of all trees was renamed *Sequoiadendron giganteum*. We know where *Sequoia* comes from, and *dendron* is the Greek word for tree, while the species epithet *giganteum* means gargantuan or giant like.

In this last name they did get it right, as the tree is the world's largest living thing. The taxonomic tinkering separating the bigtree from the coastal Californian sequoia didn't happen until well into the twentieth century. It was in 1939 when the German botanist Buchholtz, almost one hundred years after the first round of naming, gave the genus name *Sequoiadendron* to one of the great wonders of the plant world. One large specimen has a trunk circumference of 80 feet, a height of 267 feet and is estimated to weigh 2,000 tons. Truly a biii–g tree![7]

To add a little more to the redwood story, a fossil relative of the redwood called the dawn redwood or *Metasequoia glyptrostoboides* was discovered alive and well growing in eastern Sichuan province, China, in 1945. Seed was collected and brought to the botanical garden at Berkeley, California and Harvard's Arnold Arboretum where seedlings were raised. In 1948 and 1949 these were distributed to botanical gardens and parks worldwide.[8] Unlike the coast redwood this tree from the late carboniferous age is deciduous. The needles turn a rich brown in the fall and drop from the tree. In this way dawn redwood is like the larch or more like the tree David Don mistook the coast redwood for, the bald cypress. It is very hard to distinguish between dawn redwood and swamp cypress as their needles, bark and form are so much alike. The flat needles are alternate on swamp cypress twigs, and opposite on the dawn redwood. The coast redwood that Menzies discovered does not do well in the Pacific northwest, as it misses the fog of its home along the northern coast of California. But the dawn redwood from China is very successful, especially in Vancouver, B.C. both as a street tree and a park specimen. A fine avenue of them is planted in that city on Kerr Street south from 41st to 43rd Avenues and a grand specimen stands on the east side beside the drive up to the top of Little Mountain in Queen Elizabeth Park. The fossil remains of *Metasequoia* that once covered large areas of western North America before the glacial age can be found in the southern interior of British Columbia in a number of places. One location for dawn redwood fossils is near Keremeos B.C., in the roadside shales of the White Lake Basin Road on the way to the Dominion Observatory. Another is in central Washington State in the roadside cuts on State Highway 4 just south of Republic, Washington.[9]

The seeds of the tree that Menzies brought home in his waistcoat pocket had been served with dessert at a banquet in Valpariso and had come from the hills to the west of this Chilean city, at Lat. 50°S. The tree became a curiosity to grace the front yard gardens of many late Victorian and Edwardian homes. A hundred years after Menzies brought it back, the monkey puzzle or Chilean pine also found its way back to the Pacific, but to Lat. 50° N., there to grace many Victoria, Vancouver, Seattle, Port Townsend and Tacoma gardens. In Europe the monkey puzzle seems to do best in Ireland, there being many fine specimens in gardens there. In North America, however, the Pacific Northwest is the only area where it can grow well. Victoria and Tacoma have the greatest number with Vancouver and Seattle close behind. The largest specimen is in Astoria, Oregon, at the mouth of the Columbia River.[10] There is a large male specimen in British Columbia's most northerly port, Prince Rupert and there are two males and a female of these mushroom-topped trees in an old 1930s garden slowly being restored as an arboretum by Julia and Ron Moe just off the road between Holberg and Cape Scott Provincial Park on the west coast of Vancouver Island.[11]

The monkey puzzle tree is in the genus *Araucaria* and the species epithet *araucana* comes from the name of an Indian tribe, the Araucas, who inhabited the southern area of Chile where forests of these trees occur naturally. Sadly these people

The most recently discovered (1996) living fossil tree *Wollemi nobilis* joins ranks with the dawn redwood, *Metasequoia glyptrostoboides,* discovered in China in 1948 and the original living fossil tree, *Gingko biloba.*

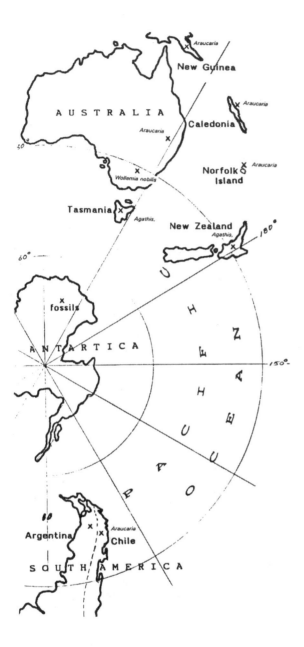

Distribution of the southern pine, in the family Araucariacae: three genera, *Araucaria* (18 species), *Agathis* (13 species); and the newly discovered 'living fossil' Wollemi pine.

are now extinct as a distinct race and only the trees are left in Chile's southern national parks. Remnant stands of this tree also occur on the east side of the southern Andes at similar latitudes and altitudes in Argentina.[12]

There are several other species in the genus *Araucaria*. These are subtropical and occur naturally on the east coast of Australia and on several nearby islands in the south Pacific. *Araucaria bidwillii* is from Queensland and is called bunya pine, while *A. cookii*, after Capt. Cook, now *A. columnaris*, is from New Caledonia and has the common name of Cook pine. The bunya pine is a familiar potted house plant in temperate climates. There is a fine avenue of Cook pine in Peradeniya Gardens, Sri Lanka's Botanical Gardens in Kandy, now over 150ft high. The hoop pine, *A. cunninghamii* is found in the high rainfall areas from New Guinea, and Queensland to New South Wales. It is grown mainly as a timber tree, and sometimes as an ornamental in Australia and New Zealand.

These trees and also the Norfolk Island pine, *A. heterophylla*, are commonly used in gardens and parks in Hobart and Adelaide in Australia and on the north island of New Zealand, and also in northern India, Malaysia and Thailand. There is an avenue of the stiff perfectly upright and formal Norfolk Island pines along the seaward side of Marine Parade in 'Art Deco' Napier, New Zealand. Unlike true pines and other trees that achieve a picturesque windblown effect, when grown along shorelines subject to heavy and constant offshore winds the branching structure and foliage form of the Norfolk Island pine is such that evenly spaced limbs and fine leaves filter the wind so that the tree stands straight and true in the face of gales and hurricanes.

The family *Araucariacae*, to which the genera *Araucaria* and *Agathis* belong, is an ancient one. The best known *Agathis* is the immense 'Kauri pine' of New Zealand. There are many fossilized species in this family that have been found in the southern hemisphere. In 1994 Field Officer David Noble of the Australian National Parks and Wildlife Service found a living fossil consisting of forty or so trees hidden away and growing in a remote gorge of the subtropical rainforest in Wollemi National Park near

Sydney, Australia. Dubbed the 'Wollemi pine', it appears to be a genus intermediate between the 'monkey puzzle' and the 'Kauri'. It has been named *Wollemia nobilis*. Since it grows in a subtropical climate this living fossil will not make it into the Pacific Northwest as has that other living fossil tree, the dawn redwood.

The *Araucaria* that Menzies brought back to England in 1795, was given this most unusual common name, monkey puzzle. The reason for this was probably because, in the tropics monkeys are trained to climb and select only the ripe fruit from the coconut palm. Botanists and plant collectors observing this selectiveness used to 'rent a monkey' to help gather leaves, flowers and fruits from many trees that in tropical areas begin their branches from fifty to eighty feet above the ground. One botanist, A. J. Corner, who wrote a famous book on trees called *Wayside Trees of Malaya* started a school in the 1930s to train monkeys to gather fruit, flowers and foliage of tall tropical trees so that he didn't have to cut them down to find out what species it was.[13]

The monkey puzzle, however, is a temperate not a tropical tree, but its lower branches do die back and fall off on older trees. These do this because they are shaded out by the dense top branches and the surrounding trees, a common phenomena in most forests of conifers. The whorls of very flat bladed leaves that end in a very sharp point are closely packed along the length of the remaining branches.

This would indeed be a puzzle for a monkey to traverse in order to reach the end of the branch where the fruit or flowers occur. In fact there is no need for a monkey or anyone to climb the *Araucaria* as the very large coconut sized cones borne way up on the top branches of the female trees fall to the ground when ripe and break up into a pile of scales and seeds. The cones, however, take two years to mature before they fall. The red brown 'foxtail' pollen cones occur on separate male trees of Araucaria.[14]

Many of Menzies' plant collections of 1788 from New Zealand remained buried away in Banks' and the Kew herbariums unnoticed and

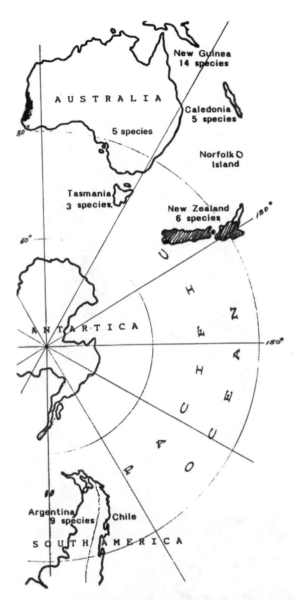

Southern hemisphere distribution of the southern beech tree, genus Nothofagus

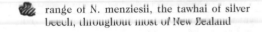
range of N. menziesii, the tawhai or silver beech, throughout most of New Zealand

the range of the western Australian endemic small tree *Banksia menziesii*

Menzies' southern beech, *Nothofagus menziesii*, female flowers and seed above, and male flowers and pollen cone, These are an inaccurate depiction, as *Nothofagus menziesii* leaves are serrate.
After Cheeseman in *Illustrations of New Zealand Flora*.

uncatalogued until 1844 when Sir Joseph Hooker of Kew Gardens described them. One of these trees was the silver or mountain beech tree, *Nothofagus menziesii*. It used to be one of the major forest trees in the mountain districts of the south island especially the eastern flanks of the Southern Alps. But silver beech has been heavily logged so there is little of the old growth left. Menzies collected *Nothofagus*, this southern hemisphere version of the northern hemisphere beech or *Fagus*, in Dusky Sound, on New Zealand's south island. The author also collected this Menzies' namesake in 1979 near Greymouth on the same island, where it occurs as second growth along streams and in areas of open forest. So it does appear to be coming back.

There are thirty-seven or more species in the genus *Nothofagus* that are found only in the southern hemisphere. Sixteen of these species are found in the cool cloud forest heights in the mountains of New Guinea; this is the farthest north that this tree occurs, reaching to four degrees south of the equator. There are five species in southeast Australia and three on the island of Tasmania. New Zealand has four or five species in addition to *N. menziesii,* the one that Menzies found.

In South America, southern Chile and Argentina, the latter in Patagonia and the islands of Terra Del Fuego, there are eight species and at least one natural hybrid of the southern beech. *Nothofagus* are monoecious, that is, it has male pollen and female seed flowers that are separate but occur on the same tree. This is like alder, birch, and Douglas fir and other Pacific Northwest conifers.

Many of the southern beeches have brilliant red, scarlet and orange fall colour; This colouring occurs in April and May in the cool and wet temperate southern hemisphere native habitats of these trees. In disturbed mineral or raw volcanic ash soils in Patagonia, *Nothofagus,* like alder in the Pacific Northwest, colonizes these bare soil areas to begin a long process toward a diverse forest environment.[15] *Nothofagus menziesii* or any of the other southern beeches have never been very successful introductions into Pacific Northwest parks or gardens. There is a group of three *Nothofagus antarctica,* the deciduous southern beech, in Vancouver's Van Dusen Gardens. They are from the Islands of Tierra del Fuego, (collectively known as Fuegia). These Pacific Northwest southern beeches are twenty-five years old and are between eight and ten inches in diameter and reach twenty feet in height with a thirty feet spread.[16] In 1995 *Nothofagus antartica* was first used as a street tree by the Vancouver Park Board.

Thus Menzies' first casual botanizing with Captain Colnett in *Prince of Wales* along the coastlines of the Pacific Northwest, New Zealand, Spanish California and Valpariso in Chile seems at the time to have produced little of ornamental value for the gardens of the English aristocracy or plant novelties for the King's garden at Kew. However, this preliminary survey, and familiarity with the Pacific Northwest, served as precursor to the voyage with George Vancouver, enabling Menzies to uncover and record the botanical and ornamental plant riches of the Northwest coast of America.

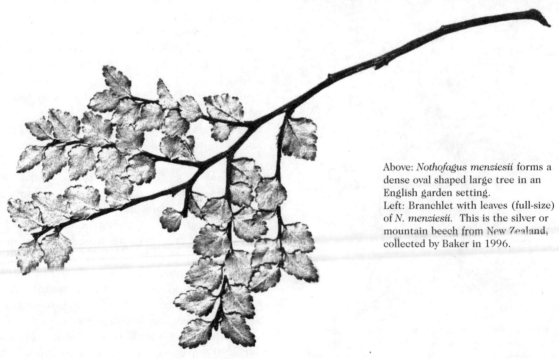

Above: *Nothofagus menziesii* forms a dense oval shaped large tree in an English garden setting.
Left: Branchlet with leaves (full-size) of *N. menziesii*. This is the silver or mountain beech from New Zealand, collected by Baker in 1996.

3

FROM PINNACE AND CUTTER

After a row of about 4 leagues we came to an Island [Protection Island[1]] *the rural appearance of which strongly invited us to stretch our limbs after our long confined situation on board & the already sameness of a tedious voyage . . . . On ascending the bank to the summit of the island a rich lawn beautiful with natures luxuriant bounties burst at once on our view and impressed us with no less pleasure than novelty. It was abundantly cropped with a variety of grass, clover and wild flowers, here and there adournd by aged pines with wide spreading horizontal/boughs and well sheltered by a slip of them densely copsed with underwood stretching along the summit of the steep sandy cliff, the whole seeming as if it had been laid out from the premeditated plan of a judicious* [landscape] *designer.* [2]

Protection Island, even though settled, still has vestiges of the flora and fauna that were here when Menzies and the crew of *Discovery* stepped ashore on 1 May 1792. This meadow landscape is a common one for islands and headlands of islands in the nearby Gulf and San Juan Island groups where a thin layer of soil overlays smooth glaciated rock. Protection Island's steep south side is now a Washington State bird sanctuary for the nocturnal burrowing rhinoceros auklet.

Thus Menzies first chance to botanize on the northwest coast after the long trip from Hawaii was in a natural pastoral-like landscape. He was probably quite familiar with this landscape of an open grass field with woodland edging. It was the common kind in the agricultural areas of England and Scotland that had been created by and for grazing animals.

Menzies, in alluding to Protection Island appearing as if 'designed' was a reflection of the contemporary style of the English landscape. This pastoral picturesque scenery aspired to by the land owning gentry of England and Scotland in the late 18th and early 19th century was exemplified in the work of Capability Brown, the first great 'improver' of landscape, and Humphry Repton, the great landscape gardener.[3]

The landscape improvements of Lancelot (Capability) Brown occurred over 30 years from 1751 to 1782. He like Menzies started as a gardener, but went on to take up improving gardens in the naturalistic manner rather than the formal (French) manner by creating non-axial views, natural scenery and prospects modeled on the landscape paintings of Claude Lorrain and Poisson.

His most famous landscape creation extant is Kew Gardens in Richmond, Surrey. His best known garden that illustrates his concepts is at Sheffield Park, East Sussex, England. It combines Lancelot Brown's basic design of 1775, with trees, grass sward and serpentine waters, with the inspired planting of the late A.G. Soames who for over a quarter century from 1909 introduced all manner of exotic trees and shrubs to this woodland garden and park that covers over 150 acres.

Humphry Repton followed on the landscape and improvement work of Lancelot Brown but was much less a flamboyant personality. His trademark was the impressive so-called Red Books he prepared for each of his client's gardens. They were bound in red Morocco leather describing and illustrating the proposed improvements by inserts tipped in to beautiful watercolour paintings of the existing landscapes. Repton practised from 1790 to 1814. Two of his 'improvements' still intact are

Sheringham Hall in Norfolk and Attingham Park in Shropshire.

Aside from admiring this pastoral scenery and landscape, Menzies made no botanical collections on Protection Island, noting only thick patches of pink seablush in bloom behind the beach – Menzies called it a valerian. It is now classified as *Plectritis congesta*. On a later visit to the island he collected the native prickly pear cactus, a variety of *Opuntia*.

He did try one zoological collection on this first visit, a skunk shot on the island by one of the crew. It smelled so highly that the crew of the cutter would not let him bring it back to *Discovery* for examination. However, Menzies finally did get his skunk, *Viverra putorius*, to examine and dissect when ashore at Fairweather Bluff, Admiralty Inlet.

Menzies got a chance to botanize the next day when he accompanied Captain Vancouver in the pinnace to the head of Discovery Inlet. Here he observed and collected several trees, the bigleaf maple *Acer macrophyllum*, the red alder *Alnus rubra* and *Malus (Pyrus) fusca*, the Pacific crabapple.

Early settlers arriving in the Pacific Northwest in the last decades of the 19th century and the first decade of the 20th to take up land in the Puget Sound, San Juan and Gulf Island groups as well as the other coastal areas and islands farther up Georgia Straits, used the Pacific crabapple as understock for grafting to the scions of apple varieties they had brought with them to start orchards. They used a novel way to transport and keep alive the dormant scions. They were stuck into potatoes to keep them from drying out on the train trip from eastern orchards in Nova Scotia's Annapolis valley, Quebec's St Lawrence valley, Ontario's Niagara peninsula and the largest fruit growing area in eastern North America, upper New York state. Some of these 1880s and 1890s apple varieties that were grafted on *Malus fusca* whips included king (of Tompkins County) from New York state, reinette and snow apples from Quebec, northern spy, golden russet, Canada red and Rhode Island greening from Ontario.[4]

Pacific crabapple, *Malus fusca*, LB/Davidsonia (above) and *Alnus rubra*, the red or Oregon alder, after Sudworth in FTPS.

Pink lady slipper, *Calypso bulbosa*, depicted using the scratch-board technique by Frank L. Beebe in the B.C. Provincial Museum handbook on the orchids of B.C.

Two days later, on 4 May 1792, in another part of Discovery Inlet, possibly on the Port Townsend side, Menzies found and collected the Pacific coast rhododendron, *Rhododendron macrophyllum* and the manzanita, *Arctostaphylos tomentosa* which Menzies identified as an Arbutus with glaucous (not shiny) leaves.

About the roots of "Pines", probably Douglas fir, grand fir and shore pine, *Pseudotsuga menziesii*, *Abies lasiocarpa* and *Pinus contorta* var. *contorta* respectively, he found a beautiful little orchid, now variously named pink, fairy or lady's venus, or false lady's slipper, and botanically called *Calypso bulbosa*.

Menzies' finding of the lovely pink lady slipper orchid *Calypso bulbosa* was not nearly so dramatic or traumatic as that for another Scot, the great nineteenth century botanist and founder of the American Conservation Movement, John Muir. One day in June 1864 while collecting botanical samples Muir pushed his way through a dense swamp, in the area of Northern Ontario along the North shore of Lake Huron. There on the bank of a stream Muir found the rare orchid *Calypso borealis*, [now *C. bulbosa* forma *alba*]; two white flowers against a background of yellow moss. *"They were alone"*, he noted, *". . .I never before saw a plant so full of life, so perfectly, spiritual, it seemed pure enough for the throne of its Creator. I felt as if I were in the presence of superior beings who loved me and beckoned me to come. I sat down beside them and wept for Joy."*

Apparently Muir years later ranked this encounter along with that of meeting the poet Ralph Waldo Emerson as the two supreme moments in his life. Aside from the emotional release it allowed him, finding *Calypso borealis*, the birds-foot orchid, in that swamp crystallized an attitude, providing the germ of an idea that would come to dominate his thinking for the rest of his life."[5]

It seems that not only was John Muir taken by *Calypso;* so also was the late Lewis J. Clark. In his monumental *Wild Flowers of the Pacific Northwest* he describes the origin of the genera epithet and the preferred habitat of this delightful Pacific Coast native orchid: *"The goddess, daughter of Atlas was Calypso, whose name means concealment, with reference to this lovely flower's habit of hiding*

*among the mosses of the forest floor, in the shade –
essential to its existence – of high forest trees...The
blossom in the wind-less air of the forest, delights
the wanderer with its heavenly fragrance – fresh
spicy and utterly distinctive...One must needs come
reverently to its native haunts there to admire it,
and go blithely away – happy in the knowledge that
others may come to enjoy it.*"[6]

The next collecting trip for Menzies was
three days later on 7 May, again with Captain
Vancouver. The route took them around the pen-
insula on which Port Townsend is located and south
along the eastern shores of the Olympic Peninsula.
Here Menzies botanized at various landings over
the next seven days: Point Wilson, Port Townsend,
Port Hadlock, Kitisat, Basalt Point, Foulweather,
Port Ludlow, Foul Weather Bluff, Harmon Point and
Hood Canal. They returned to the ships at Port
Discovery on the 14 May.

On this extensive trip along the east shore
in the rain shadow of the Olympic mountain range,
Menzies collection included several trees: the Garry
oak, *Quercus garryana*, first found near Port
Townsend; the native hazelnut tree, *Corylus
californica*; the vine maple, bigleaf maple, and the
Douglas maple, *Acer circinatum, A. macrophyllum*
and *A. glabrum*; the Cascara, *Rhamnus purshiana*;
the Pacific willow, *Salix scoulerii*; along with the
madrone, *Arbutus menziesii*.

Among eight shrubs Menzies found the
coastal form of the sticky laurel, *Ceonothus
velutinus*, and the evergreen huckleberry,
Vaccinium ovatum, along with several smaller
plants, among them spring beauty, *Montia
parvifolia*. Menzies named this fleshy leaved perennial, a member of the purslane family, *Claytonia
filicaulus*.

From Charles Newcombe's notations in the
northwest coast portion of Menzies' journal he prepared in 1923, we can establish most of the places
and areas Menzies botanized. Newcombe identified the areas with notations beside the text with
their modern place names. Fortunately, many of
these places where Menzies botanized still bear the
names Vancouver gave them. Newcombe also prepared a botanical appendix to Menzies' journal that

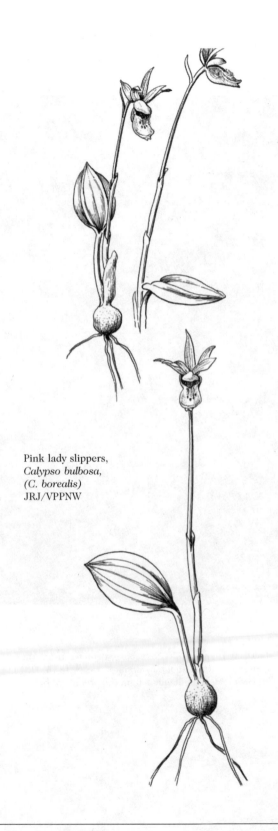

Pink lady slippers,
Calypso bulbosa,
(*C. borealis*)
JRJ/VPPNW

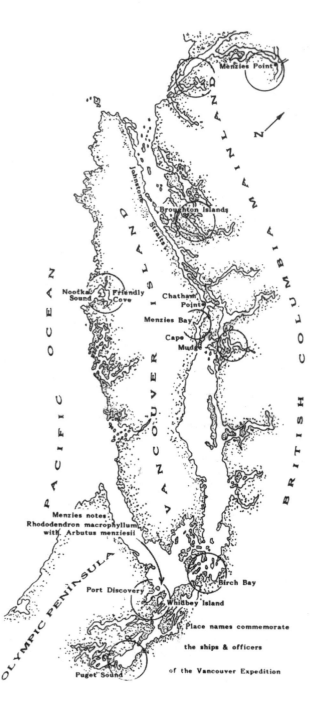

A map showing the coastal sites (circles) botanized by Archibald Menzies between May and September 1792.

lists all the terrestrial and aquatic plants he collected in 1792. Many in the list indicate the area where Menzies collected these plants.[7]

These opportunities to botanize occurred only when the boats were lowered for trips to shore for water, to explore Indian villages and encampments, to make spruce beer, to set up celestial observation posts for checking or establishing latitude and longitude measurements, and on some of the charting trips into inlets and channels along the coast that were too small, narrow or shallow to permit the big ships to manoeuvre.

While Menzies was able to botanize extensively in a few places such as Birch Bay where they anchored for repairs and at Nootka Sound, more often than not while in the ships or ship's boats Menzies was unable to pull up whenever he saw something interesting botanically along the shore. With the ships he had to wait until the cutter or pinnace was lowered to go to shore for some non-botanical purpose. When charting from the boats away from *Discovery* and *Chatham*, he could botanize when landings were made to make a meal or camp at the end of each day's mapping. This latter somewhat hurried type of botanizing occurred with the seven days charting of Puget Sound and on less hurried several daily trips to Whidbey and Fidalgo Islands while at Birch Bay.

From shipboard one can only identify shoreline plants generally, usually only the outline of trees. Also, observations taken from the launches, that usually travelled at least a cable's length [British 608 feet, US 720 feet] offshore even with the aid of a glass would be too far out to see the features or detail even if the outline was familiar, while small beach edge plants and those a bit inland would not be seen at all.

Referring to these difficulties, Menzies notes in his journal on 20 May, when *Discovery* and *Chatham* were in Admiralty Inlet where he decides to go with Peter Puget and Mr. Whidbey to chart Puget Sound:

"Two boats were now provided with arms/ provisions to go off in the morning to examine the Arm leading to the Southward [Dalco Passage] *and though their mode of procedure in these surveying*

Cruizes was not very favourable to my pursuits as it afforded me so little time on shore at the different places we landed at, yet it was the most eligible that I could at this time adopt for obtaining a general knowledge of the produce of the Country. I therefore embarked next morning before daylight with Lieutenant Puget in the Launch together with Mr. Whidbey in the Cutter who was directed to continue the survey . . . ."

In Dalco Passage, looking southeast into Commencement Bay (Puyallup River flats), Menzies notes:

"Up this Bay we had a most charming prospect of Mount Rainier which now appeared close to us though at least ten to twelve Leagues off - for the Lowland [of the Puyallup River], at the head of the Bay swelled out very gradually to form a most beautiful and majestic mountain of great elevation whose line of ascent appeared equally smooth & gradual on every side with a round obtuse summit covered two thirds of its height down with perpetual snow as were also the summits of a rugged ridge of mountains that proceeded from it to the Northward."

Capt. Vancouver gave the name of his friend, Captain Peter Rainier, at the time with the Royal Navy's Channel fleet, to the snow covered beautiful and majestic mountain of great elevation (14,408 ft.).[8]

Aside from noting the seascapes and landscapes of the Puget Sound area Menzies seems to have only collected two trees - the Oregon ash, *Fraxinus oregona* and the black cottonwood, *Populus trichocarpa*; two shrubs, the Sitka mountain ash, *Sorbus sitchensis* and the salmonberry, *Rubus spectabilis*; a grass, sea arrowgrass, *Triglochin maritima*, along with a grass-like lily with tight clusters of small bluish purple flowers on a tall stem, *Brodiaea congesta*, now *Dichalostemma congesta*. Menzies had classified this *Brodiaea*, an inhabitant of dry grassy meadows, as *Hookera pulchella* but it seems to have been renamed arbitrarily to honour James Brodie, a Scottish botanist, on his death in 1824.

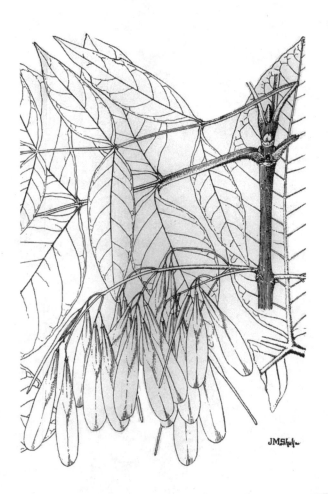

The Oregon ash, *Fraxinus oregona*, a relatively rare tree of restricted range. After Sudworth in FTPS

Left to Right, *Brodiaea congesta. B. cornaria,* and
B. douglasii , beautiful and edible. JRJ/VPPNW

The bulbs of this plant, though small, and sometimes called the false onion, are edible; that is how Menzies found it, when he observed natives on Restoration Point digging them up to eat . *"Several of the women were digging on the Point, which excited my curiosity to know what they were digging for and found it to be a bulbous root of a liliaceous plant..."* Menzies recorded. The name of this point was given to it by Vancouver when he anchored there on 29 May 1792. It honours now a rather obscure event called "Royal Oak Day", the birthday of King Charles II on his restoration to the throne in 1660.[9]

A more spectacular *brodiaea* that Menzies also discovered is *B. coronaria.* Again Lewis Clark's description of this lovely multiflowered July and August flowering grassy meadow inhabitant is the most apt: *"Coronaria is the feminine to agree with Brodiaea of the Latin adjective meaning relating to a garland' obvious by referring to the chaplet of successionally opening flowers, which are striped with vivid tones of blue, purple, and violet deliciously relieved with white at the heart of the shallow cup. Three sterile stamens add a further accent like tiny white fans."*

A more showy bluish-lavender brodiaea collected by David Douglas east of the Cascades is *B. douglasii,* now renamed, on obscure botanical features *Triteleia grandiflora.*[10]

Puget Sound was the northern limit of the now very rarely seen Oregon Ash; although reported to extend into British Columbia it has not been seen here in this century.[11] The northern black cottonwood on the other hand, the largest of the poplars, is very common, growing over 100 feet. An inhabitant of river bottoms, sand bars and sand banks, *Populus trichocarpa* forms belts and limited forests of pure growth, but is more common in mixtures with willows, alder, bigleaf maple and lowland fir. It is one of the fastest growing of coastal trees when young, easily growing three to five feet in a single season.

The leaves of the northern black cottonwood at its juvenile stage are twice the length and breadth of the leaves of the older tree. The leaves in addition have an entirely different shape; the juvenile leaf is concavely acute tipped and cordate at the petiole while the leaf of the mature tree is convexly or sharply acute at the tip and joins the petiole at a wide angle creating a diamond in shape. In spring the orange buds are covered with a very fragrant, yellowish brown gum producing a strong pungent odour that pervades the area for some distance from the tree giving it the names balsam poplar, balsam cottonwood or balm of gilead. The leaf stems (petioles) are rounded on *P. trichocarpa* with the bark thick, rough and deeply furrowed to separate it from another member of the poplar genus, *Populus tremuloides*, the quaking aspen that has smooth whitish or greenish bark and flat leaf petioles.

With its special nature and properties, *Populus trichocarpa* bark, light brown in colour, even density, textured with layered grain and inability to become water logged, had ready availability in days past, as it was found as driftwood on beaches. In the 1920s and 30s Saltspring Island beaches provided a seemingly inexhaustible supply to be collected, selected and carved by the author's grandfather (a boat builder), into model sail boats. During these decades many a flotilla of poplar bark two- and three-masted schooners, barques, with smaller cutters and pinnaces sailed out to sea with the receding tides at the end of each summer. Alas fifty years later suitable sized pieces of bark, always with a special weathered silver grey exterior, can now only occasionally be found along those same Gulf Island beaches. For grandchildren now white plastic styrofoam chunks broken from floats and buoys replace the bark along the high tide line. While this non-biodegradable plastic floats, it cannot be carved or shaped to the lines of one's dream boat.

Quaking aspen has flat leafstems (petioles) so that the leaves flutter in the slightest breeze. It is aptly named. Menzies sighted and collected *P. tremuloides* at Birch Bay. As this tree is the most widely distributed deciduous tree in North America extending right across the northern part of the continent, Menzies was far from the first to see or collect this tree. It forms an extensive belt at latitude 50° to 55° N. called the aspen parkland belt. This park-like band of trees and tall grasses extends from the Pacific Ocean in Alaska across southern

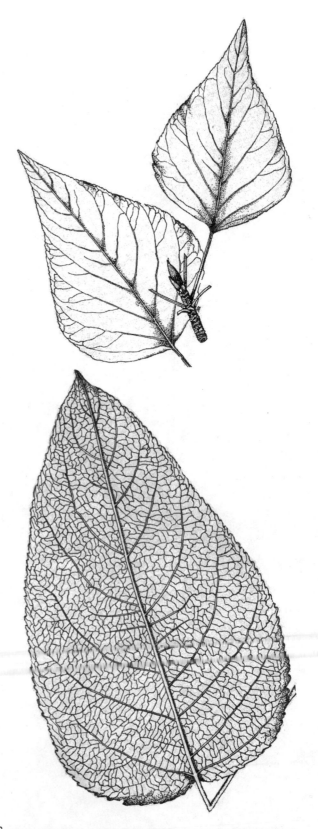

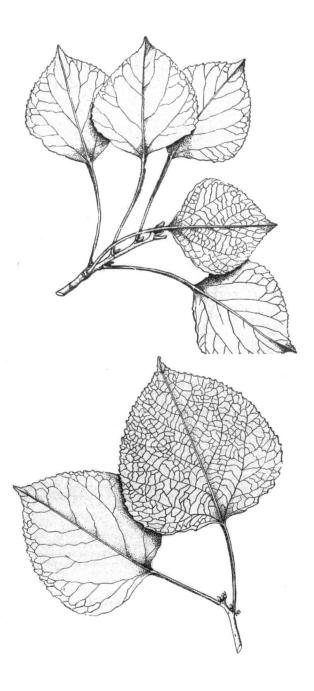

Left: Balsam boplar, *Populus trichocarpa*. Leaves of mature trees, above, with juvenile leaf, below. After Sudworth, FTPS

This page: Quaking Aspen, *Populus tremuloides*, western leaf form, above, eastern form, below. After Sudworth in FTPS.

Yukon and British Columbia to Hudson Bay, continues through northern Ontario, Quebec, Labrador and Newfoundland to the Atlantic Ocean. Groups and copses of these trees in grasslands or among spruce on hillsides are the stuff of great photography. The leaves turn a clear pure lemon yellow in September and October and with the straight clean smooth trunks make quaking aspen a most photogenic subject. It is the essential ingredient of mountain and prairie grasslands, the "typical" North American or Canadian landscape. *Populus tremuloides* shows considerable geographical variation leading some botanists, the "splitters", to distinguish several varieties. One of interest is the variety indigenous to Vancouver Island - *P. tremuloides* var. vancouveriana. It is distinguished by having hairy leaf petioles and winter twigs whereas the inland species has no hairs on the leaf stems or twigs.[12]

Menzies collection of the salmonberry, *Rubus spectabilis* in Puget Sound was the first of this purple flowered vigorous and aggressive shrub with yellow or red raspberry fruits that are made up of drupelets that in the red form resemble salmon roe (eggs). As such they are realistic enough to be used for bait in trout fishing, the use of the real thing being both unlawful as well as unsportsmanlike.

The 'grass' Menzies collected in the Puget Sound area is an inhabitant of saline coastal marshes, called sea arrowgrass, *Triglochin maritima*. It has a very wide east-west circumpolar and north-south range, from coastal Alaska to Baja California, therefore the specific epithet *maritima*. It is not a true grass, being a member of the arrowgrass family. This perennial herb is poisonous to game and grazing animals caused by the formation of hydrocyanic acid (cyanide) from two chemicals in the plant; though not poisonous themselves they combine to form the poisonous acid.[13]

The pinnace and cutter with Lieutenant Puget, Mr. Whidbey, Menzies and crews arrived back at the anchorage of *Discovery* on the evening of 26 May. As a botanical collecting trip it was reasonably rewarding for Menzies. As a coastline charting and mapping expedition it was an epic small boat voyage both in speed and accuracy and length of coastline surveyed, some 70 leagues (210 miles) in six days.

The cartographic accomplishment of Menzies' fellow officer, Peter Puget, in mapping the coastlines of the Sound that was to bear his name, would stand unchallenged for a very long time.

Seablush, *Plectreitis congesta*,
Menzies first plant discovery on Protection Island.
Leslie Bohm/Davidsonia

4

IN A NATURAL PARK.

Nature, in all her great works of Landscape observes this accommodating rule [One of neatness & elegance]. *She seldom passes abruptly from one mode of scenery to another, but generally connects different species of Landscape by some third species, which participates both. A mountainous country rarely sinks immediately into a level one,* [except along shore-lines in non pastoral landscapes] *the swellings and heavings of the earth, grow gradually less. Thus as the house is connected with the country through the medium of the Park; the Park should partake of the neatness of the one, the wildness of the other. As the Park is a scene either planted by art or, if naturally woody, artificially improved, we expect a beauty, and contrast in its clumps which we do not look for in the wild scenes of nature. . . .. We expect, that when trees are left standing as individuals, they should be the most beautiful of their kind, elegant & well balanced.* – William Gilpin, *Remarks on Forest Scenery.*

With the background ridge of the Cascade mountain range from Mt. Baker south to Mt. Rainier, Menzies describes the panoramic landscape encompassing Whidbey, Camano and Fidalgo islands with the San Juan group of Islands and the channels between:

Between us and the above Ridge and the Southward of us between the 2 mountains already mentioned a fine level country intertwined chiefly covered spots of considerable extent and interest with the various winding branches of Admiralty Inlet.[1] *These clear spots or lawns are clothed with a rich carpet of verdure and adorned with clumps of trees and a surrounding verge of scattered pines [conifers] which with their advantageous situation on the Banks of those inland arms of the sea give them a beauty of prospect equal to the most admired parks of England.*

Today this impressive panoramic view can still be experienced in the mid-channel of Admiralty Inlet from the top deck of the Washington state ferry that replaced the botanically named ferry *M.V. Rhododendron* (now newly refurbished

and plying the Tacoma to Vashon Island route), on its many daily crossings from Whidbey Island to Port Townsend and return.

Menzies continues in the poetic English Landscape descriptive tradition:

A Traveler wandering over these unfrequented plains is rewarded with a salubrious and vivifying air impregnated with the balsamic fragrance of the surrounding Pinery while his senses rivetted on the surrounding scenery where the softer beauties of Landscape are harmoniously blended in majestic grandeur with the wild and romantic to form an interesting and picturesque prospect on every side.

It is also still possible occasionally to experience this *"salubrious and vivifying air with the softer beauties blending with the sublime and picturesque views"* when travelling along the coastal areas of the islands and up inlets and across tidal flats all along the east side of Admiralty Inlet from present day Bellingham to the urbanized and suburbanized areas of Everett and Seattle. Vestiges of the natural or seemingly untouched pastoral landscape along with the managed sort of the agricultural areas are still extant on Whidbey and other islands, particularly on the north end of the former along with those in the Skagit River Estuary around Mt. Vernon. The scenic seascape–landscapes seen along Chuckanut Drive, State Highway 11, between Bellingham and Burlington and the views of Mt. Baker are best captured by the selective eye of photographers in order that the horrendously ugly elements such as the Cherry Point oil refinery and the strip development along State Highway 20 can be eliminated from the photograph and subsequent remembrances.

The pristine scenery and landscape described by Menzies did not require any screening; there was little or no human intrusion. Menzies' landscape was made up of the two main constituents of the virgin untouched landscape: natural topography and native vegetation. So that Menzies' description of the Pacific Northwest landscape vegetation will be understandable we offer the following extract from Menzies journal with the corrected Pacific Northwest common and species names given in square brackets:

The woods here were chiefly composed of Silver Fir [grand fir, *Abies grandis*], *white spruce* [Douglas fir, *Pseudotsuga menziesii*], *Norway Spruce* [Sitka spruce, *Picea sitchensis*], *Hemlock Spruce* [western hemlock, *Tsuga heterophylla*], *together with the American Arborvitae* [western red cedar, *Thuya plicata*], *and common yew* [Pacific Yew, *Taxus brevifolia*], *and beside these we saw a variety of hardwoods scattered along the banks and arms such as Oak* [*Quercus garryana*], *the Sycamore or Great maple,* [bigleaf maple, *Acer macrophyllum*], *Sugar Maple* [Douglas or Rocky Mountain maple, *Acer glabrum* var *douglasii*], *and Pennsylvanian Maple* [*Acer circinatum*, the vine maple], *The Tacamahac,* [black cottonwood, *Populus trichocarpa*] *and Canadian Poplars* [Quaking aspen, *Populus tremuloides*], *The American Ash* [Oregon ash, *Fraxinus oregona*], *Common Hazel* [*Corylus californica*], *Common willow* [*Salix scoulerii*], *and the Oriental Arbute* [*Arbutus menziesii*], *but none of their hardwood trees were*

Two of Menzies tree discoveries, Garry oak, *Quercus garryiana*, above, and the Douglas or Rocky Mountain maple, *Acer glabrum* var. *douglasi*. After Sudworth in FTPS.

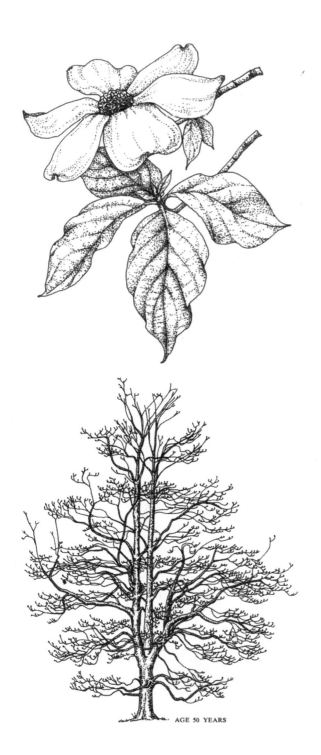

Pacific dogwood, *Cornus nuttallii*. Button of flowers with bracts and leaves, and the tree in winter. LB/Davidsonia

in great abundance or acquired sufficient size to be of any great utility except the Oak in some particular places as at Port Gardner[2] and Oak Cove."
We also met here pretty frequent, in the Wood, with that beautiful Native of the Levant the purple Rhododendron [Pacific rhododendron, *Rhododendron macrophyllum*].

This last reference is to *Rhododendron ponticum* that had become naturalized in England and Ireland since being brought from Pontic in the Caucasus by returning crusaders. It does have a purple flower while the rhododendron Menzies saw in Puget Sound, the Pacific rhododendron, has a truss of flowers that are usually pink.[3]

Menzies continues: [we met frequently with] *the great flowered Dogwood* [*Cornus nuttallii*],[4] *Common Dogwood* [*Cornus stolonifera*], *and Canadian Dogwood,* [bunchberry, *Cornus canadensis*], *the Caroline Rose,* [*Rosa gymnocarpa*], *Dog Rose,* [Nootka rose, *R. nutkana*], *but the most part of the shrubs and underwood were new and undescribed several of them I name as Arbutus glauca* [hairy manzanita, *Arctostaphylos columbiana*],[5] *Vaccinium lucidum* [huckleberry, *V. parvifolium*], *V. tetrogonum,* [blueberry, *V. ovatum*], *Lonicera Nootkagensis,* [red honeysuckle, *L. ciliosa*], *Gaultheria fruiticosa* [salal, *G. shallon*], *Spireae serrulata,* [ocean spray, *Holodiscus discolor*], *Rubus nootkagensis* [salmonberry or Menzies raspberry, *R. spectabilis*].[6]
Others from particular circumstances were doubtful and could not be ascertained till they are hereafter compared with more extensive description & C [comment], *on my return to England. The wild fruits* [collected], *were gooseberries* [*Ribes lacustre*], *Currants* [flowering currant, *Ribes sanginueum and R. laxiflorum*], *two kinds of Rasberries* [thimbleberry, *Rubus spectabilis, and* salmonberry, *R. spectabilis*], *two kinds of Whottleberries* [whortleberry, *Vaccinium uliginosum* and lingonberry, *V. vitis-idaea*], *small fruited crabs* [Pacific crabapple, *Malus fusca*], *and a new species of Barberry* [tall mahonia or Oregon grape, *Mahonia aquifolium*[7]].

On 8 June Menzies accompanied Lieutenant Broughton in one of *Chatham*'s boats to Orcas and some of the smaller islands in the San Juan Islands where he collected a small onion [*Allium acuminatum*], *"which grew in little tufts in the crevices of Rocks."* He also collected *Lilium Canadense* [now *L. columbianum*] and *Lilium Camchatense* [now *Fritillaria camschatcensis*].[8]

On 9 June 1792, Whidbey returned to the *Chatham* and reported he had gone through Deception Pass, which separates the island-like peninsula from what is now Whidbey Island. Meanwhile *Discovery* was anchored in Admiralty Inlet and the brewers had been sent ashore. The brewers would have had a choice between *Picea sitchensis*, Sitka Spruce; *Tsuga heterophylla*, Western Hemlock; *Pseudotsuga menziesii*, Douglas Fir; or even the true fir, *Abies grandis*, as all were present on the shores beside this anchorage.

Menzies spent the next several days visiting various islands in the San Juan group and mainland areas around Birch Bay, such as Semiahmoo Bay, where James Johnstone had set up a station to take astronomical observations to determine longitude.[9] Here Menzies found *"in full bloom diffusing its sweetness that beautiful shrub the Philadelphus Cornarius."* He got the genus right but not the species for this western North American Mockorange.

In 1805 Meriwether Lewis found it *"...on Mr. Claks River"* (Lewis was a terrible speller), so in 1814 Pursh named it *Philadelphus lewisii*. As Hitchcock's *Vascular Plants of the Pacific Northwest* notes: *"today the more commonly grown plant in the Pacific Northwest is the European P. cornarius. The native Mockorange is little used as it lacks the fragrant white flowers of the European species."*

The late Lewis J. Clark (no relation to either Meriwether or William), comments that *"the coastal form of P. lewisii is a shrub 10 to 12 ft. in height, while east of the Cascades it is rarely half that height and lacks any fragrance when found in full sun situations."* *Philadelphus* doesn't commemorate the city of Philadelphia; the plant and the city commemorate Ptolemy II Philadelphus, a pharoah of Egypt who lived from 308 – 246 B.C.

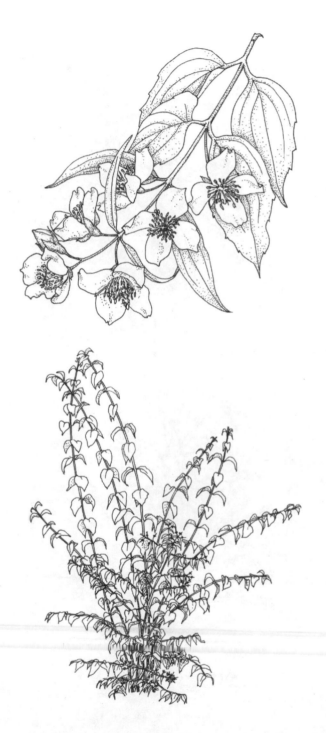

Pacific Mockorange, *Philadelphus lewisii*. Leaves and flowers with habit, a multi-stem, 1m high deciduous shrub. LB/Davidsonia

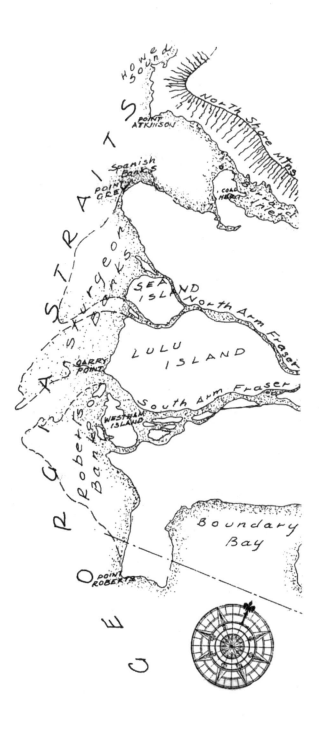

Georgia Strait, east side, Boundary Bay, Point Roberts, Roberts and Sturgeon Banks at the Fraser River delta; Point Grey and Burrard Inlet, after Capt Richards chart of 1852.

On 11 June *Discovery* anchored in Birch Bay, *"in 5 fathoms over a soft bottom about a half mile from shore."* On 12 June, Vancouver and Puget, with pinnace and launch, left for a ten day exploration north along the east side of Georgia Strait from Boundary Bay to Point Roberts (Cape Roberts) passing the Fraser River estuary, into Malaspina Strait through Agamemnon Channel to the head of Jervis Inlet; and then returning south along the outside of the Sechelt Peninsula, returning to *Discovery* and Birch Bay on 23 June.

It was on this eleven day exploration, when sailing out of Howe Sound and across Burrard Inlet, that Vancouver met and breakfasted with Dionisio Galiano and Cayetano Valdes with their ships, *Sutil* and *Mexicana*. The Spanish had a watering party at a creek near Point Grey. There is much doubt as to the exact location of the Spanish ships. Vancouver describes them as being at anchor *"under the land"*. The journal of Galiano and Valdes places the Spanish ships close to a village where they had received help from the Indians, presumably at the entrance to the North Arm of the Fraser River. From the subsequent movement of Sutil and Mexicana this seems more likely.[10]

Spanish Banks in English Bay was named by Captain George Richards of H.M.S. *Plumper* in 1859. Spanish Banks Beach Park is the most westerly stretch of shoreline and beach within the City of Vancouver's boundaries. It is part of a continuous shoreline and beach parkland extending eastward into Vancouver to include Locarno Beach, Jericho Beach and Park, some 200 acres of upland and two miles of beach. The public beach continues westward to include the eroding shoreline of Point Grey, (named Punta Langara by Francisco Eliza of the Spanish Navy in 1791 and by Vancouver in 1792 after his Navy friend George Grey).

The beach and foreshore parkland encompasses the area's nude bathing area, Wreck Beach, on the south side below the University's Botanical Gardens, and extends to the Southwest Marine Drive roadside monument commemorating Simon Fraser's epic journey in 1808 down the river that now bears his name. He reached a point near this spot on 2 July, only sixteen years after Vancouver,

Puget, Galiano and Valdes had breakfasted on the other side of the point, or more likely just below it.

North of the University Campus there is a commemorative monument locating and recording the Vancouver–Galiano–Valdes meeting. The University of British Columbia campus thus lies between these two monuments that are three miles apart.[11]

During the time Vancouver and Peter Puget were away, Menzies botanized and collected in and around the ship's anchorage at Birch Bay. He found 'Red Cedar' at several points near the water's edge. This tree is not the western red cedar, *Thuja plicata*, but *Juniperus scopulorum*, the Rocky Mountain or western juniper.

Through the San Juan and Gulf Islands this small conifer usually occurs with some dead silver grey twisted branches and portions of the main trunk killed by salt spray from winter storms or summer drought. It forms a picturesque, gnarled, and weatherbeaten tree on rock ledges or hangs out of crevices and other most unlikely places on these islands' edges. It is a tree like the madrone requiring full sun, and also like it, is easily shaded out by the more vigorous and competing Douglas fir. A requirement for juniper survival is that it occupies the sunny rock edges of these Georgia Strait islands. Junipers like the yew have 'berries' – blue for junipers, red for yews; the needles of the juniper are sharp pointed, awl shaped and when crushed have a pungent aromatic odour. The 'botanicals' used in gin have a large measure of juniper berries for flavouring.

Menzies' Birch Bay botanizing added another onion, *Allium acuminatum* to his collections along with the death camas. Menzies placed this latter lily in the genus *Melanthium*. However Hooker renamed it *Zigadensis venenosus*, which name still stands for this grass-like lily with a panicle of cream coloured flowers. Menzies dug the roots of this along with the onion he planted in the plant hutch on the deck of *Discovery*. As we already know, these plants, along with the others Menzies planted in the frame, did not make it back alive to England.

The bulbs of *Zigadensis venenosus* and a very similar variety *Zigadensis* var *gramineus* are both poisonous and not easily distinguished from

Western juniper, *Juniperus scopulorum*, in a Gulf Island habitat. LB/Davidsonia

Western juniper, *Juniperus scopulorum*, foliage and fruit, above, after Sudworth in FTPS, and stinging nettle, *Urtica dioica* var *lyallii,* below, JRJ/VPPNW

Camassia quamash, the blue camas that was dug and eaten by the local Indian people. *Zigadensis* and *Camassia* grow together and the latter are dug in early spring before either blooms. Since Menzies did not find the blue camas it is quite possible this common food item had been entirely dug up in the particular locations that he botanized and that any remaining were not of flowering size so not seen by him.

Menzies records that he found at Birch Bay all of the pines he had already enumerated. For a botanist today to use the broad term 'pines' to encompass eight genera of needle-bearing trees, only one of which is in the genus *Pinus,* would be very misleading. This is especially true in the Pacific Northwest where the dominant trees are cone and needle bearing. However, this general term is a common one still misapplied today to cover all genera and species of western North American conifers in non-botanical writings. Today's botanist would describe these trees as evergreen needleleaf conifers.

Menzies also found both black cottonwood and quaking aspen *Populus trichocarpa* and *P. tremuloides* at Birch Bay along with *Betula papyfera* var *commutata* that he called the black birch.

When young this tree does have dark brown stems. It assumes the characteristic white bark and dark horizontal lenticels only when mature. William Hooker (senior) gave it the species name *occidentalis,* so the epithet and the common name, Western Birch, did not come from Menzies' collection of this tree, but that of John Scouler, who also collected it in Birch Bay in the 1820s.[13]

Menzies found the Stinging Nettle, *Urtica dioica* var *lyallii* growing at the site of an old Indian village near Birch Bay. The Indians used this plant for making twine as well as gathering the new shoots in spring for use as a green vegetable. Another plant Menzies collected was gathered by natives for use in weaving mats and basketry; this was the bullrush or cattail, *Typhus latifolius* (*Typha latifolia*). He found large patches of it cut and set out to dry near a large swamp on Orcas Island, the largest of the San Juan islands. The cattail was the most important mat-making material of the Salish people. The mats they made from the sun-dried leaves were sometimes two meters in length. These were sewn together with nettle twine, and bound with braided cattail blades. The mats were used for insulating winter houses, for lining canoes, for drying berries, and covering doors and windows.

Menzies also found a new species of willow herb, *Epilobium*, which he didn't name; Lindley named it *E. munitum* but Pursh previously had given it the name *E. luteum* for its small yellow flowers. It grows along the borders of ponds and streams in the Pacific Northwest. However the most familiar of the *Epilobium* is the pink- or cerise-flowered fireweed, *E. angustifolium*.

Lewis Clark writing in his *Wildflowers of the Pacific Northwest* relates: *"The Indians often collected the stalks (of fireweed), then split them lengthwise and scraped out the glutinous sweet pith. The young leaves and new shoots were also used as a pot herb. Deer and elk graze extensively on this plant."*

Fireweed is the source of nectar for a dark amber fragrant honey. British Columbia mainland and Vancouver Island beekeepers annually move their hives into the extensive fireweed covered logged over areas of the province during the June to September flowering of this plant, so that the hives can produce this aromatic light honey.

Menzies also found an annual knotweed, *Polygonum*; it was given the unpronounceable and virually unspellable species name of *spergulariaeforme*, meaning like spergula, from spargo, to scatter, in reference to a plant very widely scattered in Europe and North America.

He found a saxifrage, again on one of the San Juan Islands. Menzies is credited by Hooker with eight species of saxifrage although at least two were from Bering Straits.[15] Menzies never got that far north.

The saxifrage Menzies found on the San Juan Islands is *Saxifraga ferruginea*. The rosette of leaves on this plant are up to two inches long while the white pinkish flowers are ¼ inch in diameter and born on a single or several leafless stems that branch freely and are paniculate in form. Some saxifrages, particularly the high alpine cushion or dense rosette-leaved species are highly valued as garden rockery plants. *S. ferruginea* is one of the finest. The one Menzies found is now distinguished as *S. ferruginea* var *ferruginea* to separate it from

The cattail, *Typha latifolia*, clump in flower, leaf blade left, and wind pollinated inflorescence, showing male, pollen flowers above the female seed tail. JRJ/VPPNW

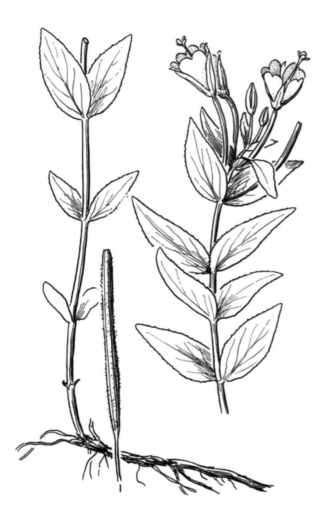

S. ferruginea var *macounii*. Lewis Clark writes of it as follows:

"On close inspection how exquisitely shaped these small flowers are! The two lower petals arc unmarked and pointed-elliptical, attenuated into a long, slender base. But each of the other three petals enchantingly remind us in chaste outline, of a Grecian vase.

The incomparable line could not be improved, two cup-marks of purist yellow are placed just so on the alabaster. A final perfect accent is provided by the plump anthers: coral before anthesis, cinnamon after."[15]

Yellow willowherb, *Epilobium luteum*, above, and the knotweed, *Spergula spergulariae*, right.
JRJ/VPPNW

Macoun's saxifrage, *Saxifraga ferruginea* var *macounii*, with rusty saxifrage, *Saxifraga ferruginea* var *ferruginea*, on the left, with flower above. JRJ/VPPNW

5

IN A SUBLIME AND BEAUTIFUL LANDSCAPE

Edmund Burke in his *Philosophical Inquiry into the Origin of our Ideas of the Sublime and the Beautiful* (1757), defines a beautiful landscape as having: *"Smallness Smoothness, Gradual Variation and Delicacy of form . . . In trees and flowers smooth leaves are beautiful; smooth slopes of earth in gardens; smooth streams in the landscape . . . Most people must have observed the sort of sense they have had, on being swiftly drawn in an easy coach* [in the company of a beautiful woman]*, on a smooth turf, with gradual ascents and declivities. This will give a better idea of the beautiful, and point out its probable cause better than almost anything else."*[1]

Walpole's comments on William Kent, a landscapist who preceded Capability Brown and Humphry Repton, reads in part: *"He leaped the fence, and found all the world was a garden. He felt the delicious contrast of hill and valley changing imperceptibly into each other, tasted the beauty of the gentle swell the concave scoop, and remarked how loose groves crowned an easy eminence with happy ornament, and while they called in the distant view between their graceful stems removed and extended the perspective by delusive comparison."*

On 24 June 1792 *Discovery* and *Chatham*, their officers and crews with ships' boats back on board, pulled up anchors at Birch Bay. They sailed past Cape Roberts, now called Point Roberts, and tacked back and forth proceeding slowly up Georgia Strait.

For the first few leagues the going was easy and wide open, but as Vancouver Island and the mainland appear to squeeze and come together there is a maze formed by a myriad of islands, arms and channels going to almost all points of the compass. Vancouver Island, Quadra Island, Marina Island, Cortes Island, Hernando Island and the mainland arm of Malaspina Peninsula effectively create a visual enclosure across the north end of Georgia Strait. If it were not for tidal flow and currents through the three main channels between and around these islands there would be no clue that there was a way through this maze. As we shall see, by keeping close by the mainland, Vancouver at first missed the only channel that was deep

enough for his ships. Quadra Island is named for Juan Francisco de la Bodega y Quadra, Commander of San Blas Naval Station and Governor of Nootka. Quadra was the Spanish official Vancouver was sent to negotiate with for the return of the Nootka settlement to England. Confirmed by the Geographic Board in 1903, Cortes Island was first named by Dionisio Galiano in 1792 after Hernando Cortez the conqueror of Mexico. Captain Alexandro Malaspina, was the celebrated commander of a Spanish circumnavigation designed to rival Cook's.[2]

By the next day they were in Malaspina Strait, between Texada Island and the mainland, having passed Jervis Inlet, which Vancouver and Puget had charted earlier from the ships' boats. They had met the Spanish ships after departing Birch Bay, at a point opposite the North Arm of the Fraser River. *Sutil* and *Mexicana* had then accompanied *Discovery* and *Chatham* to anchorage in Desolation Sound, arriving there at midnight on 28 June. Their anchorage was near Kinghorn Is-

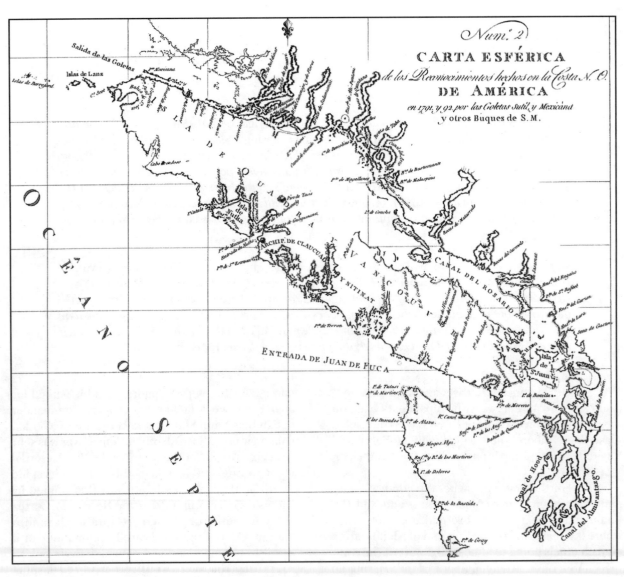

Num. 2 Carta Esferica de los Reconocimientos hechos en la Costa N.O. De America en 1791 y 92 por las Goletas Sutil y Mexicana y otres Bruques de S.M.
Dionisio Galiano, 1792.
From: *Relación... Atlas*, 1802.

The summary map showing the explorations of Galiano and Valdes in 1792.

land just inside the entrance to Desolation Sound. The next day the ships were moved to a more secure anchorage in Teakerne Arm. Galiano then visited *Discovery*, and according to Menzies, offered the services of Spanish vessels and crews

". . . to facilitate the examination of this intricate Country, saying that his Boats & Crews were ready to aid in the Execution of any plan of operation that might be devised for that purpose, & as his Vessels were of small draught of Water they might be commodiously employed on difficult & distant excursions offering at the same time the chief direction of the parties to Capt. Vancouver, which was declined, – & Capt. Galeano, then proposed to send one of his Boats to examine a large opening leading to the Northward & on his returning on board, he despatched Don Valdes Commander of the Schooner in one of the Launches upon that service."[3]

In the morning Galiano breakfasted on *Discovery* with Vancouver, presumably a return for the breakfast Vancouver had with him on board *Mexicana* on Burrard Inlet's south shore. Galiano's offer to help with the charting, according to Menzies, was declined by Vancouver. However, Galiano continued his own charting and mapping, dispatching one of the launches from *Sutil* to explore Desolation Sound.

Menzies accompanied Puget and Whidbey in *Discovery*'s launch and cutter to explore the openings that lay to the northeastward as the *"Rugged and wild appearance of the Country was likely to afford some variety to my pursuits. Mr. Johnstone in Chatham's cutter and launch left to explore to the North Westward* [in Lewis Channel]*"*.

James Johnstone, like Menzies, had previously been to this coast with Colnett in 1789 in the *Prince of Wales*; at that time he had found the western end of the narrow channel that bears his name. Johnstone's determination to find a navigable route from Georgia Strait through the many channels they encountered to 'his Straits' became an obsession with him. However, *Discovery* and *Chatham* had anchored too far to the northeast to find the navigable but narrow opening between Cape Mudge on Quadra Island and Willow Point on

Vancouver Island that connects to the Pacific. In 1788 Johnstone had come upon the channel from its western end.[4]

On 27 June they visited an abandoned Indian village or fishing camp. All they collected here, inadvertently, were fleas. *"Myriads of Fleas which fixed themselves on our shoes, stockings and cloths in such incredible number that the whole party was obliged to quit the rock in great precipitation."* After this hasty retreat

"We pulled out a little from the shore and lay on our oars before the village while Mr. Humphrys took a sketch of it, and tho I can give but a very unequal idea of its romantic appearance, yet I will attempt to follow the expressive/strokes of his Pencil in a few words. The Rock itself is somewhat round of a moderate height & projects into the cove; its face is here & there over grown with Raspberries & other Bushes, [Rubus spectabilis], while the summit is occupied with crouded, remains of the Village consisting of posts, spurs & planks crossing each other with the utmost confusion in all directions. At the Landing place which is a small Beach close to the Rock are standing Posts & Beams of a Solitary House which from its size, painted ornaments & picturesque sheltered situation seemed to have been the residence of the chief or some family of distinction." [5]

Menzies continues: *"The shore on both sides is Rocky crouded with large stones and driftwood and here and there verged with maple trees [Acer macrophyllum], whose waving branches and light coloured foliage formed a beautiful contrast with the gigantic aspect of dark verdurous hue of a thick forest of Pinery [Pseudotsuga menziesii etc.] which* spread over a high prominent mountain [Mt. Addenbrooke, 5,140 feet, on East Redondo Island, on the west side of Homfray Channel[6]], *that swelled out immediately behind to form the back ground with steep aclivity from the outer point of the cove."*

On 28 June, having boiled their clothes to get rid of the fleas the evening previously, they proceeded into Toba inlet having met Valdes in *Sutil*'s boat coming out. According to one source, a Spanish chart engraver's error resulted in the 'Canal de la Tabla', of Galiano and Valdes being changed to Canal de la Toba. It was so named, according to this source, for the 'billboard' of carved planks with Indian hieroglyphics carved on it found by the Spanish when they sailed up the long canal on 27 June 1792.[7] A much more plausible story is that Toba Inlet was named in honour of Antonio Toba (or Tova) Arrendondo, an officer from Malaspina's expedition from which Galiano and Valdes were seconded.[8]

Menzies described the sublime landscape of Toba Inlet:

"On each side were high steep mountains covered towards their summits with snow which is now dissolving and producing a number of wild torrents and beautiful cascades. As we advanced the country became more dreary and barren, large Tracts were seen without the least soil or vegetation, exposing a naked surface of solid rock, of which mass of Mountains appeared entirely composed. The woods became stunted and the trees were but thinly scattered except in Valleys and near the water side."

As for botany, Menzies continues,

"It was observable however in these stinted situations, where vegetation was making, as it were, a slow beginning, that hard woods such as Birch, [Betula papyifera var commutata], Maple [Acer macrophyllum], medlers [Amelanchier alnifolia, the Saskatoon berry], whortleberries, [Vaccinium sp]... were most predominate and not Pines, the general covering of the country."

The whortleberries are all members of the heather (ericaceae) family. Most are bog plants growing on moderately acid to high acid peat and organic 'soil' – fallen logs and stumps. In the Pacific Northwest they consist of the lingonberry, red and black huckleberries and the blueberry. A variety of this latter berry has been developed and hybridized to produce a significant commercial crop, both fresh and frozen, on some of the extensive peat bog areas of lower mainland British Columbia. This is the species *Vaccinium ovalifolium*, a two- to four-foot deciduous shrub with bluish black,

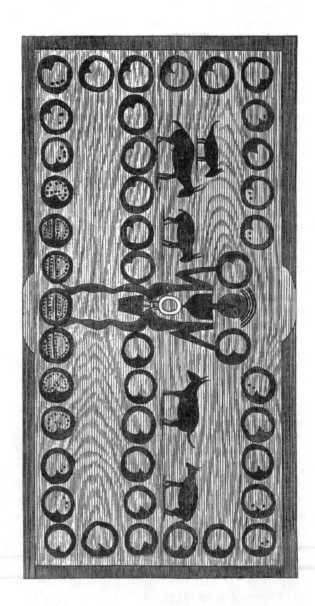

The Tabla of Toba Inlet, after Cecil Jane in *A Spanish Voyage to Vancouver and the North-West Coast of America* (Argonaut Press 1930)

Right: Western birch, *Betula papyifera* var *commutata*, above, after Sudworth in FTPS, and the blueberry, *Vaccinium ovalifolium*, after Szczawinski in HFBC.

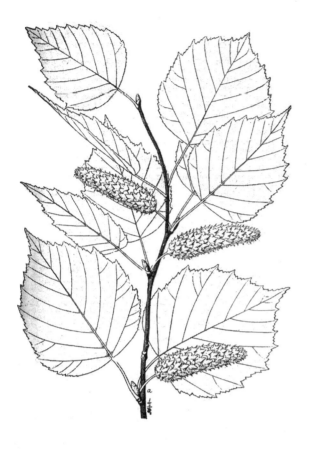

glaucous, purplish black, non-glaucous flattish berries. Being deciduous, the red fall colour of the blueberry plant is exceptionally vivid and it is effective when used ornamentally with rhododendrons. *Vaccinium ovatum* on the other hand is an evergreen shrub 18 inches to 12 feet in height. It is extensively collected from the wild in the Pacific Northwest particularly on the Sechelt Peninsula and Vancouver Island as a florist's foliage filler, along with another ericaceous shrub, salal *Gaultheria shallon.*

The evergreen huckleberry is grown occasionally ornamentally as a ground cover or filler shrub in Pacific Northwest parks and gardens particularly with other ericaceous plants like the rhododendrons. The red huckleberry, *V. parvifolium,* is an elegant deciduous shrub with bright green angular branches. It grows up to 12 feet tall but is usually seen in the wild at around 4 to 6 feet in height. In old second growth coastal forest areas, this huckleberry with almost a lace-like branch and leaf texture, often grows as an epiphyte on stumps and old fallen coniferous logs. Under garden conditions it assumes a not so elegant appearance as in the less cared for conditions found outside of the garden. The translucent red berries are edible although sour; however, if left hanging along the branches on the plant they provide a most delicate beauty when seen from below.

The combination of bright green branches and red leaves during October and November in the Pacific Northwest is an added asset of this huckleberry for the home garden or in the 'wild' in such parks as Point Defiance in Tacoma, Stanley Park in Vancouver, and other natural woodland areas and parks throughout coastal British Columbia, Washington and Oregon.

Vaccinium vitis-idaea is the lingonberry; the Pacific Northwest version of this circumpolar evergreen creeper is *Vaccinium vitis-idaea* subsp. *minus*. Lingonberry jam and a drink are made from the berries in Scandinavia, while in the Pacific Northwest it is common as a garden groundcover and rockery plant. The western North American *Vaccinium* that now bears the common name whortleberry, the name Menzies used to cover all of them, is *Vaccinium scoparium*. He could have found this almost matted red-berried shrub when he and Mudge climbed 2,826 feet to Nipple Summit on Redondo Island on 1 July. He also could have found the dwarf whortleberry there.

Vaccinium caespitosum is also a mat forming blue-berried plant from higher elevations on the coast. *Vaccinium oxycoccus* var *intermedius* is the wild cranberry[9] that Menzies found on Redondo Island. Menzies' companion on the climb, Zachary Mudge was at age 22 First Lieutenant on *Discovery*. He later rose in the ranks of the Navy to Admiral.

To return to Menzies description of the vegetation along the shores of Toba Inlet; his reference to *Amelanchier* as the medlar, *Mespilus germanica* seems odd in today's context. While both genera are in the *Rosaceae*, the rose family, they are quite unlike each other. The medlar is a fruit, a bit like a russet coloured crabapple to be eaten when dead ripe – some say it has to be half rotten to be palatable. Originally from Asia Minor the medlar is now little grown. It was a popular fruit in Northern Europe one hundred or so years ago. The medlar plant is highly ornamental when trained as an espaliered wall shrub. It has large white flowers and large furry simple leaves on a framework of mahogany brown branches.

Amelanchier on the other hand is a North American genus of several species that are highly ornamental deciduous shrubs or small trees. One from the prairie provinces and central plains states, *Amelanchier canadensis*,[10] the Saskatoon berry, has been selected from the wild and hybridized to yield a delicious small berry for the home garden which is now in commercial production in northwestern Alberta. It is sold fresh or frozen for cobblers and pies. It is a western North American specialty dish served in Alberta hotels as an accompaniment to buffalo (bison) steak.[11]

Amelanchier laevis, the shadblow or shadbush, so named, as it blooms when shad rise in the streams of New England and eastern Canada in early spring, is an ornamental shrub or small tree. The flowers are white, with petals like a witchhazel – ribbon-like, with dark purple berries. The fall colour is light pink and yellow and it is available commercially as an ornamental. There are several regional

Menzies found the huckleberry, *Vaccinium parvifolium*, above, in many places along the coast. He probably found *V. cæspitosum*, shown below, on his climb up Redondo Island's Nipple Mountain.
Both by BCN/HFBC

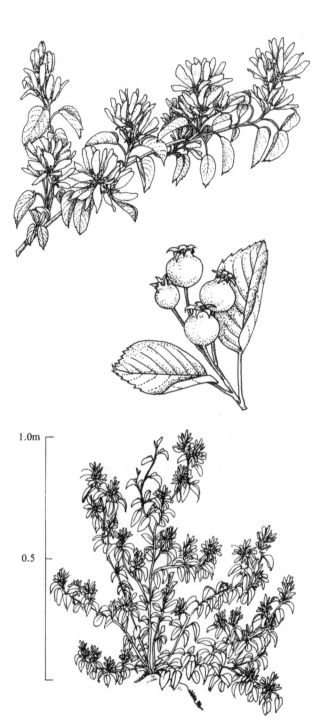

Pacific Saskatoon berry, *Amelanchier alnifolia*, branch in flower, fruit and leaves and the form of the plant, a medium sized shrub. LB/Davidsonia

variants of *A. laevis* in various parts of eastern North America.

The western alder-leaved Saskatoon berry that Menzies called a medlar is a distinct species with a range from the Pacific Ocean to the Rocky mountains. This shrub or small tree has a broad occurrence in a wide range of climates, showing a tolerance from mild heavy rainfall areas on the coast to the cold dry areas of the interior. In these dry areas it is valued for its intense yellow fall colour. A selection of *Amelanchier alnifolia* var *cucksickii* has been introduced as a garden plant by the Botanical Gardens Plant Introduction Scheme of the University of British Columbia.[12]

It is a narrow upright small tree, perhaps an alternative to the narrow upright oriental flowering cherry, *Prunus serrulata* var. 'Amanogawa', where this more floriferous but ungainly small version of a Lombardy poplar is not hardy. However the flowers of *Amelanchier*, unlike amanogawa cherry's double ice cream pink pompoms, are single, white, fertile and unfortunately very fleeting in early spring.

A double flowered *Amelanchier* would be a boon to the gardens of the colder areas (Hardiness Zones 2 and 3) in North America.

On 28 June 1792 when Menzies noted it growing along Toba Inlet's shores, *Amelanchier* would have had ripe berries. They are a favourite food of the black bear. That night they all slept on board the boats for fear of encountering not a black bear but another attack of fleas. The next night they camped on a rocky island with no vegetation, before returning to the *Discovery* on 30 June.

Menzies describes the various channels and inlets they ventured into around Toba Inlet:

"The shores in general were steep and rocky and indented forming in many places high perpendicular precipice[s] with a scarcely a sandy cover to be met with. The sides of the mountains which were high & broken with immense rocks and precipices were mostly covered with tall Pines [Douglas fir, hemlock, Thuja etc.], except their upper region which was chequered with snow and everywhere presented a dreary and gloomy aspect especially amongst the continental mountain where the Veg-

etable Creation became scanty & stinted and where lifeless tracks of huge lofty Rocks prevailed forming mountains of Immense elevation."[13]

So much for the sublime non pastoral landscape of the spectacular forest and mountain fjords of coastline British Columbia that is now so much a part of the Inland Passage cruise ship experience.

Menzies notes that Johnstone with the two other boats returned to *Discovery* the day after their return from Toba Inlet. Johnstone had been up the larger Bute Inlet which goes to the base of the south face of British Columbia's highest mountain, Mount Waddington. This mountain was named for Alfred Waddington, who conceived the idea of constructing a wagon road from the head of Bute Inlet to Fort Alexandria. He also promoted it as a railroad route. In the pursuit of the wagon road he lost almost all his fortune on the venture along with his crew and equipment when the Chilcotin Indians attacked and massacred his roadmakers on 30 April 1864.

The Canadian Pacific Railway surveyed his route but chose the Fraser River route to tidewater instead. Vancouver didn't get to name this mountain because it was one of the least obvious of the mountains of British Columbia, being almost lost or enclosed in a complex of magnificent peaks and valleys. Because these prominences and depressions extend steeply right to the sea forming a wall, and there is little or no foreground, Mt. Waddington cannot be easily distinguished from the hundreds of other peaks that surround it. This is unlike Mt. Baker, Mt. Rainier and the Olympic Range that stand isolated and enjoy the foreground of the flat Fraser River delta or the waters of Georgia Strait or Puget Sound to display their eminence.

Back in *Discovery*, day trips took Menzies to islands and coves in and about Redondo Island one of which he describes:

"In this journey the Genus Pyrola was enriched with four new Species which I met with no where else and on top of the Hill. I found two new Species of Penstemon, a new Species of Rubious, [This is a misspelling of *Rubus*, the salmonberry; it was not a new raspberry but the same one he had

Menzies missed collecting this common coastal, very early blooming shrub called Indian plum or oso-Berry, *Osmoronia cerasiformis*. JRJ/VPPNW

Bog rosemary, *Andromeda polifolia*, above, LB/Davidsonia.
Pyrola picta ,the white-veined wintergreen, left, and
P. secunda, the one-sided wintergreen, right.
Both BCN/HFBC

found in Puget Sound.] *Andromeda coerulea* [now
A. polifolia, the bog rosemary], *Pinus strobus* [west-
ern white pine, *P. monticola*], *and Pinus inops*,
[shore pine, *Pinus contorta* var *contorta*]... *and a
great variety of Cryptogamic Plants* [ferns and
mosses], *besides many other undescribed plants
which I had before met with in other parts of the
country.*"[14]

The genus *Pyrola* is in the *Pyrolaceae* or
Wintergreen family, with flowers usually on a single
stem from a basal group of fleshy leaves spreading
by slender rhizomes; it has pale pinkish and greenish flowers, five petals, with prominent style and
anthers. They are found under the shade of conifers. If it were not for the five petalled flowers,
pyrola could be confused with many of the ground
orchids occupying some of the same habitats.[15]

Newcombe lists Menzies' four pyrolas as *P.
aphylla, P. dentata, P. picta* & *P. secunda*, but he
indicates collection by Menzies in places other than
Redondo Island. The Pyrolas have a wide-spread
Pacific Northwest occurrence so Menzies could have
found them at various places along the coast.
Hitchcock classifies *P. aphylla* as a variant of *P. picta*.
Surprisingly, all the wintergreens are credited to
Menzies as first discovery.

Newcombe also credits Menzies with three
penstemons, *P. diffusus, P. menziesii* and *P. scouleri*.
Here is a genus of small shrubs and shrublets in
the *Scrophulariaceae* with pink or purple and white
tubular flowers with a three-parted lower lip that
are among some of the most sought after plants
for the rockery by rock and alpine garden enthusiasts. The penstemons or beardtongues number well
over 200 species and most are from western North
America. Lewis Clark describes and pictures a
dozen found in the Pacific Northwest.

The new species of *Ribes* that Menzies
found on Redondo's Nipple Summit was probably
Ribes laxiflorum, a gooseberry rather than a currant as it has purplish black berries that are bristly. The flowering currant of the Pacific Northwest, *Ribes sangineum* is one that made it big in
ornamental horticulture. There are two other *Ribes*
that Menzies discovered, one species that bears
his name, (given by Pursh) is *R. menziesii* and the

Californian *R. speciosum*. The former namesake is classed as a gooseberry; it has neither ornamental value nor is the berry palatable.

The bog rosemary, *Andromeda polifolia* that Menzies collected is very similar to another bog plant, *Kalmia polifolia*, the swamp laurel. The relationship between these plants is not only that they share the same habitat, bogs and swamps in the Pacific Northwest, but also a common heritage. As Lewis Clark notes: the genus name *Andromeda* was given by Linnaeus, as he observed the plant in the bogs of his native Norway *"is always fixed on some little turfy hillock in the midst of the swamps, as Andromeda herself was chained to a rock in the sea which bathed her feet as the fresh water does the roots of the plant."* Botanists are the best and the worst of romantics with their plant descriptions!

Kalmia honours Peter Kalm who was the first student and disciple of Linnaeus. The great 'classifier of Nature' named this purely North American genus of ericaceous plants after his student. The flowers of kalmia are unique; the anthers are bent back into pits in the petals so when a bee or insect lands on or disturbs the flower, they spring out, showering the intruder with pollen so it can carry it to fertilize the next flower visited.

The two true pines that Menzies collected are the only two of this genus of conifers to occur along and near the coast and islands of the Pacific Northwest. The western white pine, *Pinus monticola* is one of two five-needle pines in the Pacific Northwest while the two-needle shore pine, *P. contorta* var *contorta*, is the coastal form of the lodgepole pine.

Menzies collected many non-flowering varieties of cryptogamic plants, though probably not all from Redondo Island. They include a clubmoss, *Lycopodium complanatum*, several ferns, two of which made it into ornamental horticulture, *Polystichum munitum,* the western sword fern and *Blechnum spicant*, the deer fern, and sixteen mosses. Two moss species which bear his name are *Leucolepis menziesii* and *Metaneckera menziesii*.[16]

Menzies last journal entry at the Teakerne Arm anchorage of *Discovery* and *Chatham* reads:

The gooseberry, *Ribes laxiflorum*, above. JRJ/VPPNW swamp laurel, *Kalmia polifolia*, below. BCN/HFBC

10 cm.

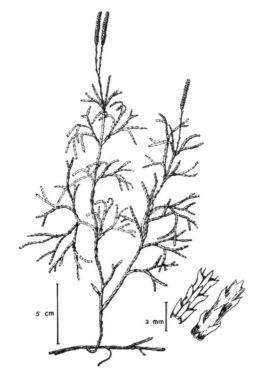

"*North East of the Ship there was a beautiful Waterfall which issued from a Lake close behind it & precipitated a wide foaming into the Sea over a shelving rocky precipice of about thirty yards high, its wild romantic appearance aided by its rugged situation & the gloomy forests which surrounded it, rendered it a place of resort for small parties to visit during our stay.*"[17]

The ideal, sublime and picturesque landscape of Uvedale Price and Horace Walpole described!

Menzies the botanist continues:

"*On the Banks of this Lake I found the Following Plants: Linneae borealis, Myrica gale, Anthericum caclyculatum, Drosera rotundifolia, Menyanthes trifoliata, Shanus albus, [Rynchospora alba] & in the Lake itself we found some Bivalve Shells which were quite new to me. It appeared to be very deep & its sides strewd with a great number of fallen trees.*"

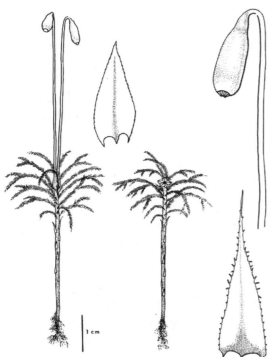

The clubmoss, *Lycopodium complanatum,* above left, the moss, *Leucolepsis menziesii,* below left. Both PDB/SMBC

Above: *Linnae borealis*, the twinflower, after Hulten.

— 65 —

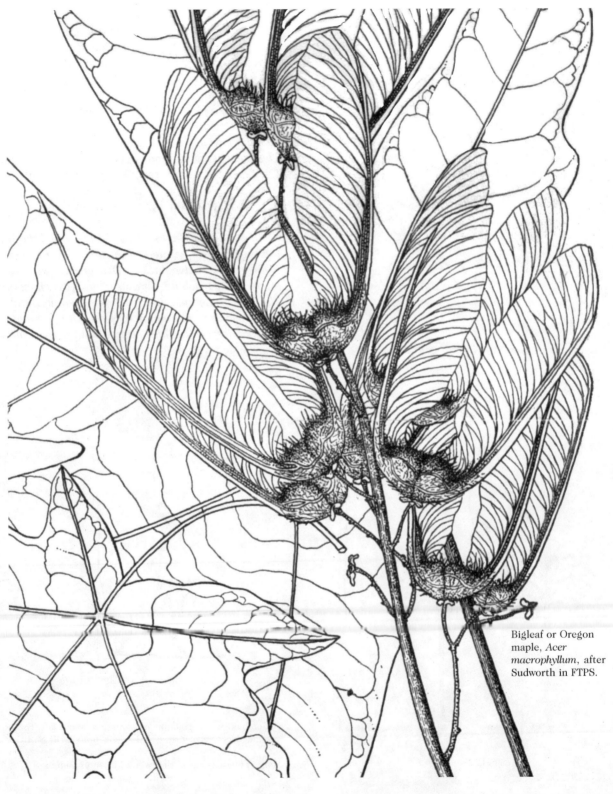

Bigleaf or Oregon maple, *Acer macrophyllum*, after Sudworth in FTPS.

6

FROM MENZIES BAY TO MENZIES POINT

The morning of 13 July 1792 we *"quitted our situation in Desolation Reach* [Desolation Sound] *which was in Latitude 50° 11´ North and Longitude 235° 21´ East from Greenwich...with a fresh breeze from the Westward with which both vessels weighed and made sail leaving the two Spanish vessels behind at anchor after taking a cordial leave of our new friends with whom we now parted but first steered to the South East for about two leagues and then hauld over between the Islands to the South West Ward till we came to the entrance of the channel where we anchord in the afternoon and Mr. Puget and Mr. Whidbey were immediately dispatched with 2 boats to prosecute their examination of it and ascertain whether it was a navigable passage for the Vessels into Johnstone's Streights."*[1]

Longitude East or West of Greenwich was determined by the map-maker, and was also generally established by the direction in which the voyage was made. Practice today is to show longitude east or west of Greenwich to 180°, so the 235° 21´ East bearing of Desolation Sound in Menzies time becomes 123° 38´ West longitude on today's maps & charts.

The anchorage Vancouver's ships reached was a half mile to the northward of Cape Mudge on Quadra Island in Discovery Passage[2] and across the narrow waters of the passage from the present town of Campbell River. Vancouver gave the name of Cape Mudge[3] to the headlands at the southern and westerly end of Quadra Island.

They came ashore at Tsqulotin (now called Yaculta), then a Salish village of 350 inhabitants with 18 canoes on the beach. Menzies notes *"The women were decently covered with garments made of the skins of Wild animals or wove from wool or prepared bark of the American Arber Vitae* [Thuja plicata] *tree."* He also describes the canoes that were also made from this tree, *"Their canoes were small with projecting prows and dug out of one piece of Timber each with four or five small thorts* [thwarts] *and some of them had their outside ornamented with rude figures painted with red ochre. Their paddles were short with round handles & painted blades."*[4] The Salish paddle has a slightly pinched waist and a spatulate- shaped blade. The

canoe lacks the high bow and thwarts of the Haida canoe as it was used mostly in the calm sheltered waters between Vancouver Island, the Olympic Peninsula, Mainland British Columbia and Washington State.[5]

Behind the Quadra Island village Menzies found a dense forest of pine trees. As we now know they were not pines but most likely Douglas fir, *Pseudotsuga menziesii.* He also found the American Cockspur Thorn *Crataegus brevispina,* now *C. douglasii.* This hawthorn or maytree has the common name of the black haw. It is a nondescript small tree with white flowers and black fruits that does not compare favourably with many fine Eastern North American species or the English introduced *C. oxycantha (laevigata),* or the deep pink flowered hybrid *C. oxycantha* Paul's Scarlet. The English maytree has now become naturalized in the Pacific Northwest. The berry of the native hawthorne is, however, a fine food for birds.

On the morning of 14 July they anchored in Menzies Bay having proceeded up Discovery Passage on an ebb tide. Menzies Bay is a uncommon type of bay or estuary along the British Columbia coastline. Richard E. Thomson in *Oceanography of the British Columbia Coast*, writes: *"There are basically two types of estuaries* [the first] *like the Fraser River downstream of Deas Island, where river runoff is large and little mixing takes place between the fresh water above and salt water below; and* [the second] *partially mixed estuaries, typical of most inlets and sounds where there is enhanced mixing between the two layers because of greater tidal action and lower runoff. A third* [hybrid] *category, well mixed estuaries, where strong tidal currents combine with low runoff to produce water that is nearly homogeneous from top to bottom...They are limited to small bays close to turbulent tidal passes such as Menzies Bay near Seymour Narrows."*[6]

Although 14 July was the third anniversary of the storming of the Bastille in Paris, the French Revolution was looked upon with much suspicion and disfavour by the English of all classes but most particularly by the British Navy. The day would have warranted little attention in this regard.

The writer's first experience with the arrogance of the French aristocracy came on viewing the garden of the Sun King (Louis XIV) at Versailles, where ordered and rigid parterres, axes, avenues, forests, sculptured figures and spaces were intentionally scaled, throughout the grounds, to make the human being seem and feel like an insignificant ant. If there was this type of intellectual and artistic oppression there must have been other types of oppression. The realization of this intellectual oppression struck home with a walk in the garden in the mild 1950s. It came as an awakening that no amount of reading or knowledge of historical events could have given. Here in the Versailles Palace grounds, were the clearly visible reasons as to why there had been a French Revolution![7]

Menzies penstemon, *Penstemon davidsonia* var *menziesii*, above, and Davidson' penstemon, *P. d. var davidsonia*. Both JRJ/VPPNW

Menzies went ashore from the anchorage in 'his' Bay with Vancouver and some of the gentlemen who made astronomical observations while he botanized: *"which I found here exceedingly barren*

Tidal flow through Seymour Narrows on a rising tide. Note the peaks of Ripple Rocks removed in 1955. After Thomson.

and met nothing new except a species of Penstemon", probably Menzies Beardstongue *Penstemon menziesii* now *P. davidsonii* var *menziesii*. This perennial forms dense mats of creeping woody stems; flowers are blue lavender to purple violet. Lewis Clark's description of this plant is: *"The common colour of is blue lavender though good pink forms are occasionally seen . . . also a beautiful white variant, forma ALBA... [it] forms dense evergreen mats on broken rock... This very beautiful rock plant blooms soon after the snow melts and continues till it falls again, often in September."*[8]

Selected darker flower colour forms that are very compact in habit are highly valued rock garden plants in Europe as well as locally.

As is often true the smallest of plants often cause the botanists the most trouble. This penstemon was named originally for Menzies, as Hitchcock notes: *"The name Penstemon menziesii, Hook, is illegitimate under the Rules of Nomenclature. Since as defined by Hooker, it (the rules that is) included the type of the earlier Gerardia fruiticosa by Pursh. He should therefore have adopted the epithet fruiticosus for his species."* Even the greatest of the botanists, which Sir William certainly was, make mistakes and are brought to task for it, one hundred years on.[9]

The robust form of *P. davidsonii* bears the sub species name *menziesii* and is chiefly found at low elevations. The epithet *davidsonii* honours John Davidson, who in 1916 established the botanical garden at the new campus of the University of British Columbia, on Point Grey.

It took *Discovery* and *Chatham* three days, from July 15th to July 18th to make it through Seymour Narrows from Discovery Passage and on into Johnstone Straits. Anchoring at night and moving with the morning ebb-tide, Menzies reported *"There was little wind – The Passage is everywhere quite narrow."*[10] It is less than one third of a mile, hardly a distance suitable for tacking against the usual summer north-westerly and northerly winds.

Mr. Johnstone had found the east end of his 'Streights' while *Discovery* and *Chatham* were anchored in Desolation Sound but the route through Lewis Channel, navigable for the smaller Spanish ships *Sutil* and *Mexicana*, was too narrow and dangerous for Vancouver's ships. Lewis Channel between Cortez and West Redondo Islands turns northwestward into Calm Channel along the northeast of Read Island. There is smooth sailing if you round Johnstone Bluff to enter Bute Inlet but should you wish to reach 'Mr. Johnstone's Straits' you must navigate the intricacies of Cardero Channel with its mid channel islets and narrows, where strong tide races and rapids occur during ebb and flow of the two-fathom-plus tides.

Once through Cardero Channel you round the top of the triangular Sonora Island and enter Nodales Channel with a southeast heading centred on Chatham Point at the west end of Johnstone Strait. This much longer and more circuitous zig-zag route has many hazards compared to the more westerly Discovery Passage – Seymour Narrows route, between Quadra and Vancouver Islands that link Georgia Strait to Johnstone Strait.

Until 1958, there was a major threat to navigation called Ripple Rock, located in mid channel at the narrowest part of Seymour Narrows. The removal of Ripple Rock rid the narrows of the only dangerous hazard that had long plagued this only channel navigable for large ships between the waters of Johnstone and Georgia Straits. There had been several previous attempts to remove the two pinnacles of rock in the narrowest part of the channel by placing explosives on them but it was not until the explosive charges were placed up and inside the peaks from a tunnel drilled under the channel from Quadra Island that the two peaks were finally removed. The explosion that did away with this navigational hazard occurred at 9:31 am on 5 April 1958, blowing rock over 800 feet into the air. This big bang event was one of the first ever live telecasts by the Canadian Broadcasting Corporation from a remote broadcast location.[11]

Today it takes about two hours to travel the distance from Cape Mudge to Point Chatham against wind and two to three knot currents.

The Dogleg around Chatham Point into Johnstone Strait from Discovery Passage, the only large ship channel in and out of the north end of Georgia Strait.

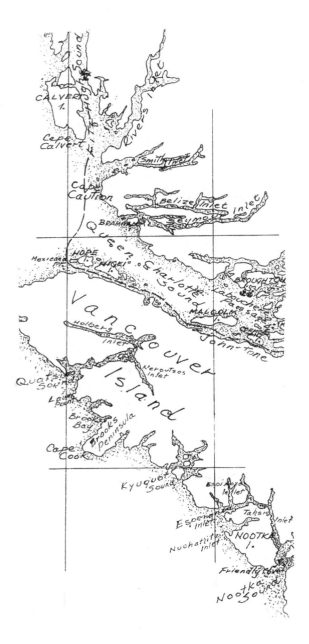

Queen Charlotte Strait, (Sound)
"a lake strewn with Islands."

In 1792 on reaching Johnstone's Straits, Menzies describes this spectacular landscape – seascape of Vancouver Island mountains and the mainland islands with their bristly outlines that occur along this narrow east-west waterway: *"The South side [Vancouver Island], rose in most places abruptly into high steep broken mountains covered with a continued forest of Pines to their summit when in some places with patches of snow."* Snow usually leaves these Vancouver Island mountains by the middle of August so Menzies caught the view just as the snow was disappearing. It is only from further down Georgia Straight at Parksville – Comox that you can see the perpetual snow covered Central Vancouver Island mountain peaks such as Moyeha and Golden Hind in Strathcona Provincial Park. Menzies continues describing the north side: *"The land on the Northside tho' hilly is of moderate height, the great chain of high continental Mountains being five or six leagues removed and extended to the North westward with elevated rugged snowy summits apparently forming everywhere an impenetrable barrier to any communication with the opposite side of the continent."*[12]

A number of islands hang like ships' hammocks between Johnstone Straits and the west end of Queen Charlotte Sound. Vancouver chose a route between these islands to enter the sound, past Hanson, Harbledown, West Caecroft, Swanson and several smaller islands, instead of hugging the Vancouver Island shore and sailing through Broughton Strait between the shore and Malcolm Island. *Discovery* and *Chatham* entered upon a wide stretch of water, an inland 'lake' strewn with groups of small islands.

To the west, Queen Charlotte Sound opened into Hecate Strait and the full force of the Pacific Ocean across the gap between Vancouver Island's Cape Scott and the Queen Charlotte's Islands' Cape Saint James. This latter point on the southern tip of Knight's Island, while the mildest spot in Canada, is also the windiest with gales reaching 120 knots regularly. Cape Saint James was named by Captain George Dixon of the *Queen Charlotte* when on 25 July 1787 he rounded this promontory, from west to east. It was St. James' day. Cape Scott was named a year earlier by the sea otter fur traders Henry Laurie and John Guise after their backer James Scott, merchant of Bombay.[13] Today in spite of these obscure origins they are very important navigational points, and both have lighthouses that define a totally Canadian, wide midpoint access to BC's inner coastline. Juan de Fuca Straits in the south and Dixon Entrance in the north are both shared with the United States.

At the east end and along the north shore of this 'lake of islands', there is a maze of channels and passages between islands that eventually lead into Knight inlet and Lougborough Sound.

On 20 July *Discovery* and *Chatham* anchored at the east end of Hanson Island before proceeding across to Fife Channel. Next morning Menzies went ashore to botanize but the densely forested islands, "...*afforded but little variety of soil or situation for Botanical researches that I made but few aquisitions during our stay at this point. Two new species of Vaccinium was pretty common in the woods and grew upward of 12 ft. high – The one had large black berries [Vaccinium ovalifolium], and the other Red [V. parvifolium], which were now beginning to ripen and as they possessed a grateful acidity we found them extremely pleasant and palatable after being so long on salt provisions. The only other which the woods at this time afforded us was a new species of Rasberry [Rubus spectabilis] that grew at least 10 feet high, and which there were two varieties, one with large red fruit and the other with a yellow that were both equally grateful and pleasant but were not met with in any great abundance.[14] These fruits with a daily supply of spruce beer greatly assisted to correct the bad tendency [of] our present mode of living. I have also met with the Menziesia ferruginea which I had not observed in any part of our more interior navigation or in new Georgia.[15] Hence it is very probably that this rare plant is only to be found toward the outer skirts of the Coast.*"

This latter observation by Menzies is not true as *Menziesia ferruginea* is neither rare or confined to the coast. It ranges as far inland in lower British Columbia as the Fraser river canyon at Yale and from the head of Howe Sound into the Pemberton Valley and Harrison Lake. This is certainly not the 'outer skirts' of the coast.

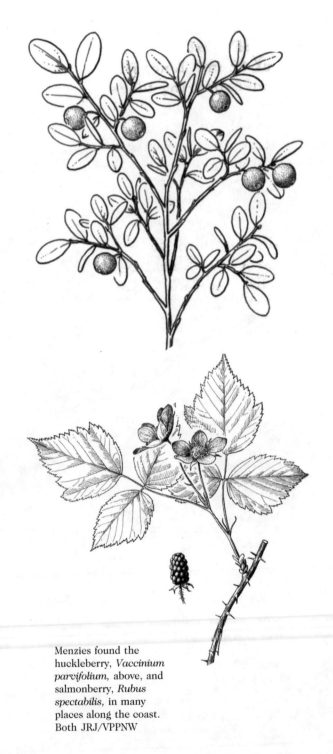

Menzies found the huckleberry, *Vaccinium parvifolium,* above, and salmonberry, *Rubus spectabilis,* in many places along the coast. Both JRJ/VPPNW

The chief ingredient of spruce beer, western hemlock, *Tsuga heterophylla*. LB/Davidsonia

From 21 July to 5 August pinnace, cutter and launches explored the intricate network of islands and passages east and north that Vancouver named Broughton's Archipelago, honouring his captain of the *Chatham*. The archipelago, although no longer referred to as such, consisted of the two large islands named Broughton and North Broughton on the north side of Fife Channel with a myriad of smaller islands: Eden, Baker, Rees, Davies and Insect Islands that form pieces of a puzzle of channels at the mouths of Knight and Rivers Inlets. Menzies did not accompany the exploration and mapping of Knight, Loughborough and other inlets of the archipelago but stayed with *Discovery* at the anchorage in Fife Passage.

Loughborough Inlet was named by Vancouver in 1792 after Alexander Wedderburn, first lord Loughborough and later first Earl of Rosslyn. He was appointed Lord High Chancellor of England, and served from 1793–1805. Fife Sound also named by Vancouver after James Duff, second Earl of Fife, Scottish landowner and improver, who twice won a gold medal from the 'Society for the Encouragement of Arts, Manufactures and Commerce.'

Knight Inlet, explored by Broughton, was named by him after Captain John Knight, R.N., afterwards Admiral Sir John Knight. Knight and Broughton were prisoners together during the War of Independence in early 1776 when they were captured trying to destroy an American sloop they had driven aground in Cape Anne Harbour, Mass. They were exchanged later that year.[16]

As we already know, it was at the Fife anchorage that Menzies was called ashore to Broughton Island as the brewers reported: *"None of that particular spruce on which they used to Brew* [was] *to be found near the landing place, on which I recommended another species, Pinus Canadensis, which answered equally well and made a Salubrious and palatable Beer."*

On 5 August, *Discovery* and *Chatham* had tacked along the north side and sailed into the island and rock strewn neck of Queen Charlotte Sound. Menzies describes the scene: *"The Great Northwest range of high mountains was not now far removed from us. Their summits were covered* with snow and their sides everywhere wooded with a continued forest of Pines down to the shore of the sound which appeared bleak and rocky."[17] This wall and roof of mountains that Menzies saw begins with Mount Waddington (3994m) in the southeast, includes Monarch Mountain,(3533m), Tachako Mountain, Stupendous Mountain with Mount Saugstad to the west in front of it, then Kalone Peak, Tsaydaychuz Peak (2769m) and ending in the northwest as a roof should, with a mountain named Gable.

The next day among these numerous islands, *Discovery* ran aground on some rocks. As the tide ebbed the ship heeled over to starboard so that the angle of the deck would not permit anyone to stand on it. They jettisoned some 17 tons of water, deck wood and ballast. With *Chatham* standing by, *Discovery* righted and floated at two in the morning on the high tide with little wind and a thick fog. They retrieved the deck wood and the masts they had used to shore up the starboard side. They anchored away from the rocks until the weather cleared and a wind allowed them to proceed northward. Menzies went ahead with Mr. Whidbey in the pinnace to find the best channel, only to look back and see the *Chatham* send up distress signals. She too had grounded on rocks on an ebb-tide and had to wait until the tide rose to float off.

From 6 August to 10 August the boats spent the time charting and sounding the myriad of islands and rocks across the entrance to Queen Charlotte Sound.

The number of these islands that grounded both ships, estimated to be in the thousands, preclude Queen Charlotte Straits as a major navigational route for any but vessels of the shallowest draft. To find a safe anchorage they hugged the eastern shore, passing Smith's Inlet until they reached the comparative safety of Fitzhugh Sound. This was named by James Hanna of the *Sea Otter* in 1786, and adopted by Vancouver. It lies between Calvert Island and the mainland. Their anchorage was a small cove called Duncan's Port Safety on the seaside of the island. While Mr. Whidbey and Mr. Puget with launch and cutter embarked back to Smith Inlet and the east shore of Queen Char-

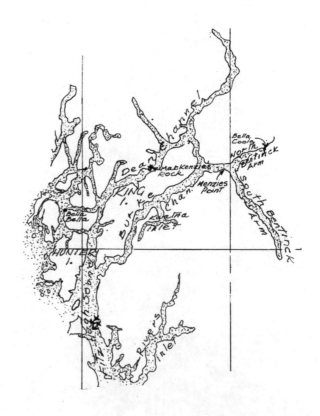

Anchors in Fitzhugh Sound locate the last charting and botanizing anchorage on the B.C. coast for 1792. *Discovery and Chatham's* anchorage for 11 to 18 August. South Bentinck arm was the farthest point reached by Menzies and the chart makers in the ship's boats in 1792. A year later, and only five weeks after Menzies was back in this area, Alexander Mackenzie came overland, down North Bentinck Arm and over to a rock on the north side of Dean Channel.

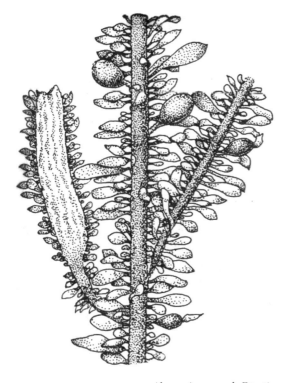

Above: A seaweed, *Egregia
(Phyllomara) menziesii.*
After LBR in *Common
Seaweeds of B.C.*
Below: Red osier dogwood,
Cornus stolonifera.
JRJ/VPPNW

lotte Sound, Menzies accompanied Johnstone on the exploration to the head of Fitzhugh Sound *"as his excursion seemed to offer a more interesting field for Botanical research."*[18]

It was 11 August when they left *Discovery* and *Chatham* at the anchorage in Port Safety. Opposite Hunter Island, Fitzhugh Sound is split by King Island with Fisher Channel on the port and Burke Channel to starboard; Menzies recounts that Burke Channel begins eight or nine leagues from the entrance to Fitzhugh Sound. The actual length is just under twelve leagues. As they entered Burke Channel a thick fog descended, with heavy rain. The next morning, 14 August, *"...had a dark gloomy unsettled appearance* [so] *we commenced our operations pretty early by first landing on the barren point we had passed so late on the preceding evening to take bearings. Here I first met on this Coast with, Empetrum nigrum, Cornus Suecica* [now *Cornus stolonifera*], *Rhodiala rosea* [now *Sedum roseum*], *and besides a new dwarf species of Vaccinium* [Now either: *V. oxycoccus,* the wild cranberry or *V. uglinosum,* the bog blueberry.]*"*

The day before he had found a blackcurrant, (probably *Ribes laxiflorum*); he found raspberries again – *Rubus spectabilis,* the Salmonberry, *"here abundant, along with red and black Whortleberries, Vaccinium parvifolium and V. ovalifolium,"* and also the false azalea and namesake, *Menziesia ferruginea.*

The crowberry, *Empetrum nigrum* is a polar species in the genus *Empetraceae* (Em = upon; petras = rock; negrum = black) in reference to the berries, which are palatable. The leaves are needle-like with a deep groove on the underside.

While there are perhaps ten species of Sedum found along the Pacific Northwest coastal areas, out of the 450 or so species in the north temperate zone, Menzies found only two. Earlier on the San Juans he found one of the three species indigenous to those islands, *Sedum spathifolium, S. oregonum* or *S. olivergens.* Here in Burke Channel he found *S. roseum.* It is a circumpolar species, so the one he found is now given the epithet *S. roseum var integrifolium.*

Plagued with thick foggy weather they entered Kwatna Inlet then on up Burke Channel passing by Labouchere Channel and turning into South Bentinck Arm.[19] Across Burke Channel and about four and a half miles from Labouchere Channel, is Menzies Point. Labouchere Channel was named after the Hudson's Bay Company paddle-wheel steamer *Labouchere*; the first steamer to arrive at the Fraser River Queensborough dock in New Westminster in 1859. The ship was named for the Right Honourable Henry Labouchere, Secretary of State for the Colonies, 1855–58. The channel was used by Alexander Mackenzie just a year later (1793) to reach Dean Channel on his way from Bella Coola to a point near Elcho Harbour.[20] At this namesake mainland feature Menzies was south by only a degree of latitude and little more than two degrees east of Banks Island which he had visited on the *Prince of Wales* some 5 years earlier. As we know he had named this island for his patron, Sir Joseph Banks.

Sailing around Menzies Point into South Bentinck Arm by hugging the south shore they passed by North Bentinck Arm. At the head of this inlet was the Indian village of Bella Coola and the beginning of a native trade route, or grease trail, into the interior. Had it not been raining and foggy on their return down South Bentinck Arm to Burke Channel they probably would have charted North Bentinck and found the Indian village. They were also short on food; conditions were bad when they came down Burke Channel to return to *Discovery* anchored at Safety Cove in Fitzhugh Sound, with both swell, wind and current against them. Cold, wet and hungry they spent the night in the open boats, reaching *Discovery* the morning of 18 August.

News had reached Capt. Vancouver via the brig *Bengal* out of Nootka that their storeship, *Daedalus* was at Nootka awaiting their arrival. They heard that the ship's captain, Richard Hergest, and Mr. William Gooch, the astronomer who was to have joined *Discovery,* and a seaman had been massacred by the natives of Woakoo (Oahu), in the Sandwich (Hawaiian) Islands.[22]

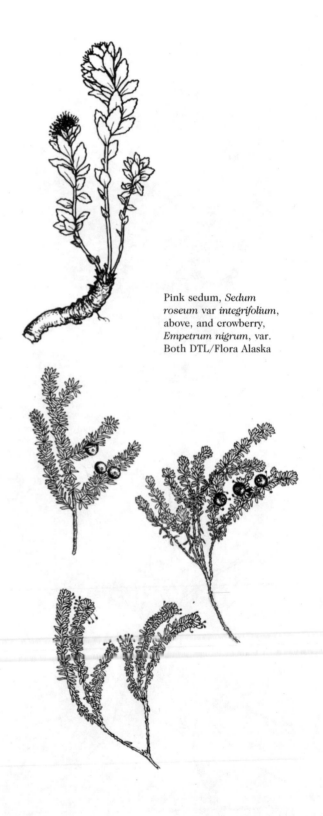

Pink sedum, *Sedum roseum* var *integrifolium*, above, and crowberry, *Empetrum nigrum*, var. Both DTL/Flora Alaska

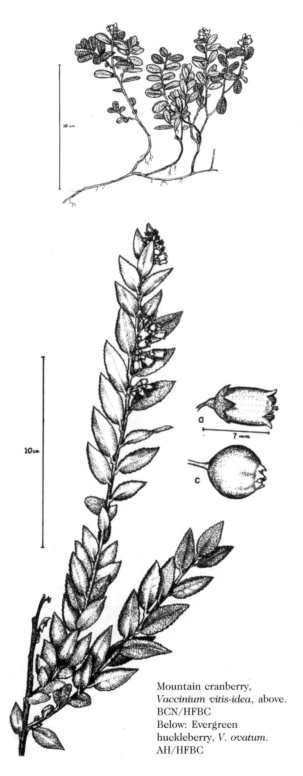

Mountain cranberry,
Vaccinium vitis-idea, above.
BCN/HFBC
Below: Evergreen
huckleberry, *V. ovatum*.
AH/HFBC

As Menzies relates it was time to call a halt for the season and head for Nootka *"for the weather was now become so cold, wet and uncomfortable that the men were no longer able to endure the fatiguing hardships of distant excursions in open boats exposed to the cold rigorous blasts of a high Northern situation with high dreary snowy mountains on everyside, performing toilsome labour on their oars in the day and alternately watching for their own safety at night, with no other couch to repose upon than the cold stony beach or the wet messy Turf in damp woody situations, without having shelter sufficient to screen them from inclemency boisterous weather, and enduring at times the tormenting pangs of both hunger and thirst yet on every occasion struggling who should be most forward in executing the orders of their superiors [to] accomplish the general interest of the voyage."*

Menzies continues, *"In short it is but justice to say that on this arduous service both officers and men were hourly exposed to various hardships and dangers, yet went through the fatiguing operations of the summer without murmur. And if we look back on the different winding channels and armlets which the vessels and boats traversed over in following the continental shore ever since they entered De Fuca's straights, it will readily be allowed that such an intricate and laborious examination could not have been accomplished in so short a time without the cooperating exertions of both men and officers whose greatest pleasure seemed to be in performing their duty with alacrity and encountering the dangers and difficulties incidental to such service with a perserveering intrepidity and manly steadiness that afforded a most pleasing Omen to the Happy issue of our future endeavours in this arduous undertaking."*[23]

Amen to that!

For Menzies, it had not been a bad four months botanizing. It is estimated he made collections of more than 250 different terrestrial plant species including mosses with an additional twenty or so lichens and an equal number of marine algae.

The shore pine, *Pinus contorta* var *contorta*, after Leslie Bohm in *Davidsonia*

7

MENZIES MEETS MOZINO

The first European to discover Friendly Cove was James Cook, in April, 1778. He mentions the incident in his journal: *"Having now finished most of our heavy work, I set out the next morning to take a view of the sound. I first went to the west point, where I found a large village before it a very snug harbour, in which was from nine to four fathoms water over a bottom of fine sand."*[1]

Walbran writes: "[it was] *named Friendly Cove in 1786 by Mr. Strange, Supercargo*[2] *of a trading expedition to this coast, consisting of the snow*[3] *'Captain Cook', Captain Lowrie Master, and the snow 'Experiment', Captain Guise Master."*

"The Indian name of the village is Yuquot or Yucuat, derived from the Indian words, "Yukwitte," to blow with the wind; "Aht," people or village; meaning a village exposed to the winds."

Discovery and *Chatham* reached the Nootka area on 26 August 1792 after 7 days sail from their last anchorage in Burke Channel. That evening it was foggy and raining when they came up on the west entry to Nootka Sound so they stood off for the night and all of the next day. On 28 August the fog did not lift until noon, delaying their entry so that *Discovery* didn't drop anchor until four in the afternoon; Chatham had preceded her by two hours.

Menzies described what he saw through the drizzling rain as they approached Nootka, *"the hazy weather...entirely obscured the inland mountains from our view, we could however observe that those nearest to us rose with an easy and gradual acclivity and were skirted along shore with a fine extended level border of Land where the luxuriant appearance of the Forest sufficiently indicated the fertility & richness of the soil. These mountains were separated by wide intervening valleys densely wooded up the sides of the mountains as the eye could discern."*[4]

On passing the Spanish fort, *Discovery* saluted it with thirteen guns, and the salute was returned from Commander Juan Francisco Bodega y Quadra's flagship *Activa*. Menzies comments: *"This Fort, if it might be called such, was no other than two guns mounted on a small platform on the outer point of the Cove, with a Flag staff on which Spanish colours were hoisted & a small guard mounted to give it the appearance of a place of defence."* Menzies continues to describe the setting of the settlement: *"The situation of the village is up on a rising neck of land which with Friendly Cove & the Shipping right before it and behind it a high beach washd by the rude surges of the open ocean & along the Verge of its bank a pleasing path was found for walking where mind could contemplate at ease the fretted wildness of the briny element foaming against Rocks & Shores without feeling the force of its fury - while on the other side huge mountains presented themselves covrd to their very summits with a continued forest of Stately Pines whose dark verdurous hue suffused a solitary gloom favorable to meditations."*[5]

This was Menzies second visit to Nootka. It was during this visit with Vancouver that he was pressed into service to act as coroner to investigate the murder of a servant of the Spanish commander Bodega y Quadra.

On matters botanical Menzies had the opportunity to meet with the two Spanish botanists Jose Mozino and Atanasio Escheverria. As Menzies relates: *"They told me that they were part of a Society of Naturalists who were employed of late years in examining Mexico & New Spain for the purpose of collecting materials for a Flora Mexicana, which they said would soon be published, and with the assistance of so good an artist must be a valuable aquisition."*[6] They were not botanists in today's meaning of the term. Jose Mozino was much more a naturalist, collecting plants, animals and fish, and in addition he was an ethnographer. Escheverria on the other hand was a *"Natural History Painter of great merit,"* to quote Menzies. While Mozino and Escheverrea were with the frigate Aranzazu under Jacinto Camano's command, the overall project was under the command of Alessandro Malaspina who had been in Nootka the summer previous in 1791. Menzies commented on this undertaking by the Spanish; *"He [Malaspina] has already examined the shores of South America & this Coast & is now surveying the Philipine Islands - He is to return by Peru & Chili around Cape Horn, to publish the results of his enquiries: so that the Spaniards mean to shake off now entirely that Odium of indolence & Secrecy with which they have been long accused."*[7]

The list of plants collected by Mozino that appears in his book *Noticias de Nutka* includes a number of Californian coastal plants that Mozino presumably collected on his way up to Nootka from Monterey along with those vegetables and weeds he found growing at Nootka. These latter 'exotics' were the result of ten years of occasional occupation of Nootka by British, American and Spanish mariners along with their animals. Mozino listed these plants as he was more interested in how people used plants than the plants themselves, perhaps more so than Menzies, and he gave equal attention to animals, fishes, insects and native customs. To give Menzies credit for more than just botanical interest, of four works published in the learned journals of the day after his return to En-

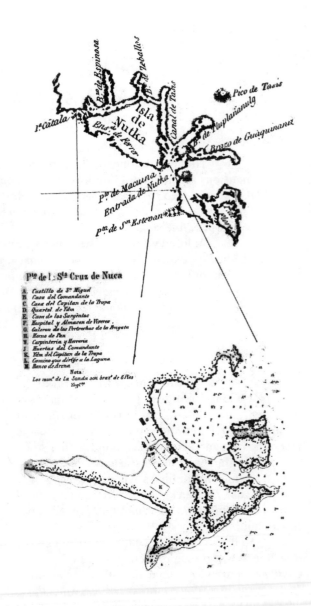

Nootka Island & Friendly Cove (enlarged) with the Spanish settlement of 1792.

Right: Barley, *Hordeum vulgare*, above, the only grain crop that ripened in Spanish Nootka. AH/MGUS
Below: the cabbage, *Brassica oleracea*

gland, two were on sea animals, and one on ferns, while the other is about an ascent of Mauna Lua on the island of Hawaii. Events after his return to England frustrated his great ambition to produce a major botanical work on the non-flowering plants, ferns, mosses and lichens – the Cryptograms.[8]

In *Noticias de Nutka*, Mozino's description of the puberty ceremony for Maquinna's daughter that he and Menzies attended together was sensitive and complete, far superior to Menzies' comments. However, Menzies was a much better botanist and scientist, being a trained surgeon and practitioner in the Linnean binomial system of identifying and classifying plants.

On 28 August Vancouver, Menzies and the other officers paid their respects to Bodega y Quadra at his quarters. Afterwards Menzies had a chance to look around the settlement's buildings, barracks, store houses and hospital along with gardens on the site of the old native village. Of the gardens he writes: *"There were also several spots fenced in,* [goats, sheep & black cattle ran free around the village], *well cropped with the different European garden stuffs, which grew here very luxuriantly, particularly in the places formerly occupied by Habitations of the Natives which by that means had been well manured & not withstanding the advantage of great utility that were thus derived from Horticulture in this Country."*

Menzies continues: *"it seems not one of the natives had yet followed so laudable an example, tho, they were very fond of the productivity of these gardens especially the different kinds of roots when they were brought to the table."* Menzies doesn't tell us what these vegetables and roots were, but we can get some idea from Mozino's list of the plants he found at Nootka.[9] Among the plants Mozino listed were the following European vegetables:

Hordeum vulgare, barley
Capsicum annum, pepper
Solanum tuberosum, potato
Beta vulgaris, beetroot
Daucus carota subsp. *sativus*, carrot
Angelica archangelica, angelica
Pastinaca sativa, parsnip

Apium graveolens, celery
Allium cepa, onion
Brassica napus, rape
Brassica oleracea, cabbage
Lactuca sativa, lettuce
Cicer ariethinum, chick pea
Cynara scolymus, globe artichoke

Along with the potato, Mozino's list includes several other *Solanum* of which one could have been the eggplant, *Solanum melongena* although this plant's preference for warm and dry climates precludes Nootka to some extent as an ideal climate for this vegetable. Nootka has a rainfall average for the six frost free growing months of 58 inches with an average temperature of 54° F, making it a cool wet climate.

These readings for temperature are averages between long term highs and lows for Winter Harbour and Tofino, the two communities with modern weather recording stations nearest to Nootka. Rainfall is the average of monthly totals for Winter Harbour and Tahsis. Winter Harbour is eighty miles north of Nootka while Tofino is forty-seven miles southeast; both are along the northwest coast of Vancouver Island. Tahsis is nineteen miles inland due north up Tahsis Inlet from Nootka.[10]

Menzies observed that *"The Activity & Industry of the Spanish on this remote infant settlement was more than they* [the English] *were led to believe."*[11]

On 1 September *Sutil* and *Mexicana* arrived in the cove at Nootka. Menzies relates: *"We were pleased to see our friends of Desolation Sound, Capt's Galiano and Senor Valdes all well."* They had little time with their friends as the next day the two Spanish ships left for the journey South to Monterey and San Blas.

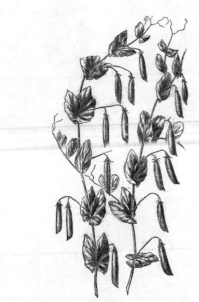

On 4 September an entourage of Spanish and English officers and men led by Quadra and Vancouver, in the *Discovery*'s pinnace and launch along with *Chatham*'s cutter and a large Spanish launch, all went on an excursion, complete with fife and drums, to Tahsis, at the head of the western arm of Nootka Sound. The purpose: an 'offi-

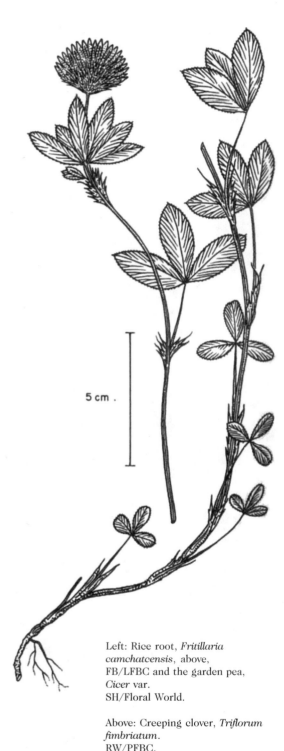

Left: Rice root, *Fritillaria
camchatcensis*, above,
FB/LFBC and the garden pea,
Cicer var.
SH/Floral World.

Above: Creeping clover, *Triflorum
fimbriatum*.
RW/PFBC.
The thread like roots are edible.

5 cm.

cial' visit to Maquinna, the Nootka native chief.

Menzies described the outing: *"We then
pulled along the western shore of the Sound, which
in an eminent degree posessed the general dreary
rocky aspect of the Country & every where coverd
with a forest of Pines down to the Water's edge. We
did not go above two leagues when we put on shore
to breakfast at a small harbour called Maweena,
[Marvinus Bay], & soon after setting out again we
enterd a considerable branch leading to the North
West Ward & winding inland by a deep valley between very high steep mountains. The water was
smooth & the day was uncommonly favorable for
our excursion."*

They delayed their 'official' visit until the
next day, camping for the night at a meadow down
the beach from Maquinna's House. On a part of
the meadow Menzies observed females digging what
he thought at first was *Fritillaria camschatcensis*,
the rice root, but found it to be instead, a species
of clover, *Triflorum fimbriatum* (now *T.
wormskjoldii*), with a creeping root about the size
of a *"pack thread, which they always dig up at this
time of year for food. After washing it clean they
mix it with a quantity of oil & eat it with their Fish
or Animal Food in the same manner as we do
Sallad."*

During the festivities and visit to
Maquinna's long house, Menzies recognized a friend
from his visit to Nootka five years earlier in 1787.
She was the wife of Maquinna's brother and daughter of an elderly chief of the Nootkas. Menzies related: *"She and her sisters were then very young,
yet they frequently shewed so much solicitude for
my safety, that they often warned me in the most
earnest manner of the dangers to which my Botanical rambles in the Woods exposed me & when they
found me inattentive to their entreaties, they would
then watch the avenue of the Forest where I enterd,
to prevent my receiving any insult or ill usage from
their Countrymen. But it was not until after I left
them that I became sensible to how much I owed to
their disinterested zeal for my welfare by knowing
more of the treacheries & stratagems of the natives
on other parts of the coast."*

On 1 October Menzies sent a collection of seeds to England with Zachary Mudge, who took passage on the brig *Fenis* sailing under Portuguese colours and bound for Macao and then on to England with dispatches from Vancouver for the government. The seed collection was addressed to Sir Joseph Banks and was for Kew. Menzies related that: *" I was afterwards happy to find that Mr. Mudge had taken great care in their preservation by which some valuable plants were added to the great collection at his Majestie's Garden, [Kew], through the uncommon skill & Industry of Mr. Acton, in rearing them."* Menzies was referring to either William Aiton, the King's gardener at Kew, or to his son William Townsend Aiton who succeeded the elder William in 1793. There seems to be no record of the plants Aiton, Junior or Senior, raised from the seeds sent to Sir Joseph.

On 12 October, in true botanical tradition, Menzies went on shore to do some last minute collecting to retrieve the *"seeds of several Plants which I had left to ripen on the bushes to the very last moment."* On the morning of the 13 October, Menzies left Nootka Sound bound for a winter in the Sandwich Isles (Hawaii).[12]

His last look at the landscape about Nootka he recorded as follows: *"The land about Point Breakers is everywhere covered with a forest of Pines & is very low for several miles back, it then swells into those huge mountains which form the interior & whose summits were now seen in many places covered with snow apparently fresh laid during the late stormy weather."* The winter of 1792–93 had just begun to settle in on the northwest coast of America.

Flower and foliage of *Banksia menziesii*, a small tree native to western Australia. See map on page 32

MENZIESIA AND OTHER NAMESAKES.

The herbariums that receive a botanist's or a collector's plant specimens, classify these plants and make any corrections to the collector's guesses as to the plant's correct botanical name. These institutions and their taxonomists also select the genus and species under the strict international rules of nomenclature. The plant that you as a collector have found you cannot name after yourself; someone else must do it on your behalf.

Sir Joseph Banks, Sir Joseph Hooker and Sir William Hooker along with other botanists classified and named the plants collected by Menzies. This 'old boys' network of taxonomists gave Menzies a genus of plants in the family Ericaceae, commonly called the false azalea. The one species of this genus he discovered on his first visit to the Pacific Northwest, *Menziesia ferruginea*, is one of seven species. Five occur in Japan, and one in eastern North America. *Menziesii ciliicalyx, M. multiflora*, and its variety *M. multiflora* var *longicalyx* have pink flowers while *M. pentandra, M. pilosa* and *M. purpurea* have bright red flowers with the last, *M. purpurea*, has the species epithet for its flower colour. The lone eastern North American species is *M. pilosa*. It ranges from Pennsylvania into Georgia and Alabama.[1]

The common name false azalea is apt because *Menziesia* has branches and foliage that are look-alikes for its true azalea cousins in the genus *Rhododendron*. Unlike deciduous azaleas, *Menziesia* lacks their large and bright flowers. The blooms on *Menziesia* are tiny urn-shaped cream-coloured flowers. These are like many of the heather family that include such diverse plants as salal, kinnikinnick, manzanita and heather. The flowers of *Menziesia* are insignificant. In addition they are not very easily seen as they are hidden away beneath the leaves. However, false azalea does have fine fall colour and is a great accompaniment to heavy dark green coniferous trees and broad leaf evergreen shrubs both for natural settings and in gardens using native plants. Because of its less than spectacular floral attributes false azalea has never been introduced or sold as a commercial garden plant. It is grown in some Pacific Northwest native plant enthusiasts' gardens.

As if to compensate for this 'insignificant' genus the botanical taxonomists and the classifiers at Kew gave Menzies' name – as species epithets – to some very outstanding trees that he collected. These are *Arbutus menziesii* and *Pseudotsuga menziesii*, both from the westcoast of North America, along with *Nothofagus menziesii* previously mentioned. This latter tree, southern beech, is also from a west coast, that of South Island in New Zealand.[2] All three of these trees are standouts in one or more of their physical and botanical features. In 1791 on the way out to the north coast of America, Menzies had several days of botanizing when *Discovery* put in at what is now Albany, leeward of West Cape Howe on Western Australia's south coast. Captain Vancouver, always mindful of his duty, gave the name of King George Sound to those sheltered waters where he anchored at the west end of the Great Australian Bight. Among Menzies' finds here, were plants in the genus named for his patron Sir Joseph[3], however the *Banksia* which bears his epithet was given by Robert Brown for a medium sized scraggly tree with crumbly bark, typically 3 to 10 metres in height.

Banksia menziesii is indigenous to the coastal plain of Western Australia north and south of Perth. Quoting Alexander S. George, the leading authority on banksia: "B. menziesii is a common component of woodlands and shrublands on deep sandy soils from Kalbarri southwards to Waroona... The flowering period is March–August when the conspicuous flowers attract birds such as the New Holland Honeyeater, Brown Honeyeater, Western Spinebill and Wattlebirds." Menzies banksia has large spectacular reddish pink, sometimes lemon yellow, cones or bottle-brush-like flowers. The leaves are evergreen and strap-like with sawtooth edges and are between six and twelve inches long. The woody fruit or cone requires fire to open it. This is similar in some respects to the much smaller cones of the North American lodgepole pine, Pinus contorta and the closely related jack pine, P. banksiana that also requires fire to open the cones in order to germinate the seeds.

Menzies also botanized in the Hawaiian Islands during the winter of 1792–93 before Discovery returned to Nootka for the conclusion of the Vancouver–Quadra negotiations. He had previously botanized here with Captain Colnett. Hawaii's most stately tree fern bears the Menzies epithet, Cibotium (Dicksonia) menziesii. This name was conferred by Hooker in 1846.

Joseph Rock in his 1913 book The Indigenous Trees of the Hawaiian Islands, describes this component of the Hawaiian forests, particularly on the windward slopes of Mauna Kea, as follows: "The fibrous trunks of these immense ferns have often a diameter of three feet and reach a height of about 24 feet or so, not including the almost erect fronds, which measure occasionally more than 12 feet, giving it a total height of sometimes 36 feet. Thanks to the hardiness [toughness] of these ferns, they were able to withstand attacks from cattle, and even uprooted by wild pigs, and laid prostrate, they continue to grow." Along with tree ferns there is another Hawaiian native tree with the Menzies epithet, Raillardia menziesii, a small tree in the Compositae family with the Hawaiian name naenae tree.

The overhead pattern of a tree fern similar to the Cibotium menziesii, discovered by Menzies in Hawaii, after Piggott.

Right: The occurrence of *Arbutus menziesii*, in dense stands, isolated groves and groups. Showing discovery dates for Pacific Madrone by Archibald Menzies.

There are a number of Abutilons variously called flowering maple or Chinese bellflower from South America that are used as shrubs in frost-free gardens and as house plants in the Pacific Northwest. These plants along with hibiscus and the hollyhocks are in the family *Malvaceae*. The red flower of one species of *Hibiscus sinensis* is claimed by at least three nations as their floral emblem, Hawai, Fiji and Malaysia. The bellflower with the Menzies epithet is one of the Hawaiian Islands' endemic flora.

Menzies collected the Abutilon called Koolaoula on "the Sandwich Islands" giving no specific location but later collectors found it on the islands of Hawaii, Lanai, Ewa and Oahu.[4] However, the Hawaiian plant that was the first to be named an endangered species by the United States government was collected by Menzies on his climb of the island of Hawaii's Mauna Kea. It is the Hawaiian wild broadbean or Hawaiian vetch, a perennial vine in the *Leguminosae* with red flowers. *Vicia menziesii* was given endangered species status in 1978 and the next year was one of four species appearing on the US Postal Service endangered flora stamp issue. It is claimed that there are only several hundred plants in existence. The demise and severe reduction of the numbers was caused principally by loss of habitat.[5]

Aside from the eucalypts of Australia, perhaps no other tree in the north temperate zone is as colourful or as picturesque in its features of colour, form and visual quality when seen in its natural coastal and island habitats than the broadleaf evergreen member of the heather family, the Pacific Madrone, *Arbutus menziesii*.

Menzies first saw this most picturesque of trees on 1 May 1792, when he went ashore with Capt. Vancouver on their second landfall on the north coast of America. The place was Port Discovery at the northwest end of Washington's Olympic Peninsula.[6] However, it was the Spanish priest Fra Juan Crespi in 1758, taking part in a trek up the California Coast from San Diego, who first noted this tree with its peeling red bark, rhododendron-like leaves and orange red berries.

Friar Crespi gave it the name madrone because it resembles very closely the strawberry madrone, *Arbutus unedo*. It is native to Spain and Portugal and is also found native in the counties of Cork, Kerry and Sligo in Ireland. In California it has long been available as an ornamental shrub or small tree ideally suited to hot dry sites & soils. In the winter-wet Pacific Northwest, however, strawberry madrone is at the limit of its suitability and hardiness (USDA Zone 8) to get into the top ten broad-leaved evergreens for Pacific Northwest gardens.

There are four cultivars of this narrowly-serrate-leaved shrubby tree growing to 10 metres: *Arbutus unedo* var *compacta* is more shrub like, while *A. unedo* var *integerrima* has narrow non-serrate leaves, *A. unedo* var *microphylla* has very small leaves and *A. unedo* var *rubra* has deep pink flowers instead of the very pale pink of all the others. In southern Portugal a cottage industry has developed using the fruits of this species to flavour a 45 proof liqueur called Medronhio.

The coat of arms for Spain's capital city, Madrid, has a tree with big red fruits and a big black bear as a centrepiece. The tree is the Strawberry Madrone, *Arbutus unedo*, which, among other places, still grows wild southwest of Madrid in the Sierra de Gaudalupe, east of the town of Madroniera or farther south in the Sierra Moreno on the Sierra Madrona. The big black bears have long disappeared.

Juan Crespi recorded in his journal for 12 July 1758, *"At the end of the day we came upon many Madrone* [arbutus] *but the fruits were smaller than the same species in Spain."*[7] The Spanish liked to keep all their plant and geographical discoveries very secret, so to Menzies goes the credit as the discoverer of this tree, as his was the first description to be published.

Menzies' discovery of *Arbutus menziesii* at the northeast end of the Olympic Peninsula was about eighty miles short of its northern limit, Malaspina Straits on the mainland side and Discovery Passage on the Vancouver Island side, both at the head of Georgia Strait, at about 50° N. Father Crespi twenty three years earlier had found the southern limit at 33° N., just a few miles out of San Diego near the coast at the latitude of Mt. Palomar.

The Canary Island's madroño, *Arbutus canariensis*, above, from a Spanish source and the Southwest US and northern Mexico native *A. xalapensis*, after Sargent in MTNA.

The range of populations of *Arbutus* species: *A. menziesii* 🖌 along the Pacific Coast and the varieties of *A. xalapensis*, var *arizonica* 🍐, from southern Arizona and the SW corner of New Mexico, S into Mexico in the Sierra Madre Occidentale, with var *texana* 🦋 ,in the Chisos Mts on the New Mexico-Texas border, south into western Texas in Big Bend National Park and the slopes of Sierra Madre Orientale including the disjunct occurrence of *A.m. peninsularis* at the tip of Baja California.

There is however, a disjunct occurrence of Pacific madrone at the southern tip of Baja California in Mexico where it is found among oaks at 5000 feet on the slopes and in the arrroyas of Sierra Victoria. It has been given the name (by botanical splitters) *Arbutus menziesii* var *peninsularis*. This occurrence is separated by 700 miles of the narrow Baja peninsula from Juan Crespi's discovery of the species just north of San Diego.

The leaves of Pacific madrone are simple in shape, oval, thick and leathery, dark glossy green on the upper surface, pale grey green on the underside with entire edges. Leaves on seedlings and regenerating shoots from stumps have sharply toothed edges. This juvenile serrated leaf persists for at least three growing seasons. In the Pacific Northwest new growth and leaves appear in late February and early March. When these leaves are mature in July and August all the previous year's leaves turn butter yellow and fall. Menzies' oriental strawberry tree is unlike many other broadleaf evergreens which lose their leaves over a much shorter period of time.

One could argue that this is a very practical response by the madrone to the climate of the Pacific Northwest where there is a surfeit of moisture in soil and air in the early spring while there is an almost complete absence of moisture in soil and air in July and August.

The flowers of Menzies' madrone also appear with the new leaves in early spring, coming in grape-like clusters of creamy white flowers at the ends of the branches. Should conditions be right, each flower will be visited by a honey bee and fertilized to form into a round granular coated orange-scarlet berry. Conditions are only right one out of every four to six years so usually only 10 to 20 percent of the flowers form fruit. In that one year in five or six when the crop is heavy, Pacific madrone is a magnificent sight especially when coupled with branches and trunks that have lost their papery thin red bark to show a smooth olive green new skin. Often there are dead branches on the older trees that have a bleached white appearance adding to arbutus' reputation as the most picturesque of Pacific Northwest trees. It is the most dramatic seen from a boat or on a walk along the shoreline, hanging out over the rocky bluffs and beaches of the islands and channels in Georgia Straits and Puget Sound.

Pacific madrone usually grows 10 to 15 metres in height with an equal or a greater spread, single, straight and multi-trunked, up to one and a half metres in diameter, but usually less than seventy-five cm. Menzies' arbutus requires well-drained porous soils in full sun. It is resentful of summer watering and shade. *Arbutus menziesii* is a pioneer on disturbed mineral soils and logged-over coastal and island Douglas fir forest areas.

In the Pacific Northwest, extensive logging, clearing for housing and highway development in the areas where Pacific Madrone occurs has resulted in opening to full sun many suitable gravelly mineral soil areas and sloping sites that are ideal for this tree. The result has been a quantum increase in the area and numbers of the species in the decades of the sixties, seventies and eighties.

Pacific Madrone seedlings have established themselves in cleared areas on roadside cutbanks thickly enough to produce large blocks or fringes of ground cover; also there are locations where some seedlings continue to grow on into pure stands of an acre or more. If conditions are right, seedling conifers, particularly those of Douglas fir, establish and grow up in among these stands shading out all or most of the arbutus. Since the madrone is intolerant of any shade all or part of a tree will die in competition with Douglas fir.

It is rare to see western arborvitae, Sitka spruce or western hemlock with Pacific madrone but it does occur, with the conifers eventually winning out, primarily because they are more shade and poor drainage tolerant. The native conifers that are more appropriate to use with arbutus are the shore pine, *Pinus contorta* var *contorta* or the western juniper, *Juniperus occidentalis*. Areas where these regeneration and succession processes have occurred within the purview of the author include: northern California on roadside cuts along California State Highway 299, Willow Creek to Weaverville (Trinity Mtns); north on State Highway 3 to Yreka and from Crescent City on US 199 through the Siskiyou Mountains to Grants Pass; in southern Oregon, Interstate 5 from Ashland to Roseburg to Oakland, Oregon; and in Washington State in the Olympic Peninsula, east Puget Sound

Pacific madrone, *Arbutus menziesii*, the only broadleaf evergreen tree indigenous to the southern part of coastal B.C. Foliage and fruit below. LB/Davidsonia

The Douglas fir, *Pseudotsuga menziesii*.
Needles and cone with the unique
trident scale, above. LB/Davidsonia

along US 101 at the Hood Canal area, Port Townsend–Discovery Junction areas and Whidbey Island, Anacortes, San Juan Islands and the Bellingham areas on the west side of Puget Sound.

Areas of significant arbutus regeneration on the British Columbia mainland include suburban housing developments and the Upper Levels Highway from 22nd Street to Horseshoe Bay in West Vancouver, continuing on up the Sechelt Peninsula and across Jervis Inlet to the Powell River area.

Across Georgia Strait on the east coast of Vancouver island there are large increases in stands of Arbutus along the Island Highway from Nanaimo to Nanoose Bay and on to Parksville as well as around housing, resort and recreational developments in and around these communities.

The clearing for recreational housing, logging of the young second growth to pay off the mortgage on many of the larger and smaller of the Gulf Islands, has improved the edges and increased the diversity of the shorelines and roadsides with these colourful and picturesque trees. Visiting or cruising among these islands is an enhanced visual experience, equivalent if not superior to the more advertised and heavily touted, Greek, Caribbean and Indian Ocean islands.

When Menzies first saw *Pseudotsuga menziesii* he called it a spruce or fir, comparing it to the spruce of Nova Scotia, *Picea rubens* or *P. glauca;* the red or white spruce are both important lumber and pulpwood species. Red spruce is so called because twigs and bark are reddish brown, while the bark and twigs of the white spruce are whitish to greyish brown. The former, *Picea rubens,* has a very restricted range: Nova Scotia, New Brunswick, southeastern Quebec and scattered occurrences east of Lake Huron.

Picea glauca, the white spruce and *P. mariana*, the black spruce, are both trees in the boreal forest region extending from Newfoundland, Labrador, Quebec, Ontario, Manitoba, the nonsouthern grassland areas of Saskatchewan and Alberta, north to the timberline in the Northwest Territories and westward into the mountains of Yukon and British Columbia.

Picea sitchensis, the Sitka spruce, is a species confined to coastal areas in the Pacific Northwest, while the other B.C. native spruce, *P. engelmannii*, is confined to the southern Canadian Rockies, interior wetbelt and the alpine areas of the Kootenay, Monashee, Okanagan and Cascade mountains.

With the exception of a selection of the white spruce, *P. glauca Albertina* or *P. glauca Albertina 'Conica'*, a dwarf conifer called the Alberta white spruce, there has been little or no use of these spruce species ornamentally. *Picea pungens,* from the U.S. Rocky Mountains area, has glaucous blue-green foliage, (needles), that have made it a favourite single specimen or paired front lawn planting throughout suburban North America. The bluest and most widely planted is 'Koster' blue. Fortunately or unfortunately, depending on your like or dislike for this striking conifer, in our mild wet Pacific coast environment the tree does not do at all well and is subject to a disease that attacks and kills the older needles.[8]

The Douglas fir honours another Scotsman, Botanist–Collector, David Douglas. In the late 1820s he introduced *Pseudotsuga menziesii* to England and Scotland from seed sent home via various Hudson's Bay Company ships. For many years it was classified as *P. douglasii*, then *P. taxifolia*, (false hemlock with yew-like leaves). David Don had seen and noted Menzies' collection of this tree prior to Douglas's introduction of it. So eventually the rules of nomenclature prevailed, that the name first published was used for the species epithet while Douglas, the one who introduced it to cultivation, getting the common name. All told a fair compromise; however, the botanical nomenclature and common names of many other western North American conifers leaves much to be needed as a rational or objective exercise in botanical classification.[9]

Douglas collected this conifer from his base at the Hudson's Bay Company post at Fort Vancouver on the Columbia River, across from present day Portland. He dispatched seed back to England and Scotland where it was introduced as an ornamental to gardens and arboretums there and in northern Europe. In the Pacific Northwest we know Douglas fir not as a garden plant but as

The Sitka spruce, *Picea sitchensis*, LB/Davidsonia

Right: top to bottom, *Pseudotsuga wilsonii*, *P. forrestii*; after Flora Sinensis; and the Californian species, *P. macrocarpa*. After Sudworth in FTPS.

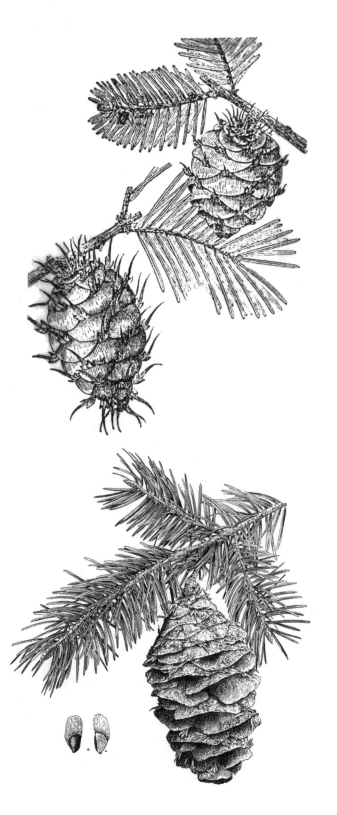

one of our most important and valuable coastal timber and lumber trees.

In lumber classification terms, Douglas fir is classified as a softwood species. It is far from this in actuality if anyone has had to recycle Douglas fir lumber and timbers, in particular edge grain flooring or 2x8 and 2x12 joists milled in the 1920s. On a hardness rating of 1 to 10, dry 40- to 50-year old milled Douglas fir is at least a 9!

There are six other species of the Douglas fir, seven if you are a botanical 'splitter'. There are three species of this pseudo, (false) tsuga, the Japanese name for another westcoast conifer species the hemlock. These three occur at inland mountain locations in China.

These Chinese species are: *Pseudotsuga sinensis, P. forrestii* and *P. brevifolia.* The last named, short-leaved pseudotsuga, from Yunnan-Kwangsi, is very rare. There is a species, *P. gaussenii*, the East China pseudotsuga, that is cultivated. *Pseudotsuga wilsonii*, the Taiwan pseudotsuga, is found in the central mountain ranges at elevations between 800 and 1500 metres on this island off the coast of mainland China, while *P. japonica* is endemic to the islands of Japan.[10]

Pseudostuga gaussenii, the East China pseudotsuga, can be seen in the Mt. Huangshan Arboretum and the Hangchow Botanical Gardens, and at the UBC Botanical Garden. It has been suggested that *P. wilsoniana* and *P. forrestii* are not distinct species, nor *P. gaussenii* and *P. wilsonii.*

Californian foresters and botanists distinguish another species, *Pseudostuga macrocarpa*, bigcone Douglas fir that has larger cones than *P. menziesii*, as the epithet and common name indicate. Bigcone Douglas fir has a limited occurrence in California, from Banner and San Felipe Canyons in San Diego County northward to the Mount Pinos region in Kern County. This is a little over two hundred miles, with an elevational range from 300 metres in chaparral up to 2400 metres in the mixed conifer forest.[11]

The species *P. menziesii* var *glauca* is an environmental variant from the eastern side of the Rocky Mountains from Montana to Mexico. It has the common name blue Douglas fir. This form is considerably more hardy than the coastal form discovered by Menzies as is evident from the following experience: in 1975 a single specimen of *Pseudostuga menziesii* var *glauca* was discovered among a row of *Picea glauca*, white spruce, along the south perimeter of the legislative grounds portion of Wascana Centre Park in Regina, Saskatchewan. This row of conifers was planted in 1922–25. The trees had been dug from the wild on the eastern slopes of Rocky Mountains west of Calgary, near Banff National Park, if not in it, and shipped by train to Regina. In 1975 the single fir was 8 metres in height while the spruce in the row were 2 to 3 metres taller. Unfortunately it failed to survive being moved to make way for a new entrance. However, the white spruce that were moved with the Douglas fir did survive the move.[12]

The Douglas fir is used occasionally as an ornamental in the Pacific Northwest, particularly when it is young and Christmas tree-like in appearance. This latter visually suitable image has led to the growing of a crop of considerable proportions of this species, for Christmas trees on cut-over forest lands, particularly on the Olympic Peninsula, lower Puget Sound area and the northern part of Vancouver Island's east coast. Because of this Christmas tree industry there has been an increased use and planting of the Douglas fir in Pacific Northwest gardens and parks. In the past it had not usually been available in ornamental plant nurseries.

By the turn of the century there were a number of horticultural forms of *P. menziesii* developed for ornamental use in England and Northern Europe.

Among the cultivars were *Pseudotsuga menziesii pendula,* with weeping branches, *P. menziesii stairii* a rare dull golden needle form, *P. menziesii standishii* and *P. menziesii fletcherii.* This last cultivar, which seems to be the only one still available, is a dwarf, spreading, dark green flat-topped irregular formed shrub. Murray Hornibook in his classic *Dwarf and Slow Growing Conifers,* published in 1938, describes and pictures the myriad dwarf, weeping, prostrate and foliage colour forms of conifers past and known in Northern Europe prior to the second world war. Among them is the only known listing in English of the dwarf, witches broom, golden foliage and prostrate varieties of Douglas fir.

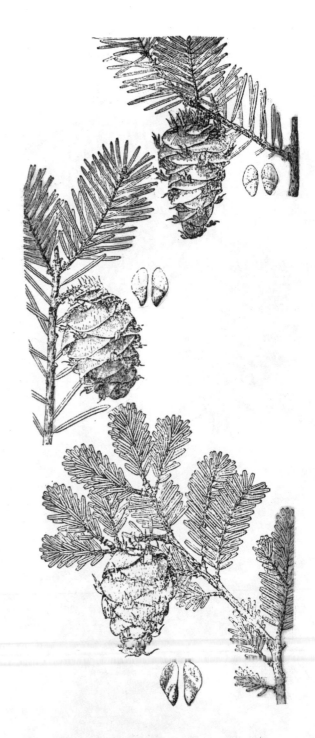

The Chinese species, from top to bottom, *Pseudotsuga sinensis, P. gaussenii and P. brevifolia.* After Flora Sinensis

The ground orchid,
*Habenaria (menziesii)
orbiculata.*
JRJ/VPPNW

Thankfully, in this writer's opinion, the use and planting of myriad 'cute little pointy plants' has gone out of vogue. Fortunately also, in the Pacific Northwest the climate, so suitable for conifers, results most of the time in the so called dwarf and slow growing becoming, very large, very fast.[13]

Some other, non-garden, Pacific Northwest plants that bear the *menziesii* epithet include a number of plant families aside from *Ericaceae*. They include mosses, lichens and ferns that were a special interest of Menzies. Aside from the lichens, mosses and ferns, the cryptogams, (meaning hidden seed) also include the marine algae. One marine alga that he collected at Nootka was *Phyllosmara menziesii*. This large kelp or brown algae occurs in intertidal and subtidal moderately exposed waters from British Columbia to California. It was later reclassified as *Egregia*, but it retained the discoverer's epithet for the species. *Egregia menziesii* was one of more than twenty marine algae that Menzies collected while in the Pacific Northwest.[14]

The one species of lichen that is named for Menzies is *Zambelina menziesii*. He did much better with the thirty-four or so mosses he collected. Two species bear his name: *Leucolepsis menziesii* and *Neckera menziesii*. *L. menziesii* is a western North American endemic moss that grows in damp shaded low swampy soil areas near water and is sometimes an epiphyte on trees and fallen logs. *Neckera menziesii* is now *Metaneckera menziesii*. When the genera was reclassified the species epithet, for Menzies, remained unchanged, following the international rules of nomenclature. This moss forms light green mats and is mainly epiphytic on deciduous trees. It is frequently found in coastal forests and is similar except for colour to *Metaneckera douglasiana* that forms golden or dark green glossy mats.[15]

Among the genera of flowering plants Menzies collected in the Pacific Northwest that initially had the Menzies epithet but lost it due to "taxonomic tinkering" are the following: *Echium menziesii* changed to *Amsinkia intermedia*, the sedge *Juncus menziesii* changed to *J. falcatus*, the orchids *Goodyera menziesii* reclassified as *Goodyera oblongifolia*, with *Platanthera menziesii* becoming *Habenaria menziesii*, then changing to *H. orbiculata*. This latter ground orchid occurs throughout North America. *Pinus menziesii*, not a pine at all, became the fir, *Abies grandis*.

One of the raspberries, the salmonberry that Menzies kept rediscovering each time he botanized, named *Rubus menziesii* became *R. spectabilis*.[16]

Western snake root, *Sanicula menziesii* was found to be *S. crassicaulis*. This perennial in the family *Umbelliferae* is supposed to have healing properties (from *sanare*, to heal, and *crassicaulis*, thick stemmed).[17] *Eutoca menziesii* was reclassified to a *Phacelia*, a much nicer sounding genus name, but the species epithet was invalid as the prior valid name for the species was *Phacelia linearis*. Most of the 114 or so species of these southwestern American herbaceous perennials and annuals have intense blue flowers.

Menzies would have had another tree species, the Sitka spruce, named for him had his collection of it been looked at before 1833. In 1832 a German botanist at the Acadamie des Sciences de St. Petersburg, August Heinrich Gustave Bongard, placed Sitka spruce in the genus *Pinus* with the species epithet *sitchensis*. This species epithet was for Sitka the capital of Russian Alaska located on the Baronoff Islands, part of the Alexander Peninsula in the Alaskan Panhandle. It is possible that this spruce was collected here before Menzies found it in the Admiralty Inlet area in May 1792.

In 1833, the English botanist John Lindley examined David Douglas' collection; also knowing of Menzies' collection, he placed it in the genus *Abies* but gave it the species epithet *menziesii*, for the tree's first discoverer. Seventeen years later, Lindley, as a horticultural writer now aware of Bongard's work in St. Petersburg, still held to this fir genus but accepted the species epithet *sitchensis*. Finally a nurseryman rather than a botanist put things straight by placing this tree in its correct genus, *Picea*. In 1855 Elie Abel Carriere, Director of the Jardin des Plantes nurseries in Paris, listed both species names, *sitchensis* and *menziesii*, claiming they were two different spruce species. Nurserymen are fond of splitting in order to have

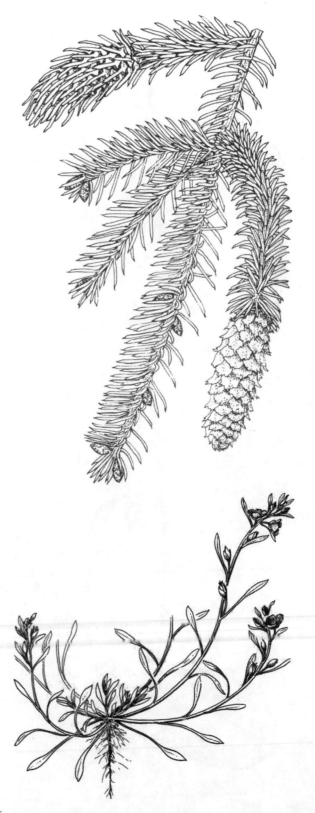

more 'varieties' to list and offer for sale. A year later eminent botanists Carl Anton Meyer and Ernst Rudolph von Trautvelter at the St. Petersburg Botanical Gardens decided correctly that the two were the same species and confirmed the priority of the *sitchensis* epithet. So Menzies Spruce was not to be.

Among the plants Menzies collected that retain his name as species or subspecies, (ssp), or variety, (var), are two in the *Compositae* or daisy family; *Arnica menziesii* is one among a great many yellow flowered herbaceous plants; the smallest and most common is the six inch high, bright yellow, *A. mollis*. The largest flower is on the largest *Arnica, A. cordifolia*.[18] The other is *Aster menziesii*, which Canadian botanist C. F. Newcombe postulated was collected by Menzies in a California location as it is not present in the Pacific Northwest.[19]

Calandrinia ciliata var *menziesii* is a diminutive plant with three-quarter inch rose-coloured five- to seven-petalled flowers. The leaves closest to the ground have the longest stems (petioles), and these get shorter further up the stem. Menzies' variety of *C. ciliata* is one of very few in a genera of a hundred or so species that finds its way into the Pacific Northwest; most are found in South America. The species name honours the Swiss botanist F.N. Calandrini from a generation before Menzies.[20]

Chimaphila menziesii is in the Heather, or *Ericaceae* family. While Newcombe called it 'Menzies' Wintergreen', a more appropriate Pacific Northwest common name for it is 'Menzies' Pipsissewa'. This distinguishes it from the Pyrolas that are also commonly called Wintergreens and the adjective Menzies to distinguish it from the more common, *C. umbellata* var *occidentalis* or Pipsissewa. As Lewis Clark notes; *"Pipsissewa, is an adaptation of the Cree name for the plant – 'pipisisikweu'; the name has a charming euphony quite fitting for this curiously attractive plant."*[21]

The nodding creamy to pink flowers, of 'Menzies' Pipsissewa', rise two to an umbel above a mat or cluster of dark green elliptical serrate-edged leaves. It differs from *Chimaphila umbellata* var *occidentalis* in having smaller darker green and less waxy leaves. The evergreen leaves alone warrant it

Left: Sitka spruce, *Picea sitchensis*. Needles and seed cones, above, after Sudworth in FTPS, and *Calandrina ciliata* var *menziesii*, JRJ/VPPNW

Above: Menzies pipsissewa, *Chimapala menziesii*. AH/HFBC

as a delightful plant for the garden. Pipsissewa should be raised from seed rather than transplanted from the wild as it is both difficult to transplant and endangers the continuance of wild populations. It is a plant to combine with the twinflower or the twinberry and among the larger hellabores or asarums in partial shade under deciduous azaleas or small-leaved open leggy rhododenrons.

Leo Hitchcock in his *Vascular Plants of the Pacific Northwest* distinguishes a northern and a southern race of Menzies delphinium, *Delphinium menziesii* var *menziesii* and *Delphinium menziesii* var *pyramidale*. The former has hairy stems, and has a range from the Puget Sound area north to Vancouver Island and eastward into the Fraser River Valley, while *Delphinium menziesii* var *pyramidale*, which lacks hairs, has a range that is south of the Columbia River but west of the Cascade Mountains. Both Menzies delphiniums have three to twenty flowers to a raceme in early summer, in various shades from light to dark, of purest blue on the sepals, petals and spurs of each flower.

The delphinium is a major component in the background of the English herbaceous or perennial border. Gertrude Jekyll, the great late Victorian–Edwardian exponent of the flower border, had a favourite delphinium with beautiful grey green foliage as well as small pale, clear, blue flowers and an open habit with grace and charm that she used in many of her border layouts.[22] There are over two hundred species of delphinium in North America and the old world! Gardens in the Pacific Northwest provide a most suitable habitat for the garden varieties of delphinium that have been developed from this rich North American plant heritage.[23] Developed in California just after the turn of the century, Pacific Hybrid Delphiniums are particularly favoured for Pacific Northwest Gardens. Seed of this eleven-month perennial is available in a mixture of colours or in separate colours.

Menzies campion, *Silene menziesii* is a widespread Pacific Northwest low-growing much-branched perennial plant with clusters of small white flowers on the ends of the sticky hairy stalks with narrow opposite leaves. It is in a vast and variable genus of over 300 species. The most common garden campion is the annual used for bedding dis-

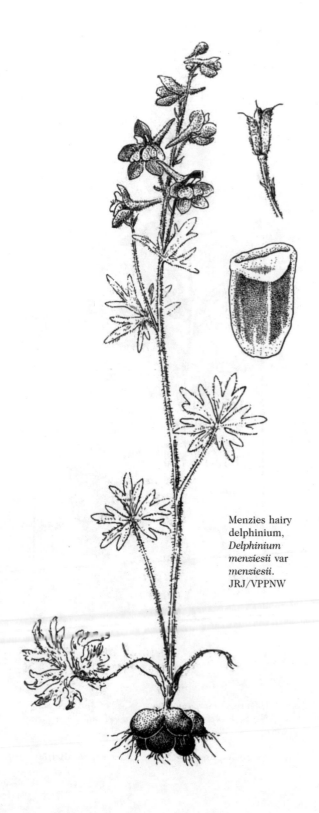

Menzies hairy delphinium, *Delphinium menziesii* var *menziesii*. JRJ/VPPNW

Hesperis menziesii, now *Phoenicaulis cheranthoides*, above and Menzies gooseberry, *Ribes menziesii*. JRJ/VPPNW

play, *Silene pendula*, with white, dark to light pinks and a salmon. Menzies campion gets very straggly under good care and attention; whereas on a dry gravel roadside cut it forms a compact grey-green drift with myriad white wavy-edged half-inch flowers. It differs from the old world weedy species common on the Pacific coast, *S. gallica,* which is taller with a whiter more hairy appearance. This common wayside flower is the namesake of the '1930s gifted' amateur detective in the PBS Mystery series shown on television in the late 1980s that was adapted from the stories by Margery Allingham.[24]

   Spiraea douglasii subsp. *menziesii* is distinguished from the more southern coastal subspecies *douglasii* by never having the conspicuous greyish-tomentose hairs on the underside of the leaves. 'Menzies' spiraea' extends from the Alaskan panhandle south including the Queen Charlotte Islands, Vancouver Island, coastal British Columbia, Washington, Oregon and occurring again in the interior wetbelt of western Idaho.

   Douglas' spiraea has a range from southwestern British Columbia to north coastal California. This two- to four-foot high shrub honours its first discoverer and the one who introduced it to ornamental horticulture. It has dense rose-pink panicles of flowers that quickly turn a rich dark brown and persist well into the winter. The shrub suckers easily to form dense thickets at the edges of lakes and swamps, the preferred habitat of this member of the rose family.

   There are many spiraeas used in ornamental horticulture. By far the most widely grown shrub in Canadian gardens is the hybrid *S. X vanhouttei* or the bridalwreath spiraea. Frank Skinner of Dropmore, Manitoba developed a low growing compact variety of *Spiraea douglasii menziesii* with six inch spikes of deep rose flowers that is hardy in Canadian hardiness zone 2b. This spiraea is available commercially under the name, *Spiraea menziesii* 'Dropmore'. Menzies' spiraea, as a subspecies of Douglas' spiraea, was distinguished as such and combined by botanists Calder and Taylor in 1965. Up until then, these two plants had been considered separate species.[25]

   Two plants with the Species epithet *menziesii* in the *Cruciferae,* cabbage-mustard family (if you are an agriculturist), or the wallflower–arabis family (if you are a gardener or horticulturist), are *Lepidium virginicum* var *menziesii*, pepper grass; and *Parrya menziesii*. This latter plant was reclassified from the name Menzies gave it to *Hesperis menziesii*, and later again to *Phoenocaulis cheisanthoides*, losing the Menzies' epithet completely.

Ribes menziesii, unlike *Ribes sangineum* has little or no garden value. It is a three- to seven-foot high, very spiny unpalatable gooseberry of northern California and southern Oregon. The small reddish-purple berry is eaten by both blue and sooty grouse and is the alternate host of the fungus that kills western white pine. Menzies or canyon gooseberry has a range which overlaps that of the five needle pine, *Pinus monticola*. This gooseberry along with others and the spineless *Ribes,* the currants, are the alternate hosts for the fungus *Cronartium ribicola* which causes white pine blister rust. This disease, an arch destroyer of white pines is common over much of the white pine, (*Pinus strobus*), region in eastern North America and has now become established in many parts of the range of *P. monticola* in the Pacific Northwest.

So, two hundred years after Menzies was in the Pacific Northwest, the plant score for Menzies reads: one genera, twenty-four species in hand to eight species lost; three subspecies were gained. This score will probably hold as the botanists have at last finally caught up with their revisions and taxonomic tinkering on those plants Menzies found on the northwest coast of America.

Two species, tall mahonia or Oregon grape, and the redflowering currant made it into the English garden directly, while others required some measure of horticultural tinkering, such as hybridizing with hardier species, breeding to get brighter or deeper flower colour, compactness of habit and other characteristics to give the plant more adaptability to a variety of conditions that are met with in the garden.

Red flowering currant, *Ribes Sangineum*, foliage, flower and fruit. A native plant that made it into the garden.
LB/Davidsonia

MENZIES' PLANTS FOR THE GARDEN

There are some fine garden plants that Archibald Menzies found in the spring and summer of 1792, as he and Captain George Vancouver made their way up the waters of Georgia Strait. Menzies found these trees, shrubs and groundcovers while botanizing from the longboats and launches of Discovery and Chatham during the course of surveying and charting the shorelines and islands in and around the waters of Admiralty Inlet, Puget Sound and Georgia Strait.

Most notable of Menzies' discoveries are the broadleaf evergreen *Mahonia (Berberis) aquifolium*, the Oregon grape, with its low growing variant *Mahonia nervosa;* and the deciduous flowering currant, *Ribes sanguineum*. These two Pacific Northwest originations are a shiny green, prickly-leaved, evergreen shrub with bright yellow flowers and blue berries; the other a deciduous shrub with bright pink to red flowers. Both of these plants first found by Menzies, along with another, *Forsythia viridissima*, brought back from China by a later plant explorer, Robert Fortune, combined to become the standard early harbingers of spring, (along with daffodils of course!) for the English late-Victorian and Edwardian suburban garden. These plants, however, were not popular or used in Pacific Northwest gardens or parks until well after 1960.

The author's professional landscape architectural practice, begun in the 1950s, initiated the extensive use of flowering currant, *Ribes sangineum*, and Oregon grape, *Mahonia aquifolium*, in gardens and parks in the lower mainland and coastal areas of British Columbia. Before the 1960s these native plants were not available locally, and had to be imported from European grower nurseries, mainly in Holland.

Tall mahonia is the common name used in horticulture for *Berberis aquifolium*. However in the Pacific Northwest gardening and horticultural circles, this broadleaf evergreen shrub still retains the genus epithet *Mahonia* and the common name Tall Oregon Grape or just Oregon grape. Before the mid-1960s, an exotic evergreen, a very spiny barberry from China, *Berberis julianae*, via Dutch grower nurseries, filled many of the places in the garden later taken by the native tall mahonia, when it was reintroduced to the man-made landscapes of the Pacific Northwest.

Tall mahonia makes a fine informal hedge and combines well with bigleaf and lacecap hydrangeas or the deciduous pink-flowering shrub, *Rhododendron schlippenbachii*. The shiny dark green leaflets, intense yellow clusters of flowers and the greyed-blue berries, display year round interest in this plant. The leaflets, (seven to nine pairs make up a leaf), become bright red over winter when there are a few nippy November days. If the non-prickly stems of *Mahonia* are cut to the ground it will renew and grow back to three to five feet in height in the space of two or three years. While it withstands clipping and shaping well, this form of topiary tidiness, completely destroys the irregular natural character and beauty of this native plant.

Mahonia nervosa has a longer leaf and a lower growing, more spreading habit than tall mahonia. The leaves fan out from a single short stem like the fronds of a small tropical palm tree. It is best used as it occurs and grows in nature, as a ground cover among the trunks and in the open but deep shade of second-growth conifers. It is also a fine accompaniment to the western swordfern and hellabores under tree-trained rhododendrons.

Gaultheria shallon, with its coastal indian common name, salal, is another Menzies discovery. Salal has tough leathery leaves with the heather family's urn shaped flowers that are light pink, and turn into blue-black 'berries'. Although it is a prized garden plant, it played another role when first introduced to Great Britain and northern Europe. It was planted on moorland, along the edges of woods and in open woodland areas as cover and food for pheasants and grouse on the estates and the hunting parks of England, Scotland and Germany. Salal is still in use for this purpose today. While the word Salal is a language sound taken from the Chinook Indians of southwest Washington for *Gaultheria shallon*; their name for the black edible fruit is 'kikwsala'.[1]

Menzies's botanizing was just a bit too far north to discover the non-urn shaped flowers of another shrub in the heather family, *Rhododendron occidentale*, or the western azalea. The most northerly occurrence of western azalea is along the Pacific coast just south of the Columbia River. Heavy fog and rough weather prevented Vancouver from landing south of, or near the mouth of the Columbia while beating up the coast from a landfall at Cape Mendocino.[2]

Rhododendron occidentale has flowers with various shades of pink with a yellow blaze in the Pacific Northwest, whereas in the southern Sierra Nevada Mountains near Yosemite, where western azalea grows around the base of the worlds' largest living things, the bigtrees, *Sequoiadendron giganteum,* the flowers are always white with the same yellow blotch.[3] Menzies did discover the other western North American rhododendron that is now the state flower of Washington – the Pacific rhodo-

Oregon grape or tall mahonia, *Mahonia aquifolium*, branch with berries above and the plant below. LB/Davidsonia

Right: Western azalea, *Rhododendron occidentale*, two views; above from USDA Range Handbook and below JRJ/VPPNW.

dendron, *Rhododendron macrophyllum* (the species epithet means big leaf). Menzies found it growing along with *Arbutus menziesii*, the Pacific Madrone, that first May day in 1792, when he and Vancouver made their second landfall after leaving Hawaii.[4] These two members of the heather family still grow in the same spot today near Port Discovery beside US Highway 101, where Menzies and Vancouver found them 200 years ago.[5]

It is quite in order that Menzies would have a genus and a species in the *Ericaceae* named after him because he also found, in addition to the rhododendron, another member of that family growing with the madrone and the rhododendron on that May day. This discovery was a manzanita, *Arctostaphylos columbiana*, with the common descriptive name hairy manzanita. The hairy adjective refers to the hairs on the underside of the evergreen leaves. The word manzanita is the Spanish name for 'small apple'.

This five- to six-foot high shrub, which is still found growing with madrone and Pacific rhododendron at Port Discovery, looks a little like a small arbutus with dark-brownish-maroon, not red, peeling bark, smooth stems, the same urn-shaped (urceolate) pink flowers that form into brown, not orange, berries. The fruits on this particular species of manzanita, however, do not resemble very closely, 'little apples'. Menzies confused *Arctostaphylos columbiana*, with the Spanish madrone, *Arbutus unedo*. Had it been later in the year, July or August, and he had seen the "little brown apples" - he probably would not have made the mistake.

He called the arbutus that bears his name, the oriental strawberry. This apparently was a reference to a Chinese tree, *Arbutus kiangsinensis*, of Kiangsi Province in south-central China, but there is no documented confirmation.

The hairy or Columbia manzanita (after the Columbia River) extends into coastal British Columbia on Vancouver Island as far north as the dry open rocky outcrops on the mountain sides along the Alberni Canal. All the other "little apples" do not range this far into the Pacific Northwest, but occur in southern Oregon and throughout California. These form a group of non-prickly shrubs and brush that make up the chaparral on the slopes of the Sierra Nevada and the other mountains of California.

Chaparral is a western North American term, from the Spanish for a dense tangle of brushwood. The shortened form of this word is the term chaps, a split apron of leather worn while astride a horse to protect the rider's legs from being scratched and torn when travelling through brush. Menzies was one of the first to observe the use of this apron by the Spanish in California. In October and November 1792, as we know, after leaving Nootka *Discovery* and *Chatham* sailed south to Spanish California, visiting San Francisco and Mission Santa Clara, as well as Monterey and the adjoining mission before sailing to the Sandwich (Hawaiian) Islands.

While at Monterey, Menzies describes in his journal the garb of the Spanish soldiers garrisoning these outposts of Spanish Empire: *"Their Body is defended by a quilted buff coat of several folds of leather that is impenetrable to Arrows. They have a kind of Apron of thick leather fastened to the pummel of the Saddle and falling back on each side covers the Legs & Thighs/& affords considerable defence either in passing through thorny brush woods with which the Country abounds, or from such Weapons as the Indians generally make use of."*[6]

The main chaparral manzanitas include the whiteleaf manzanita, *Arctostaphylos viscida*; woolly manzanita, *A. tomentosa*; greenleaf manzanita, *A. patula*; and the more tree-like Parry manzanita, *A. manzanita*.[7] Neither the Pacific madrone, Pacific rhododendron or the Columbia (hairy) manzanita or its California kin made their way into the English garden. The madrone and manzanita, particularly the latter, are difficult to grow in the damp, cool climate of northern Europe. These plants do best in areas with hot dry summers and on poor sandy but well-drained soil. If you were a traditional gardener of the period it would have been an anomaly to grow these plants particularly in poor or unimproved non-agricultural or non-horticultural soils. Improvements to the fertility and tilth was a *sine qua non* of the English garden.

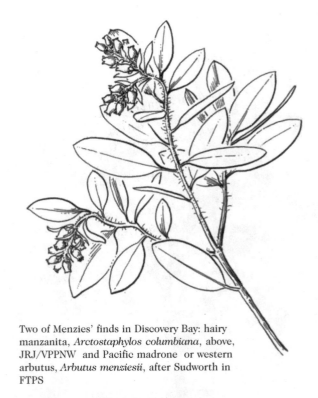

Two of Menzies' finds in Discovery Bay: hairy manzanita, *Arctostaphylos columbiana*, above, JRJ/VPPNW and Pacific madrone or western arbutus, *Arbutus menziesii*, after Sudworth in FTPS

Salal, *Gaultheria shallon*, above. BCN/HFBC Pacific rhododendron, *R. macrophyllum*, the state flower of Washington. LB/Davidsonia.

The Pacific rhododendron was also by-passed, largely because its introduction coincided with the more colourful and larger-leaved Himalayan species that Sir Joseph Hooker brought back from his travels in India in the mid 1840s.

These eastern exotics were, along with the rosebay, *Rhododendron maximum* and the catawba *R. catawbiense,* both from eastern North America, with *R. ponticum* used as the understock for grafting to the newly developed hybrids. They became the darlings of the plant connoisseur, amateur plant enthusiast–collector and the mainstay of the large estate and private rhododendron collections of the Victorian and Edwardian gentry.

The faded or washed-out small pink of the Pacific rhododendron just couldn't compete with the larger intense clear red of *R. arboreum* and *R. thompsoni*, the yellow of *R. falconeri*, the pure white of *R. dalhousiae* and large clear pink of *R. griffithianum*, so it was overlooked in the early rhododendron sweepstakes of the mid- to-late- 19th century.

It was not until the 1920s in the eastern United States that a nurseryman, Joe Gable of Stewartstown, Pennsylvania, received pollen of Menzies rhododendron, *R. macrophyllum* from another nurseryman and rhododendron grower, George Fraser of Ucluelet on the west coast of Vancouver Island. Joe used the pollen George Fraser sent him on the native eastern Rhododendron, *R. maximum* to produce a hybrid that he called Albert Close, after a friend in the United States Department of Agriculture. It was introduced as a hybrid for the gardens in the Pacific Coast and the milder areas of the east coast in the late 1950s.[8] The flowers of *R*. 'Albert Close' are borne in a tight deep pink ball (truss), with dark purple spots in the throat of each flower.

No one since the Fraser-Gable east-west encounter appears to have used *R. macrophyllum* in hybridising. However, the species in the wild is being rediscovered and reassessed for the rich diversity of both colour and flower forms now appearing in the logged-over areas of the Pacific Northwest. Pacific rhododendron like the Pacific madrone is a pioneer on open mineral soils on logged-over hillside areas.

There have been population explosions in

the last two decades in such areas as western Oregon, and locations near Port Townsend and Whidbey Island in Washington's Puget Sound, along with an increase in the numbers but not the diversity of the several populations of *R. macrophyllum* on mainland British Columbia and Vancouver Island.

Much of the renewed interest in the Pacific rhododendron, which became the state flower of Washington in 1955, is recorded in the pages of the *Journal of the American Rhododendron Society*. A recent article documents the flower colour, size and spotting variations of a population of this rhododendron in a large logged-over area in Western Oregon.[9] There are two populations of *R. macrophyllum* that occur on the mainland of British Columbia. The most well known is at mile 19 from the west gate of Manning Provincial Park on Highway #3, while the other is around the North end of Ross Lake. Both are in the upper or Canadian end of the Skagit River valley.

There were three populations of the Pacific Rhododendron on Vancouver Island: the ecological reserve at Rhododendron Lake; on Macmillan Bloedel's Parksville tree farm area; and near Weeks Lake on the Shawnigan Lake to Port Renfrew highway. The upper Nanaimo lakes had a population of *R. macrophyllum* until they were flooded out by the dam constructed in the 1950s that raised the lake level. The water in the lake is piped to Macmillan Bloedel's Harmac pulp mill near Naniamo for use in washing bleach from the paper produced there. The Nanaimo lakes area is overlooked by Mt. Hooker. The writer is sure neither father or son would have approved. At Rhododendron Lake ecological reserve there is the unusual association of Pacific rhododendron with *Chamaecyparis nootkatensis*.[10] This fine tree of the Pacific Coast was first discovered by Menzies. Non-gardeners, foresters, native carvers and boat builders know it as yellow cedar.

The replicas of the ships' boats of the *Discovery, Chatham, Sutil* and *Mexicana* made for the Discovery Re-enactment Voyages of 1992 have had frames and transoms made, and been planked, sides and bottom, with the beautiful, clear, even-grained, yellow, pungent smelling wood from this tree. It is

The Pacific rhododendron, *Rhododendron macrophyllum*, *R. californicum* of Hooker.
Adapted from USDA *Range Plant Handbook*.

Right: Nootka falsecypress, Alaska cedar or yellow cedar, *Chamaecyparis nootkatensis*. A weeping form is a fine garden tree. LB/Davidsonia

5   10   15m

sometimes called Alaska cedar. For gardeners there is an ornamental weeping tree form of Nootka falsecypress that was rare in Pacific Northwest gardens and parks until it was re-imported from Europe in the 1950s, over 100 years after it had been introduced there.

Menzies' falsecyparis discovery made it into the garden another way, by the back door, so to speak. It did this by being part of a natural hybrid with a closely related genera, the Monterey cypress of California, *Cupressus macrocarpa*.

This bi-generic marriage occurred in England first in 1888 then again in 1911 and again in 1940, producing a fast growing, dense fine foliage, disease free, bright green conifer the taxonomists called *Cupressocyparis leylandii*. Leyland cypress has found a wide use in the Pacific Northwest gardens as a dense informal and formal hedge, as it withstands severe shearing, shaping and pruning, and also as a screen and windbreak. For this latter use the shallow roots need lots of room to spread in order to anchor the tree securely as it can be easily blown over.

While the Nootka falsecypress was discovered by Menzies, it was introduced as an ornamental to English gardens in the 1840s when that other Scottish botanist David Douglas sent seed back to Scotland. He also sent seed of another west coast falsecypress that Menzies missed seeing by not being able to land on the Coast between Bodega Bay and the Columbia River on his way up the coast in April 1792.[11] Confined to a 200-mile long strip along the Oregon – California Coast between Cape Mendocino and Cape Blanco it is known locally as the lumber tree, Port Orford cedar, botanically as *Chamaecyparis lawsoniana*, and horticulturally as Lawson's cypress. Port Orford cedar is no longer the important timber tree it once was in Oregon–California. Most of the old growth has been logged and the tree is not used for reforestation in its old range.

James Lawson was a farmer and friend of David Douglas. When Lawson received the seed of this tree from Douglas about 1835 , he gave it to his father's nursery in Edinburgh and from that day forward this nursery and others in Britain, like the sorcerer's apprentice, produced varieties of Lawson's cypress in many foliage colours, blue, golds, light greens and dark greens. Myriad fastigiate and upright forms of these many colours were also developed from this west coast, genetically unstable conifer species, so that by 1940, a hundred years after it was introduced, there were over 150 distinct forms and colours of this conifer named, all directed to ornamental use in gardens and parks.[12]

There is a magnificent row of these trees along 16th Avenue in Vancouver between Burrard Street and Arbutus Street; while along 15th Avenue between the same two streets there is a narrowly upright golden colour form of Lawson's cypress that is used as a boulevard tree with birches. These golden spires are now up to 50 feet in height. These and the trees on 16th Avenue were all planted around 1911 about the time this Vancouver city residential area was being developed. In 1984 this block long avenue of Lawson's cypress were included as a heritage grove in Vancouver's heritage tree inventory.

If Menzies missed Lawson's cypress he did discover several other northwest conifers. One was the mainstay for totem poles, rain capes and longhouse construction of the Indian peoples all along the shores where he botanized. Hilary Stewart in her book *Cedar* presents a complete documentation of the Pacific Northwest Indian peoples' use of this tree.[13] We generally call this tree by its lumber name: western red cedar; the botanical name is *Thuya* but with the Spanish spelling with a soft 'j', *Thuja*. The species epithet is *plicata*. While western red cedar is the lumber name, western arborvitae (tree of long life) is the botanical or horticultural common name for *Thuja plicata*.

The Lummi people – the Clallum tribe who lived around Port Discovery and Port Townsend, near where Menzies and Vancouver made their first landfall and saw this tree, called it H'cha-chiltsh.[14] Menzies failed however to record it or any other local name as Joseph Banks had requested. Selections of this tree for garden and park use that are available in the Pacific Northwest include the European developed cultivar *Thuja plicata* 'Excelsa'; it has a more compact habit and deeper green winter foliage than that usually seen occurring naturally.

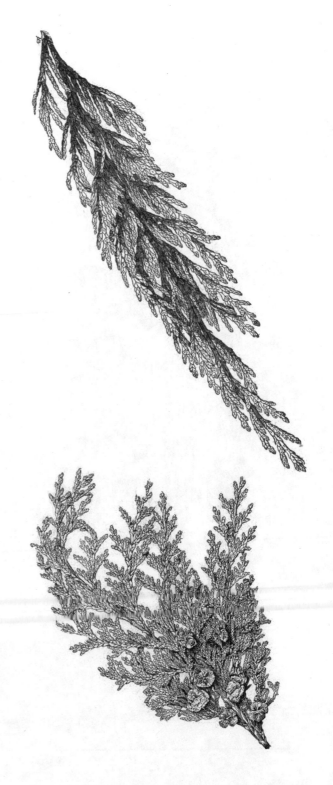

Left: Lawson's cypress (Port Orford cedar),
Chamaecyparis lawsoniana, foliage above,
foliage and seed cones below.
After Sudworth in FTPS.
There are many garden forms of this tree.

Western arborvitae (western red cedar),
Thuja plicata, foliage above and seed cones below.
After Sudworth in FTPS

Thuja is usually yellow-green in appearance, and it also drops its old branchlets in late summer giving it a somewhat scruffy appearance which quickly improves when new growth appears in the fall and winter.

There are a number of golden or yellow foliage forms; *Thuja plicata* 'Aurea' is the most well known. Because of this leaf variegation, where Carotin replaces chlorophyll causing the yellowing of portions or some of the needles, the trees are slower growing and considerably smaller than the all green needle forms. One writer has noted that the fragrance of these crushed needles is fruity, while another has said that no crushing is needed to produce a smell of pineapple.[15] The writer, who has lived with these trees, claims that the smell of *Thuja plicata* is unique!

With the passing of an act of the Provincial Legislature in 1949, *Cornus nuttallii*, the Pacific or western dogwood, became the official floral emblem of British Columbia. The Dogwood Act also included the protection of this tree by forbidding the cutting or removal of it from provincial crown lands and imposes fines for its removal or destruction. It is the earliest official protection and conservation measure for a single species in the Province. Menzies' discovery of the Pacific Dogwood along the shores of Admiralty Inlet was the first on the Pacific Northwest coast.[16]

The range of western dogwood is extensive, from British Columbia south along the coast and inland to the Yosemite valley in California plus a disjunct, isolated population in Idaho. This permitted other western explorers the opportunity to discover it, notably, Lewis and Clark in 1805 in the Idaho location and John Charles Fremont in the Yosemite location. As we have learned, dogwood was given the species epithet *nuttallii* by fellow ornithologist James Audubon for the sometimes Harvard professor and English–American naturalist, Thomas Nuttall. This and the other discoveries were well after Menzies' discovery, but because Menzies' collection was not classified until the 1830s he is not credited with the discovery of the Western Dogwood.

The flowers of Pacific dogwood are very small and appear button-like; then they enlarge to 'strawberry' or cluster of 'clove' shaped seeds. The feature that makes the tree spectacular, eye catching and a candidate for the most beautiful of Northern Hemisphere spring flowering trees is the five to six large creamy white bracts that surround each 'button'. Pacific dogwood has been used successfully as a boulevard tree in Vancouver.

In the city *Cornus nuttallii* is used on the wide majestic treed centre median of King Edward Avenue from Cambie Street just below Queen Elizabeth Park, west for two miles to Arbutus Street. The major reason they are successful is that they receive no summer watering. It is a characteristic shared by many native plants. The dogwoods in many-stemmed clumps share this wide grass boulevard with large blue-green Lawson falsecypress that are also very successful because they too, resent any summer watering. There is also a two-block planting of *Cornus nuttallii* along 62nd Street west of Ontario Street in south Vancouver.

The Pacific dogwood has always been a contender for the most beautiful of spring flowering trees. Other, non-native contenders that grow successfully in Pacific Northwest gardens and parks and along its streets include the Chinese dove, pocket handkerchief or kleenex tree, *Davidia involucrata* and the eastern dogwood, *Cornus florida*. Both of these and the dove tree have the large bracts that surround the button like umbel of tiny flowers. One of the largest dove trees in North America is also located in Vancouver. It has a trunk diameter of 2 feet and a height of 65 feet. This tree is on north side of Southwest Marine Drive between MacKenzie Street and 49th Avenue.

Menzies' discovery of the Pacific or western dogwood *Cornus nuttallii*, differs from the eastern dogwood *Cornus florida* in being less floriferous but with more (*C. florida* has four bracts) and larger bracts for the Pacific coast tree. The Pacific dogwood has a bolder and coarser form, is taller growing and wider spreading and is more often seen with multiple trunks than its eastern cousin. The Pacific dogwood is really only successful where the temperature highs and lows are not extreme; USDA Zones 6 and 7 suit it best. Its thin bark precludes its general use in paved urban situations unless surrounded by thickets of snowberry or mahonia or in among other trees.

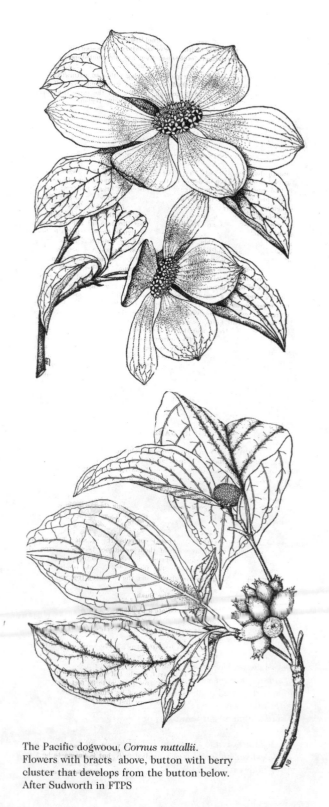

The Pacific dogwood, *Cornus nuttallii*. Flowers with bracts above, button with berry cluster that develops from the button below. After Sudworth in FTPS

Eastern dogwood, *Cornus florida*, above, LB/Davidsonia, and below, *C. canadensis*, with white stamens or *C. unalaskensis* with black stamens that occurs west of the Rocky Mountains.
After Virginia Howie *Alaska-Yukon Wildflower Guide*

There is a variegated form of *C. nuttallii* with yellow edged and blotched leaves, *C. nuttallii* var. Eddieii, or *C. nuttallii* 'Eddie's Goldspot', which adapts better as an urban tree. It will consistently bloom well, once in April – May and again in late September just as the coastal Indian summer turns the variegated leaves multicoloured. This spotted leaf form was found in the wild in the 1920s on the north face of Sumas Mountain in the lower Fraser valley by Henry Eddie, pioneer B.C. and Pacific Northwest nurseryman of Sardis, B.C. *Cornus nuttallii* var. 'Goldspot', was a similar find in Washington State. There is a fine boulevard planting of *C. nuttalli* 'Eddie's Goldspot' south of King Edward Avenue along both sides of Cambie Street to 41st Avenue in Vancouver. Here this irregularily yellow blotched-leaved tree is alternated with the golden Japanese falsecypress, *Chamaecyparis pisifera aurea* to provide the yellow gold colour to brighten the blue-grey aura of Vancouver winter landscapes. *Cornus nuttallii Eddieii* has pink autumn colour in association with a second early October bloom and red fruits.

Some of the finest shades of pink have been seen on the leaves of goldspot dogwood when they turn in late Autumn. The spring bloom, although there is usually a second bloom in fall, provides the most spectacular show. The bracts, blooms and leaves usually appear together, create an explosion of life, while at other times the flowers will appear before the leaves for a more delicate effect.

In its natural environment, along both sides of Georgia Strait and throughout Puget Sound, Pacific dogwood is an edge-of-the-forest tree that appears as an individual or in small groups of three or four among other deciduous tree and conifers in second growth woodlands. When clearing these woodland areas for homesites and other developments the dogwood can be retained with the tall unsupported trunks cut off at the ground. New trunks will sprout from the roots to form a handsome small tree in a short three to five years.

There are some lesser members of the *Cornaceae* genus on Menzies' discovery route; *Cornus stolonifera* has non-bracted flowers and white fruits in umbels on a large ungainly shrub that occurs from the Great Lakes eastward to the Pacific coast. There is a variety, *C. stolonifera flaviramea*, which has bright yellow stems. This is an effective shrub for the garden that enjoys winter snow or needs contrast in plantings of dark green evergreens. Pollarding of the two year old stems maintains a good shape and size to this shrub.

Menzies discovered *C. stolonifera* in the Admiralty Inlet area growing presumably in its preferred habitat close to and in a swamp or other wet ground. Menzies, also, first collected what is now classified as *Cornus unalaschkensis*, the west of the Rockies variant of the cornel or bunchberry, *Cornus canadensis* of eastern Canada.

There are two Pacific Northwest discoveries of Menzies common in the areas he botanized that have received little attention ornamentally. One is a large deciduous shrub, ocean spray, *Holodiscus discolor;* the other a deciduous tree: cascara, *Rhamnus purshiana* whose bark produces a potent laxative.

In early summer, *Holodiscus discolor* has many irregular heads or fluffy plumes of creamy white flowers that cover the multi-stem, eight to ten feet tall plant giving it the appearance of splashes of white water when waves wash up and around a rock, hence the common name for it, ocean spray. Too large for average suburban gardens, ocean spray is a valuable vandal proof, drought resistant, maintenance-free shrub for the hilly and rocky poor soils of Pacific Northwest seaside parks and large gardens. Ocean spray has never been available as an ornamental mainly because of its very ordinary appearance and the availability of substitutes, several species of Spireas like the most widely known and grown of all, bridal wreath, *Spiraea X vanhouttei.* On Vancouver Island, the Gulf Islands and other coastal areas with less than 35 inches annual rainfall, on seaside hillsides overly dry for alder to grow, *Holodiscus discolor* seems to play an initiation role in the succession process to regenerate Douglas fir.

The cascara, *Rhamnus purshiana* is a medium size tree that grows in association with alders, maples and birches as an understorey and edge-of-the-conifer-forest member. Menzies found cascara growing in this habitat in the Puget Sound coastal areas. It also grows in the British Columbia interior wet belt, the Kootenays and in northern

Ocean spray, *Holodiscus discolor*, above, from USDA Range Handbook, and the cascara tree, *Rhamnus purshiana*, LB/Davidsonia

Right: Northern, above, and southern leaf forms of *Rhamnus purshiana*. The black berries are favoured by pigeons. Both from Sudworth in FTPS

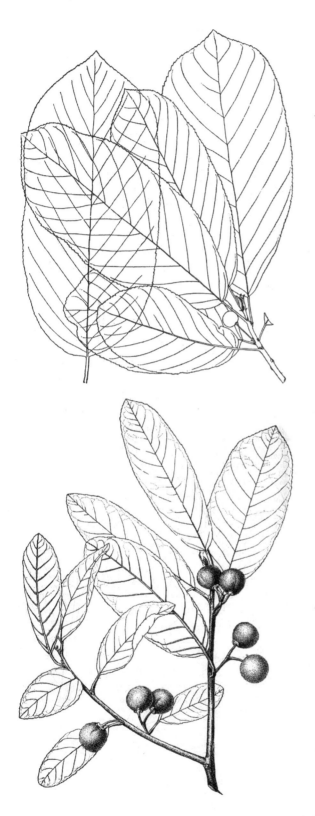

Idaho. In the 1920s and 1930s the little black round berries used to attract flocks of the wild grey pigeons who spread the seeds. Alas, the pigeons are now greatly reduced in their numbers. In the late thirties most of the large cascaras on lower Vancouver Island and the Gulf Islands were harvested by itinerant Japanese cascara bark collectors, who peeled the thin greyish brown bark from the stems and branches for sale dried, for the extraction of the drug *Cascara sagrada*. These large trees, some 40 feet in height and 3 feet in diameter, had grown up as part of the second growth regeneration, replacing the old growth forests that had been logged the decade before and the decade after the turn of the century. Fortunately many of the trees regenerated from the stumps and roots that the bark collectors felled, forming multi boled trees of attractive shape and size. The heavily veined leaves are light green and provide vivid yellow fall colour.

Before 1939 the price of dried cascara tree bark, sacked, was 7 cents a pound. At the outbreak of World War II it rose to 20 cents a pound. By 1942 there was no market for the bark as the drug had been synthesized in the laboratory.

The cascara along with the bigleaf or Oregon maple, vine maples, the red or Pacific alder, the Pacific crabapple, Pacific willow, white birch and Pacific dogwood, played a different forest role quite unlike the role of the hardwoods of eastern North America. These eastern trees formed and dominated great climax forests themselves, while on the Pacific coast the deciduous hardwoods became the nursery for initiating the process of succession to the climax species of the coastal coniferous forest.[17]

Douglas fir, Sitka spruce, hemlock and western red cedar, all of which Menzies discovered, gave, he wrote *"...a dreary and gloomy aspect...a rich carpet of Verdure...a forest of stateley Pines whose dark verdurous hue diffused a solitary gloom –favorable to meditations."*[18] These trees also came to provide forest products: timbers, lumber, plywood and pulp for the homes and newspapers of half a continent, only to return, at least partially, to the visual attractiveness and value as landscape that it had two hundred years ago.

By far the most maligned of these regenerators and renewers of the coastal forest and perhaps one of the most important biological links in the succession process is *Alnus rubra*, the red or Oregon alder, which Menzies noted on the shores and islands of Admiralty Inlet. It is a fast growing tree with nitrogen fixing bacteria nodules on its roots permitting it to put this essential growth element into the soil to supply both nutrient, shade and drainage for the emerging seedlings of Douglas fir and hemlock that will supplant it in the ensuing fifty to eighty years. Along the coast an attractive visual aspect and element of the forest landscape of this alder succession in its first stages is the late winter and early spring display of the emerging buds of the tree. These provide pink smokey swaths across hillsides, identify the mountainside streams and drainage courses as well as showing the perched hillside terraces and the traces of old logging road routes. In spring the yellow flowers of the bigleaf maple and the yellow fall colour of it and the willow, and the red and yellow of the vine maple, provide visual improvements and enhancements to the coastal forest landscape that would please even those contemporary 'Improvers' to Archibald Menzies, Capability Brown and Humphrey Repton, as well of course, the Surgeon-Botanist himself.

Two B.C. fritillarias. Left: *Fritillaria pudica*, right, *F. chamschatcense*. After JRJ in *Vascular Plants of the Pacific Northwest*.

10

MENZIES MISCELLANY

Today when we think of wild flowers we envisage meadows and open pastoral areas, filled with buttercups, bluebells, and butterflies, cowslips, columbine, daisies and Lilies. This was also the romantic concept held by Menzies. He collected at least a dozen wild flowers in the lily family along those coastal areas and islands he botanized on the *Discovery* voyage. These lovely plants, include the onions and camas, *Allium* and *Camassia*, fawn lilies and chocolate lilies, *Erythronium* and *Fritillaria* and the tiger lily and and false lily of the valley, *Lilium* and *Maianthemum*.

Onions were a special interest of Menzies, but their heads of showy but small pink flowers are such that we do not usually think of them as lilies. Lewis Clark lists six species of onions on the coast in all, including the one Menzies found on the rocky shores of Orcas Island, the largest island of the San Juan Group. Menzies notes in his Journal for 8 June:

"The shores were almost every where rugged and cliffy which made Landing difficult & the woods were in many places equally difficult of access from the rocky cliffs & chasms / with which they abounded, but I was not at all displeased at the change & general ruggedness of the surface of the country as it produced a pleasing variety of objects of my pursuits & added Considerably to my Catalogue of Plants. I here found another species of that new genus I discovered at Village Point in Admiralty Inlet. [Triandra later Brodiaea also in the Liliaceae], & a small well tasted wild onion [Allium acuminatum], which grew in little Tufts in the crevices of the Rocks with a species of Arenaria both new. I also met with the Lilium Canadense, [Fritillaria affinis], & Lilium Camschatcense, [F. camschatcense], the roots of the latter is Sarana so much esteemd by the Kamtchadales as a favourite food."[1]

The "Kamtchadales" are the indigenous people from Alaska's Aleutian chain of islands, now known as Aleuts.

The most famous of the fritillarias is the Crown Imperial, *F. imperialis* of gardens. Six orange bell-like flowers with six petals in a circle around a crown of leaves, (in *Liliaceae* things come in threes and sixes), on a stem fully three feet high. Even with its size, colour and grandeur, *imperialis* is no match in size for the fritillarias Menzies collected, the chocolate lilies, so named for the rich purplish brown of the flowers. On *F. lanceolata* they are shaped like bells with no flare while *F. camschatcensis* has flowers that are shaped more like trumpets with a flaring out at the end of the six petals. Both are lovely wild flowers to see and to photograph, but not *ever* to pick, should you want to see them again! They occur on sunny grassy headlands and shores of Puget Sound and Georgia Straits. As it occurs east of the Cascades, not on the coast, Menzies did not find the yellow bell, *Fritillaria pudica*. This beautiful little single-flowered lily is an inhabitant of interior open sagebrush areas where David Douglas collected it on his travels up the Columbia River in 1820.

Two species of the sky blue camas occur in the Pacific Northwest, *Camassia leichtlinii* and *C. quamash*. The genus name is the latinized Indian name for the edible bulb that the native people of the West and Northwest dug as food. It is quite possible that the Indian people selected and established the very large natural fields of this lily that the early explorers in the west saw and reported in their journals.[2] In May 1792 the bloom was over for the camas in the areas Menzies botanized and we will never know for sure whether he collected Camas bulbs and had them in *Discovery*'s afterdeck plant case, with his onion collection. Leichtlini's or the great camas, blue, pink and cream forms, is a common garden plant in Europe while only rarely in the Pacific Northwest and only if a garden or park has a deep soil headland or a grassy patch between rock outcroppings that is sure to dry out in summer. There are several examples of this ideal camas habitat in Beacon Hill Park in Victoria on the southern end of Vancouver Island.

Camas shares these park habitats with what some consider to be the most beautiful of the Pacific Northwest coastal area lilies, *Erythronium*, the fawn or Easter Lily. Menzies collected two of the five that Lewis Clark lists and pictures in his *Wild flowers of the Pacific Northwest*[3], the white fawn lily and the pink fawn lily, *Erythronium oregonum* and *E. revolutum*. Beside the white and pink fawn lilies there are the high elevation yellow and white avalanche lilies, *Erythronium grandiflorum* and *E. montanum,* and Henderson's fawn lily, *E. hendersonii*, from the Siskiyou Mountains.

Beacon Hill Park and a few other Victoria and Oak Bay parks and gardens are representative of the hundreds of sites that once existed, where thousands of these bulbs with their leaves provided a rich mottled light and dark green carpet on the ground below a spring display of beautiful white demure flowers. These natural garden areas in the 1920s and 1930s occurred on Whidbey Island, the San Juans, the Gulf islands both large and small, as well as southern parts of Vancouver Island.

In the Gulf Islands during these years the first spring picnics of the year were planned to coincide with the blooming of the 'Easter lilies' as these fawn lilies were then called. The picnickers would travel by boat to one of the many small unin-

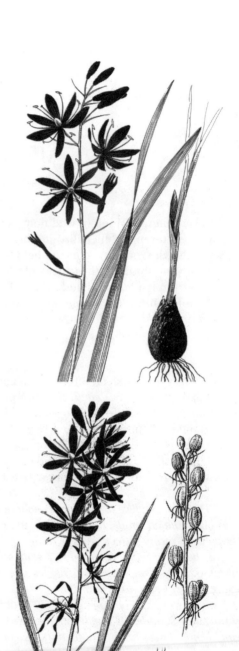

Camas, *Camassia lietchlinii*, above, and *C. quamish*
Both after Frank L. Beebe in *Lily Family of B.C.*

The white fawn lily, *Erythronium oregonum*. JRJ/VPPNW

habited islands or a picturesque park-like headland on one of the larger islands; there to land and joyfully pick handfuls of the lilies. There would usually be a group photograph of this 'rite of spring', with all participants holding armfuls of the lilies as if to record the catch of a big game safari or to show that nature's beauty or bounty was boundless! No one ever seemed to remember that the picked flowers only lasted three or four days in a vase in the house and no one realized that picking the blooms and the leaves not only weakened and killed the bulbs but also wiped out seed formation so that there would be no bulbs to take the place of those that died at the end of their 5–7 year life.

The few that survived this devastation in the wild were now further decimated on such places as the Gulf Islands by loss of habitat to another type of human activity, the bulldozer and subdivision.

Those gardeners who have captured this lily by raising it from seed for their gardens find it is one of the finest of spring groundcovers at the front of rhododendron plantings or under the light canopy of deciduous trees.

Menzies' other *Erythronium* find, the Pink Fawn Lily, was seen in "King George's Sound," [Nootka Sound]. Charles F. Newcombe who also botanized extensively on this coast and retraced much of Menzie's route, notes under *E. revolutum* in the list of plants Menzies collected: *"A purple flowered species of wide range along the coast of Vancouver Island and reaching the mainland at Kingcome Inlet."*

Newcombe continues: *"Specimens from the following localities touched at by Menzies have been seen: Nootka, Cape Mudge, and near "Cheslakees" at the mouth of the Nimkish River."*[4] The flower of this fawn lily is very clearly pink, not purple. The mottled leaves are very much like those of the White fawn lily, however. As Clark notes: *"they each favour a different habitat the Pink preferring fine sandy soil in open or semi shaded habitats that are subject to flooding while the White Fawn Lily prefers a soil rich in humus and an upland habitat."*

The writer first found the beautiful pink *Erythronium* in an alder wood just north of Menzies Bay on the east coast of Vancouver Island in the late 1950s. By the mid-seventies suburban residential development had overrun the site wiping out the lilies. The Alpine Garden Club of B.C. consistently has both the pink and white fawn lilies on their annual seed list. The members of this club and its American counterpart, the Northwest chapter of the American Rock Garden Society, do yeoman service in growing many of our native wild flowers; our most serious concern is the loss, by development, of many of the natural habitats of these and others of our Pacific Northwest's unique flora.

Much of the habitat destruction we have experienced in Mr. Puget's Sound, Captain Vancouver's Admiralty Inlet, King George's Straits, and the islands, lagoons, peninsulas and coastlines they encompass, could have been largely avoided had we clustered and grouped our houses so as to share a beautiful view, preserve intact a wild flower headland or a picturesque madrone and pine along a rocky shoreline. Instead we chopped the land all up in little bits so that everyone got a little of this paradise.

It didn't take long to discover in doing this we broke up and violated the view with powerlines and poles, destroyed the wild flower meadow or headland with septic tank fields, driveways and parking areas and plunked houses among the pines and madrones – those few that were left, that is – to create an alien shoreline of suburban houses and gardens with mown grass, golden junipers and pink roses. We destroyed our natural heritage for a mess of potage in the sacred name of private property and selfish greed!

Menzies collected the tiger lily, *Lilium columbianum* [*canadense* of Menzies, *parviflorum* of Newcombe], with orange flowers and maroon spots on 'laid back', recurved, petals. It is classified in garden terms as a Turk's cap lily. These caps are borne along a stem, which at the top can be five feet high and have up to thirty flowers on it; more usually, half the height with one fifth the flowers. This easily grown native lily has been used in Pacific Northwest gardens that have been raised from wild collected seed. However, the lilies most likely to be seen in these gardens today are complex hybrids.

The pink fawn lily, *Erythronium revolutum*.
JRJ/VPPNW

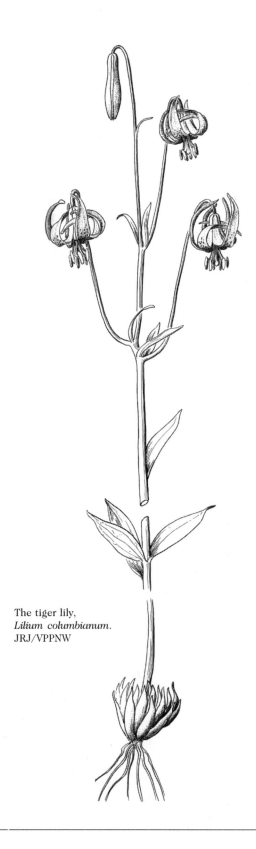

The tiger lily,
Lilium columbianum.
JRJ/VPPNW

Among the first of the tiger lily type hybrids for gardens developed in the 1920s were the Bellingham hybrids, named after the city in northern Washington State where they were grown and first flowered. Although the original seed for these hybrids came from a grower in northern California, it is almost certain that *L. columbianum* was not one of the parents or grandparents. These Bellingham hybrids developed by Dr. David Griffith of the USDA enriched parks and gardens in the Pacific Northwest and Great Britain up until the second world war. In the early 1950s new hybrid lily groups like Fiesta and Dr. C. F. Patterson's Harlequin hybrids appeared to replace the earlier strains. These are American hybrids in Division 4, one of the nine Divisions into which all hybrid and species lilies are classified by type of flower.

The writer was privileged to use Professor Patterson's Harlequin (Saskatoon) hybrid lilies as a massed landscape element among drifts of the grey foliage low-growing form of the Saskatchewan native snowberry, *Symphoricarpos orbiculatus,* along the edges of the grass swards at the campus of the University of Saskatchewan in Saskatoon.

The multi-coloured turkscap tiger lilies, yellow, orange and red with multi-coloured spots, are a fine herbaceous border plant with delphiniums or among fluffy masses of gypsophylla, (baby's breath) in coastal gardens.

In her book *Garden Lilies,* Isobella Preston, who was the ornamental horticulture propagator and hybridizer with the Central Experimental Farm in Ottawa in the 1920s and 1930s, recommended growing lilies in a separate bed with columbine, *Aquilegia* spp. She notes that *L. columbianum* was tried in Ottawa but lived only two seasons. Miss Preston developed the Stenographer series of lilies, crossing *Lilium dauricum X L. maculatum* with *L. davidii.* These hybrids lilies are of the upright facing type.

Two of the best in her Stenographer series are 'Lillian Cummings' and 'Brenda Watts', a yellow and a red-orange. I have it on good authority that these first class lilies' namesakes were also top notch stenographers in the Canadian federal government civil service. *Lilium philadelphicum,* the prairie lily, is the Saskatchewan provincial flower; it is also an upright type.

Some of other plant hybrids Miss Preston developed are the Preston lilacs and the Rosybloom crabapples. Along with lilies, she hybridized lilacs, hemerocallis, ornamental crabapples and other herbaceous perennials that produced many fine hybrid ornamentals for Canadian prairie and eastern gardens. Her contribution to Canadian gardens has yet to be completely documented or fully recognized.[5]

The Shasta or Mt. Hood lily, *Lilium washingtonianum*, and its various subspecies is a trumpet type lily that is native south of the Columbia River and into California. The name honours George Washington, first President of the United States, and was bestowed by Dr. Albert Kellogg who set up a herbarium of California plants in the old Academy of Sciences in San Francisco in the 1860s.[6] It is a fragrant, pink, dark purple or white multi-flowered, five- to six-foot single stem plant occurring in open woods, grassy meadows or chaparral. The white shorter stem form, var. minor, the one called Shasta lily, is usually grown in gardens while the others have been used in hybridizing to produce some of the very complex garden lilies of today.[7]

The coastal forest native in the *Liliacea, Maianthemum dilatatum,* as Clark writes, has a number of confusing and inappropriate common names, false lily of the valley, two-leaved Solomon seal and deerberry are a few names for what is a marvellous ground cover for use in Pacific Northwest gardens, under the shade of large rhododendrons. There is a fine planting of *Maianthemum* under them in Meerkerk gardens on Whidbey Island. In this member of the lily family it is not the flowers that are the attraction but the pairs of bright green parallel-veined, heart-shaped leaves that have long pointed drip tips. Like many leaves in the tropical and temperate rain forests, the leaf of *Maianthemum* catches water that is funnelled to the tip to drip off to the ground away from the plant centre where it might cause drowning of the plant. The small white flowers that are borne on two- or three-inch stems are unique in the *Liliaceae* in having flower parts in twos not threes, two petals, two sepals and four stamens. Fruit is a mottled brown berry.[8]

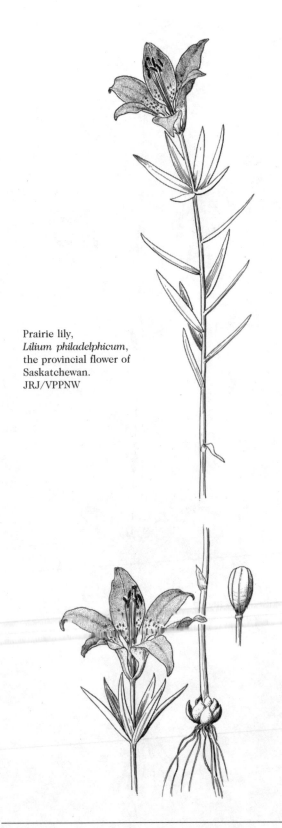

Prairie lily,
Lilium philadelphicum,
the provincial flower of
Saskatchewan.
JRJ/VPPNW

Shasta lily,
Lilium washingtonianum,
above.
JRJ/VPPNW

Deerberry,
Maianthemum dilatatum,
below.
LB/Davidsonia.

The plant Menzies collected as an *Epimedium*, and Sir William Hooker later named for the captain of *Discovery, Vancouveria hexandra,* is a member of the *Berberidaceae* along with one of the Pacific Northwest's best known shrubs, tall mahonia or Oregon grape. *Epimedium* are foot-high herbaceous, colourful, persistent-leaved perennials, and have long been used as partial or complete shade ground covers or foreground border plants in European gardens. The advantage that *Vancouveria*, with its fern-like foliage has for Pacific Northwest gardens over many of the garden *Epimedium* varieties is that it seems to be more adaptable to differing conditions. *Vancouveria hexandra* is vigorous, suppressing weeds and multiplying by underground rhizomes to cover areas thickly as a good groundcover should. Some people classify it as a weed, a great compliment for any plant that reduces the need for watering, weeding and cultivating in today's garden. It has little white tutu-shaped flowers while another variety, *V. chrysantha* has lemon yellow flowers. *Vancouveria* is usually available at specialist west coast nurseries.

Another group of flowers that evoke great feelings of romance and visions of flamboyant colour and beauty are the orchids. Unlike the majority of tropical orchids that are epiphytic, that is, growing on the limbs & trunks of trees or rocks with air roots rather than roots in soil, the native orchid species of the Pacific Northwest are terrestrial. They live on the ground in soils rich in organic matter. One of Menzies first plant discoveries in the woods at Port Discovery was the beautiful pink ground orchid or fairy slipper, *Calypso bulbosa,* of which there are two colour variants, *C. b. subsp occidentalis,* a translucent white, and *C. b. subsp bulbosa,* a bright yellow.

This latter fairy slipper occurs on the east side of British Columbia's coast range but the white one is a coastal variety. The writer remembers vividly finding this pure translucent white fairy slipper in the woods above Crofton on southern Vancouver Island in the late 1930s, only to be deeply embarrassed the next spring when desperately trying to impress a young lady, to find it had completely disappeared. The beauty of the young lady is not remembered, the beauty of orchid and the embarrassment remain to haunt and humble.

Menzies collected six other orchids, four in the genus *Habenaria*, one *Epipactus*, and *Listera convallarioides*. Orchid flowers often mimic the shape or part of an insect to attract that insect to visit the flower and so to fertilize it. Some orchids produce a scent to attract specific insect pollinators while others can only be pollinated by a specific moth, butterfly, bee, wasp or fly. Orchid seeds also need a fungus in order to provide sustenance or trigger germination for the minute, wind distributed seed. In the South Pacific, some islands have quite recently gained new species of orchid from seed swept up into high atmosphere air currents then caught and dropped by tropical rain storms onto suitable island habitats where the seed germinated and a new orchid becomes established.[9]

These occurrences of an entirely new species, where it has never been observed or recorded before, are a torment to those botanists who thought they had compiled complete and definitive island floras. Outside of tropical areas few orchids are grown in gardens as landscape plants. There are at least two orchid species that have made a place in temperate landscapes. The Japanese *Calanthe* and its natural hybrids are grown as goundcovers under red pine with variegated cream and white leaved *Hosta baileyii, now H. undulata.*

The eastern North American lady slipper, *Cypripedium acaule*, has been used as ground cover under pines and in pine woodlands. Many other lady slipper or moccasin flowers are grown in rock gardens and plant collections by native plant and alpine garden enthusiasts.

It is hoped that in the Pacific Northwest we will continue to set aside parks and forest areas and provide protection for the habitats of our diminutive but beautiful native orchids.

Menzies did not collect a native plant that is found in the Pacific Northwest coastal forests, perhaps because these plants have the largest leaves of any on the coast and had flowered too early to be noticed. In botanizing it is difficult to press and dry intact, a fleshy forty- to fifty-inches-long and twenty- to thirty-inches-wide leaf. This is the size of *Lysichitum americanum*, the yellow arum

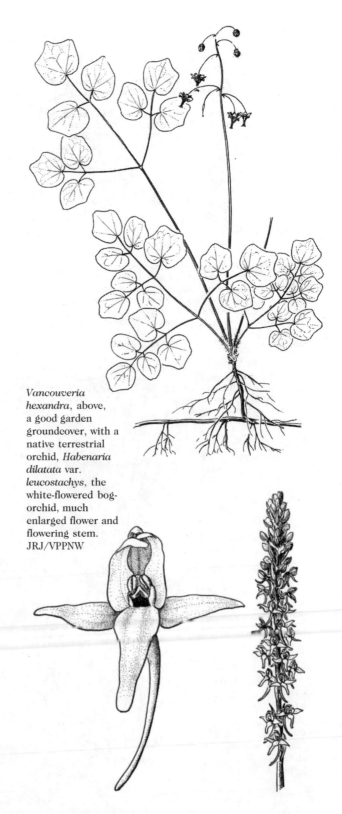

Vancouveria hexandra, above, a good garden groundcover, with a native terrestrial orchid, *Habenaria dilatata* var. *leucostachys*, the white-flowered bog-orchid, much enlarged flower and flowering stem. JRJ/VPPNW

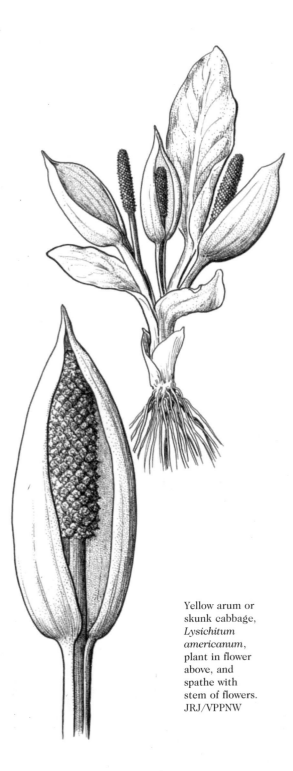

Yellow arum or skunk cabbage, *Lysichitum americanum*, plant in flower above, and spathe with stem of flowers. JRJ/VPPNW

with the more common, but inappropriate name of skunk cabbage. The swamp habitat of *Lysichitum* with its great yellow-green elephant-ear leaves and butter-yellow spathe, like the flame of a primeval torch rising out of the black muck, combine to create an illusion of some prehistoric jungle scene where any minute you expect to see a woolly mammoth or triceratops come thrashing through the undergrowth. Or, if knowledgable in oriental mythology, *Lysichitum*, like the lotus, would permit the viewer to marvel at the pristine purity, delicacy and clarity of colour of leaf and flower rising from such dirty black muck. Even the smell the viewer would associate as coming from the muck, not the beautiful aura of the Buddha.

Menzies, who probably knew nothing of woolly mammoths, dinosaurs or Buddha's auras, probably would have thought of it as a type of taro from the South Seas. While taxonomists still argue whether the North American yellow spathe and the Asiatic white spathe are the same or separate species, gardeners in England have produced a cream spathed hybrid between the two.

Lysichitum are highly valued stream and waterside plants in English and European gardens and parks. Attempts to use it in similar areas in the Pacific Northwest have been met with much derision. Up until the late seventies where it had occurred naturally in park areas, its habitat was almost always eliminated as part of development. Now, however, certain of these swamp habitats have been retained and incorporated into the park's design with the indigenous plants along with the watershed and forest surround that maintains the conditions necessary for the viability of *Lysichitum* and other waterside plants.

Oplopanax horridus, the devil's club, Menzies collected as *Fatsia horrida*. It has a leaf twelve to fifteen inches across that has petioles, mid veins and stems densely covered with poisonous spines! This too would seem a difficult plant to collect, press and mount but Menzies seems to have 'subdued' this devil of plants, for he did collect it.

The devil's club is another plant that is found in a wet ground, shaded forest habitat. Of this environment, soil condition or the combination in the coastal garden, only the shade is mandatory to the use of this native plant. Devil's club (*Oplopanax horridus*) has furry, foot-wide, palmate leaves on spiny angular six- to eight-foot stems with spikes of white flowers that turn to bright red berries. It is an effective and strong textured plant to enrich a tall north wall or a north entry stairway corner. Combined with swordfern, blue-leaved *Hosta, Helleborus, Aconitum* and *Aquilegia*; with *Enkianthus* or *Menziesia* it provides a rich blend of textures, year round greens, with the yellows and rusts of autumn.

As mentioned earlier, one of Menzies' interests was the families of non-flowering plants, in particular the genera in the *Polypodiaceae* or the Fern family. He collected a number of ferns on the *Discovery* voyage. This was before 'cryptomania' swept the mid Victorian conservatory scene, which saw entire glass houses devoted to the growing of tropical and subtropical New Zealand, Malaysian and south seas ferns and treeferns.

Dr. Ward's 'closely' glazed cases in squares, octagons and bell shapes became miniature ferneries and primeval terrarium landscapes on stands in the heavily draped bay windows of Victorian parlours. While they didn't make it into the nineteenth century fernery or terrarium, several of Menzies' fern collections did become fine landscape plants for gardens. There are at least three that make fine groundcovers for shaded and woodland areas in northwest gardens.

The most well known is the western swordfern, *Polystichum munitum*. It is also the fern cut in the wild for use by the florists for greenery. The hilted sword-like pinnae (leaflets) that make up the fronds are ranked each side of the stipe (stem) to form a feather. These fronds can be four feet in length, but eighteen to twenty four inches is more common. The swordfern plant forms clumps that individually or massed provide a bold green sea-like texture to the winter deciduous woodland landscape. There is much variation in plant size and serration patterns of the 'leaflets' for this fern in the Pacific Northwest. This keeps the taxonomists busy!

The swordfern available from nurseries is the form with linear frond and overlapping "leaf-

The devil's club, *Oplopanax horridum*, a dramatic plant for a north side of the house planting.
JRJ/VPPNW

Right: The two types of fronds of the deerfern, *Blechnum spicant*, above, and the maidenhair fern, *Adiantum pedatum*.
MB/F&FABC

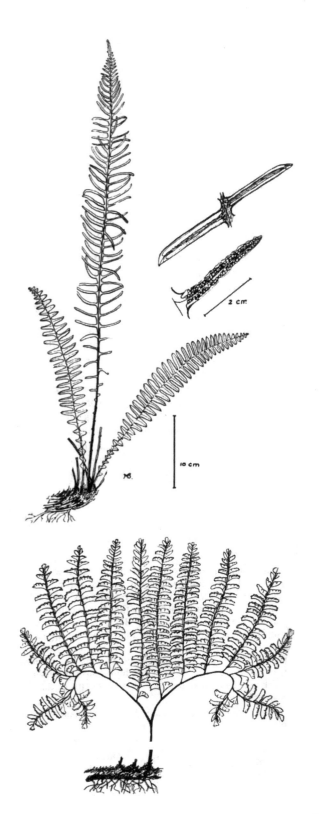

lets" (pinnae) that occurs on Vancouver Island and the mainland shores of Georgia Strait. In these locations it is often a common massed natural groundcover in large areas under open hemlock and Sitka spruce woodlands. The fern genus *Polystichum* is highly variable (polymorphic) within the three species, four subspecies and several forms that occur in the Pacific Northwest.[10]

Adiantum pedatum is the native maidenhair fern. It has delicate sprays of fronds that are a fine accompaniment with the native false lily of the valley, *Maianthemum*, or the real lily of the valley, *Convallaria*, in a shady and damp area of the garden.

While *Adiantum* is deciduous, *Blechnum spicant* or deerfern is a fine evergreen clump fern that bears upright fertile antler-like fronds quite different from the whorl of fronds at the base that spread out at ground level. Deerfern is much smaller than the swordfern but it likes the same conditions.

Athyrium filix femina, the ladyfern, and *Woodsia obtusa oregana*, both have bipinnatifid fronds so they appear more lace-like and finer textured than the sword or deer ferns; however, the fronds of these two are deciduous.

Menzies seems to have missed seeing and collecting two beautiful native *Primulaceae* that are commonly found growing with *Erythronium* and *Camas* in mossy meadows and rock bluffs on the islands of lower Georgia Strait and Mr. Puget's Sound. These are the lovely shooting stars or pheasant's eyes, *Dodecatheon pulchellum*, (*pauciflorum*) the few-flowered shooting star, and *D. hendersonii*, the broad-leaved shooting star.

The words of Lewis Clark's descriptions and observations of these striking natives are worth repetition:

"The showy corolla [of Dodecatheon hendersonii] is extremely variable, so that one sees within the space of a few yards individuals that are palest pink, light orchid, rose-purple, deep purple, and even (occasionally) white... This is a well-proportioned plant of refined beauty. It is easy and admirable in the rockery, though the gardener needs to be forewarned that in August the plants shrivel to

a small nub that is easily overlooked; diligent search will usually reveal a few tiny bulblets on this un-promising nubble... The leaves [of D. pulchellum] may be glabrous to rather densely pubescent, they may be more ovate-lanceolate, or the whole plant may be glandular hairy. The staminal tube varies in colour from yellow, through orange, to reddish-purple. The corolla lobes are generally bright rose-purple, flushed with more intense colour at the base, then above this ringed with deep yellow on which is stitched a beautiful zigzag trim of rose purple. Pulchellum indeed! A lovely thing." [11]

There are two other shooting stars in the Pacific Northwest, the white shooting star, *Dodecatheon dentatum*, and Jefferies shooting star, *D. jefferyi*. Dodecatheon is of Greek derivation: dodeka, twelve, and theoi, gods, both alluding to the cluster of flowers that crown the stem.

As we turn into the twenty-first century we see before us a select and diverse group of native and exotic trees and shrubs, groundcovers and flowers for our park and garden landscapes.

The 'improvements' made to our native coastal plants, first seen in a garden and landscape context by Archibald Menzies, as well as those collected from other temperate areas around the world will give us a continuing legacy that is rich and wonderful, bringing us a beautiful and enriched environment in which to live.

Shooting stars or pheasants eyes.
Left: *Dodecatheon dentatum*.
Right: *D. jefferyii*.
JRJ/VPPNW

NOTES

CHAPTER 1

1. Cox, E.M.H. *Plant Hunting in China, A History of Botanical Exploration in China and the Tibetan Marshes*, Collins London, 1945

2. Lyte, Charles, *Sir Joseph Banks 18th Century Explorer, Botanist and Entrepreneur*, David & Charles, Newton Abbot, London, North Pomfret (VT) 1980. In 1791, while on their way the Pacific Northwest of North America, Menzies with Capt. Vancouver in Discovery put in on the Southwest Coast of Australia (Albany) and spent two weeks botanizing the unique flora of this area of Western Australia. Among the several species of *Hakea, Grevillea, Drysandra* and *Banksia* he collected were five of the latter genus. The red and yellow flowering banksia with long strap-like toothed leaves that is endemic to a more northern coastal part of Western Australia; Menzies did not collect. It was later named for him. Menzies banksia, *B. Menziesii*, is a medium to tall tree in the coastal plain woodlands from Albany to Geraldton. See: Chapter 8 Note #3 and *Flowers & Plants of Western Australia,* by Erikson, George, Marchant and Morcombe, Reed Books Pty Ltd. Sydney NSW, 1991 reprint.

3. Bligh, William, *A Voyage To The South Seas*, Griffin Press, Adelaide, 1975.

4. Lord Ernest E., *Shrubs And Trees for Australian Gardens*, Lothian Publishing Co. Pty. Ltd. Melbourne and Sidney, 1972 reprint of Fourth Edition.

5. Louis-Antoine de Bougainville,(1729-1811) was a French navigator who gave his name to the largest of the Solomon Islands that was a battle site in World War II. The very common tropical shrub/climber with the colourful bracts most commonly royal purple, dark maroon or bright mauve, *Bougainvillea,* comes not as you might expect, from Bougainville Island in the South Pacific but from Brazil in South America.

6. Lysaght, A. M., *Joseph Banks in Newfoundland & Labrador, 1766 His Diary, Manuscripts and Collections*, University of California Press, Berkeley & Los Angeles, 1971, pages 120 & 139-40.

7. Newcombe, C.F., *Menzies Journal of Vancouver's Voyage,* Memoir No. V, Archives of British Columbia, William H. Cullen, Kings Printer, Victoria, B.C. 1923.

8. The greatest of the collectors and discoverers of ornamental plants was Ernest Wilson. In 1926 he described some of his travels and the garden plants he found in a book, now a classic, with the title: *China Mother of Gardens*.

9. Fairchild David, *Garden Islands of the Great East, Collecting Seeds from the Philippines and the Netherlands India in the Junk "Cheng Ho"*, Charles Scribner's Sons, New York, 1943

10. *Reliquiae Houstounianae*, (1781).

11. California Historical Society Quarterly, VOL.II, NO. 4, January, 1924, Menzies' California Journal, Page 317.

12. Ibid, Menzies' California Journal, Page 338.

13. Olson, Wallace M. (ed.) *The Alaska Travel Journal of Archibald Menzies 1793–1794.*

CHAPTER 2

1. Quote is from John Forsyth's Biographical Note in *Menzies Journal of Vancouver's Voyage*, page ix., op cit.

2. Naish, John, M.D., *Archibald Menzies: Surgeon and Botanist,* International Dendrology Society Yearbook 1988, London, pages 123-128.

3. Walbran, John,T., Capt., *British Columbia Coast Names*, University of Washington Press, 1976, Reprint of the 1905 original.

4. Ibid, Page 402

5. Lyte, Charles, *Sir Joseph Banks 18th Century Explorer, Botanist and Entrepreneur,* David & Charles, Newton Abbot, London, North Pomfret (VT) 1980 . Page 124.

6. See McClintock, Elizabeth - *Trees of Golden Gate Park*, 41 - The Sequoias, Pacific Horticulture, Vol. 50, No 1, Spring 1989, Pacific Horticultural Foundation San Francisco and also The World's Tallest Tree Discovered, National Geographic Magazine. 1-9, July 1964.

7. Griffin, James R., and William B. Critchfield, 1972 *The Distribution of Forest Trees in California*, Berkeley, Calif., Pacific SW. Forest & Range Exp. Stn. 114p., illus.(USDA Forest Serv. Res. Paper PSW-82) (Reprinted with Supplement, 1976).

8. The author and his wife participated in this Dawn Redwood distribution in 1949 by bringing two Metasequoia seedlings by Greyhound bus from Berkeley California to Victoria's late Park Superintendent, Herb Warren. These trees are now in British Columbia's capital city, Victoria, in Beacon Hill Park.

9. Joseph A. Witt, Former Curator of Plant Collections, Univ of Washington Aboretum, Personal Communication. For those who are interested in the paleobotany of the Dawn Redwood, *Metasequoia glyptostroboides,* consult the Burke Museum on the campus of the University of Washington, Seattle, Washington.

10. Mrs. Molly Thompson, Victoria, B.C., Personal Communication 1987

11. Dorothy Gibson, Tofino B.C., Personal Communication, 1988

12. Goodspeed, Harper, *Plant Hunting in the Andes*, Univ of California Press, 1940 & MacMillan, H.F., Tropical Planting & Gardening, 5th Ed. MacMillan, London, 1952.

13. Corner, E. J. H., C.B.E., F.R.S., F.L.S., *Botanical Monkeys,* The Pentland Press Limited, Edinburgh, Cambridge, Durham. 1992

1414. Mrs. Molly Thompson, of Victoria has observed the monkey puzzle over many years. She reports having found a tree in Victoria bearing both male and female cones. Personal communication, 1988.

15. J. Wood, an Argentinian dendrologist, has written about this little known southern hemisphere genus, *Nothofagus*, the southern beeches and those species occurring in South America in: *The 1989 Year Book of the International Dendrology Society*, London, 1990, pages 99-106.

16. Moore, David M., *Flora of Tierra del Fuego*, Anthony Nelson, England, 1983.

CHAPTER 3

1. Protection Island so named by Captain Vancouver as it guards the mouth of Port Discovery Inlet. The cornucopia shaped inlet is about eight leagues from mouth to end. It lies on the west side of the peninsula where Port Townsend is located and east of Port Angeles on Washington's Olympic Peninsula.

2. Protection Island landscape, a premeditated plan of a judicious designer, *Menzies Journal of Vancouver's Voyage April to October 1792*, C.F. Newcombe MD. Editor, Archives of British Columbia Memoir No. 5, Kings Printer, 1923 page 18.

3. See the Four Volume Limited Printing of: *The Red Books Of Humphrey Repton*, Basilisk Press, London, 1976. Also Stroud, Dorothy, Humphrey Repton, Country Life Ltd., London, 1962.

4. Author's maternal family records - The Beddis's of Saltspring Island, 1880 cf.

5. Fox, Stephen, *John Muir And His Legacy, The American Conservation Movement*, Little, Brown and Company - Boston - Toronto, 1981, pages 43-44.

6. Clark, Lewis J., *Wild Flowers Of The Pacific Northwest,* Gray's Publishing Limited, Sidney, B.C., 1976.

7. Newcombe C.F. Md., Botanical & Ethnological Appendix to *Menzies Journal of Vancouver's Voyage*, William H Collin Printer to Kings most Excellent Majesty, Victoria, B.C., 1923.

8. Walbran, op cit, pages 414 -416.

9. Walbran, op cit page 421.

10. C. Leo, Cronquist, Arthur, Owenby, Marion & Thompson, J.W., *Vascular Plants of the Pacific Northwest*, University of Washington Press, Seattle, Wash., Second Printing 1971, page 1:801.

11. Oregon Ash in British Columbia, see: Taylor Roy L. and MacBryde, Bruce, *Vascular Plants of British Columbia, A Descriptive Resource Inventory,* Technical Bulletin No. 4, The Botanical Garden, The University of British Columbia, The University of British Columbia Press, Vancouver, 1977.

12. Dr. Roy Taylor, Personal Communication.

13. *Range Plant Handbook*, Forest Service, U.S. Dept of Agriculture, U.S. Govt Printing Office, Washington D.C., 1937, Page GL17.

CHAPTER 4

1. Admiralty Inlet is the name given by Captain Vancouver to the stretch of water that is the mouth of Puget Sound. The inlet begins at Port Townsend, (also named by Vancouver), South to Foulweather Bluff at the entrance to Hood Canal, (also a name given by Vancouver), that is across from Double Bluff on Whidbey Island. These two promontories mark the northern end of Puget Sound.

2. Port Gardner was named by Vancouver for his patron Commodore Sir Alan Gardner under whose command Vancouver served while on the Caribbean Station 1781-89. See Anderson, Bern, Rear Admiral, U.S. Navy (Ret.), *Surveyor of the Sea, The Life and Voyages of Captain George Vancouver*, University of Toronto Press, Toronto, 1960. pages 19-28

3. The Pacific rhododendron is the official flower of Washington state. For a full discussion of the this and the other ericaceous plants Menzies discovered see Chapter 8.

4. The Pacific dogwood is the official flower of the province of British Columbia, see also Chapter 8.

5. The hairy manzanita. This ericaceous plant is discussed in Chapter 8.

6. Huckleberry, salal, ocean spray and salmonberry; All these shrubs are discussed and referred to more fully in Chapter 8.

7. Tall mahonia or Oregon grape, See Chapter 10.

8. The chocolate lilies; See Chapter 9 for a discussion and description of these lilies.

9. Longitude was determined by a complicated series of sighting of stars and measurements of the distance between them and the moon. This was first developed by a German astronomer by Johannes Werner in 1514 and refined in the late 1700s in England by the King's Astronomer Nevile Maskelyne. This complicated lunar distance method for determination of longtiude was supplanted by the early years of the nineteenth century by the accuracy of Harrison's and other clock makers ship's chronometers. For the story of this problem of finding your ship's position at sea, see: Sobel, Dava, *Longitude*, Walker and Company, New York, 1995.

10. J.E. Roberts, personal communication.

11. Walbran, op cit, pages 71, 212 & 466. Also: *The Letters & Journals of Simon Fraser 1806 - 1808,* Edited by W. Kaye Lamb, Dominion Archivist, Macmillan and Company, Toronto, 1960.

12. *Menzies Journal*, Page 64.

13. John Scouler was the Surgeon and amateur Botanist on the Hudson's Bay Company vessel *Prince William*, which brought David Douglas, the plant collector for the Royal Horticultural Society, to Fort Vancouver on the Columbia River. It sailed back and forth between the Pacific Northwest and Hawaii on HBC business.

14. By Nelson, who was the botanist who lost his life to fever after surviving the epic Bounty longboat trip from Tahiti to Timor with Capt Bligh. See Chapter 1.

15. *Sedum ferruginea* described. Clark, *Wildflowers of the Pacific Northwest*, op cit, page 213.

CHAPTER 5

1. Watkin David, *The English Vision, The Picturesque in Architecture, Landscape and Garden Design*, John Murray, London 1982.

2. Walbran, op cit, pages 113, 313 & 406,

3. *Menzies Journal*, opcit, page 64 65, and J.E. Roberts personal communication.

4. *Menzies Journal*, op cit, page 65.

5. J. E. Roberts, personal communication. The Landseer engraving in Vancouver's Journal of an Indian Village in Bute Inlet was taken from an on the spot sketch by Tom Heddington, a Midshipman who was a member of Chatham's crew. Meany, op cit, page 225.

6. Addenbrooke is a name given by Vancouver to a point of land in Fitzhugh Sound. Why or when it was transferred to a mountain on East Redondo Island is not known. Homfray Channel was named by Daniel Pender of the surveying vessel *Beaver*, for Robert Homfray, an eccentric civil engineer residing in Victoria, 1860-1902. See: Walbran, op cit, pages 12 & 245.

7. Walbran, op cit, page 490 & *Menzies Journal*, op cit, p. 70.

8. J. E. Roberts, personal communication.
9. The cranberry, from crane-berry as the stalk of the berry is supposed to look like a crane's neck. Several botanists classify this plant in another ericaceous genus, *Oxycoccus*, see Szczawinski, Adam F., *The Heather Family of British Columbia*, Hndbk #19, B.C. Provincial Museum Victoria, 3rd Printing, 1975.
10. The Saskatoon berry, like the unpalatable, *Arctostaphylos uva-ursi* or kinnikinnik, was also used in pemmican.
11. Commercial cropping of the Saskatoon berry. Dwain Foster, Peace River Small Fruit Growers Association, Beaverlodge, Alta., Personal communication.
12. See Chapter 11.
13. *Menzies Journal*, op cit, page 71.
14. *Menzies Journal*, op cit, page 75
15. Menzies orchid discoveries are discussed in Chapter 9.
16. Schofield, W.B., *Some Common Mosses of British Columbia*, Handbook No. 28, B.C. Provincial Museum, Victoria B.C. 1959.
17. *Menzies Journal*, op cit, page 76.

CHAPTER 6

1. *Menzies Journal*, op cit, page 81.
2. Discovery Passage probably named for Vancouver's Ship Discovery although there is no record of who named it.
3. Cape Mudge was named by Vancouver for Zachary Mudge, Ist Lieutenant, *Discovery*. see note 12, Chapter four. also Walbran, op cit, page 345.
4. *Menzies Journal*, opcit, page 83.
5. Durham, Bill, *Canoes of the Northwest Coast*, 1960 reprint, Shorey Publications, Seattle, Wash., n.d., also Stewart, Hilary, op cit, pages 48 through 59 and Shadbolt, Doris, Bill Reid, Douglas and McIntyre Ltd., Vancouver, B.C., 1986.
6. Thomson, Richard E., *Oceanography of the British Columbia coast*, Can. Spec. Publ. Aquat. Sci. 56:291 p., 1981 reprinted 1984.
7. Author's personal experience.
8. Menzies Penstemon, Clark, Lewis J., *Wild Flowers of the Pacific Northwest*, op cit page 472.
9. Sir William Hooker's taxonomic error. Hitchcock, et al, *The Vascular Plants of the Pacific Northwest*, in 5 parts, University of Washington Press, Seattle, Second Printing, 1971. Page 379.
10. *Menzies Journal*, op cit, page 84.
11. Author's personal experiences.
12. *Menzies Journal*, op cit page 86.
13. Walbran, op cit, page 446 and 471.
14. A new raspberry? Menzies must have inadvertently called this a new species of *Rubus* although he had already found it in Admiralty Inlet - Puget Sound area.
15. New Georgia is usually considered to have encompassed the area of the Pacific Northwest from the Columbia River, latitude 46° N to latitude 55° N. Prince Rupert is 54°10" N.
16. Walbran, opcit, pages 291-92 & pages 178 & 305.
17. *Menzies Journal*, op cit, page 94.
18. *Menzies Journal*, op cit page 98.
19. Bentinck, North and South Arms were named by Capt Vancouver for William Henry Cavendish Bentinck, 3rd Duke of Portland (1738-1809), Leader of the Whig Party, and had been Prime Minister. Ten years before Vancouver honoured him with two narrow mid B.C. coastal channels. His ducal title was also honoured by Vancouver with another Vancouver chart name in Portland Canal. The duke distinguished himself as Home Secretary in charge of Irish affairs under Prime Minister Pitt. His son Lord William Cavendish Bentinck, a soldier, became Governor General of India in 1833. There is a monotypic (one only) genus of palm, *Bentinckiana nicobarca*, found only on the Nicobar and Andaman Islands between Latitude 5°-14°N and between 92°- 94° East Longitude in the Bay of Bengal south of Burma and north of Sumatra and east of the upper part of the Malay Peninsula. See Walbran, *Chambers Biographical Dictionary*, Editor: Magnus Magnusson, Chambers Harrap Publishers Ltd, 1990 and Rao, P.S.N. *Phytogeography of the Andaman and Nicobar Islands, India*, The Malayan Nature Journal, Vol50/prt2, November 1996.
20. Walbran, op cit, page 295.
21. Menzies Journal, op cit, page 107.
22. Menzies Journal, Page 103.

CHAPTER 7

1. *Cook's Third Voyage*, Vol., 4, page 279.
2. A supercargo is a merchant ship's officer who is in charge of the cargo - from the Latin, sobrecargo.
3. A snow is an old type of square rigged sailing ship with single topsails, two main masts and a third short mast attached to the stern mast. This short mast is called a snow mast to which a gaffed trysail was rigged and flown. See A.B. Nordbok, *The Lore of Ships*, Crescent Books, New York, 1975.
4. Menzies describes the shoreline landscape of Nootka Sound. Ibid, page 106.
5. *Menzies Journal*, op cit, page 108.
6. *Menzies Journal*, op cit page 126.
7. *Menzies Journal*, op cit, page 128.
8. See Newcombe's preface to Menzies Journal.
9. See, Appendix B in Mozino, Jose, Mariano, *Noticias de Nutka, an Account of Nootka Sound in 1792*, translated and edited by Iris Higbie Wilson, McCelland & Stewart Limited, Toronto/Montreal, l970.
10. *Climate of British Columbia*, Report for 1976, B.C. Ministry of Agriculture, Victoria.
11. *Menzies Journal*, op cit, page 112.
12. *Menzies' California Journal*, California Historical Society, Vol.11, No.4, January, 1924.

CHAPTER 8

1. Bailey, L.H., Hortus Third, Macmillan, New York, 1976
2. Menzies southern beech, See Chapter 2.
3. Menzies collected five banksias during his botanizing along the coast of King George Sound and hinterland of Princess Royal Harbour and Oyster Harbour and Vancouver Peninsula. *Discovery* spent twelve days, (28 September to 10 October 1791, anchored in the Sound with crews going ashore for wood and water while Menzies explored for plants. These are *Banksia*

ilicifolia, holly-leaved banksia, *B. grandis*, bull banksia, *B. coccinea*, scarlet banksia, *B. littoralis*, the swamp or river banksia and the Albany banksia, *B. praemorsa* along with a number of western Australian plants including three that bear his epithet, *Urticularia menziesii*, a bladderwort or pond weed, *Drosera menziesii*, an Australian sundew and *Caladenia menziesii*, a western Australian endemic ground orchid. When they put in at Sydney, Menzies sent his plant collections and seed, from western Australia, home to Banks and Kew Gardens where they arrived 19 months (June 1793) later. The Albany banksia, *Banksia praemorsa*, a large shrub to 12ft, was described and named from the plants raised and flowered at Kew that came from the seed sent by Menzies. See Alexander S. George, *The Banksia Book*, Kangaroo Press, Dural Delivery Centre, NSW 2158/Timber Press, Portland OR.

4. Hillebrand, W.F., 1965 reprint ed., *Flora of the Hawaiian Islands*, Hafner Publishing Co., New York & London., 673 pp.

5. Kimura, Bert Y., and Nagata, Kenneth M., *Hawaii's Vanishing Flora*, Oriental Publishing Co., Honolulu, Hawaii, 1980, page 57.

6. *Menzies Journal*, op cit page 15.

7. Palow, *Noticias de California*, Vol.1, Bosqui, San Francisco, 1873, Page 205.

8. Hosie, op cit, page 82, Bloom, Adrian, op cit, page 95.

9. See also Chapter 10.

10. Wang, Chi-Wu, *Forests of China*, Maria Moors Cabot Foundation Publication Series No.5, Botanical Museum Harvard University, Boston, Mass., 1961.

11. Griffin, James R., and William B. Critchfield, *The Distribution of Forest Trees in California*, Pacific SW., Forest & Range Exp. Stn. 114 p., illus. (USDA Forest Serv. Res. Paper PSW-82), Berkeley, Calif., (1972), Reprint with Supplement, 1976.

12. Author's personal experiences.

13. Hornibrook, Murray, *Dwarf & Slow Growing Conifers*, Country Life Ltd, London, Second edition, 1938 or for a more up-to-date treatment in colour see Bloom, Adrian, *Conifers for Your Garden*, Floraprint Ltd, Calverton, Nottingham, 1974.

14. *Menzies Journal*, op cit pages 151 & 152. Scagel, R.F., *Guide to the Common Seaweeds of British Columbia*, Handbook #27, B.C. Provincial Museum; Waaland, Robert J., *Common Seaweeds of the Pacific Coast*, J.J. Douglas, Vancouver, 1977, page 60.

15. The Mosses of British Columbia are described in Scofield, op cit. Menzies collected 16 mosses in the Pacific Northwest, see *Menzies Journal*, op cit, Appendix II, page 149.

16. Menzies raspberry, *Menzies Journal*, op cit.

17. Clark, Lewis J., op cit, page 348.

18. Clark, Lewis J., op cit, page 521 et sec.

19. *Menzies Journal*, op cit, Appendix I page 133

20. Clark, Lewis J., op cit, page 115.

21. Clark, Lewis J., op cit page 372

22. Jeckyll, Gertrude, *Colour in the Flower Garden*, Country Life Ltd., London, 1908.

23. Hitchcock et al, op cit, Part 2 pages 346-66. and Pizzetti, Ippolita & Henry Cocker, *Flowers, A Guide For Your Garden*, Harry N. Abrams, Inc., Publishers, New York, 1975.

24. Pizzetti & Cocker, op cit.

25. Calder, James A., and Roy L. Taylor, *Flora of the Queen Charlotte Islands*, Research Branch, Canada Dept of Agriculture, Ottawa, Monograph #4, Part 1, 1968.

For available spireas suitable for Pacific Northwest garden use see Sherk, Lawrence C., and Arthur R. Buckley, *Ornamental Shrubs for Canada*, Research Branch, Canada Dept of Agriculture, Ottawa, Publication 1286, 1968

CHAPTER 9

1. Turner, Nancy, *Plants in British Columbia: Indian Technology*, British Columbia Provincial Museum, Handbook No. 38, Victoria, 1979.

2. *Menzies Journal*, op cit, pages 4-14.

3. Author's personal experience.

4. *Menzies Journal*, op cit, page 18.

5. Author's personal observations at Discovery Bay, Washington, in 1980.

6. *Menzies California Journal*, California Historical Society Quarterly, Vol II, No 4, January 1924, pages 294-95.

7. USDA., *The Range Plant Handbook*, op cit, pages B15 et sec.

8. George Fraser's letters to Joe Gable 1929-39, Archives of British Columbia, Victoria, B.C.; also author's personal experiences.

9. Boge, Dallas, The Ross-Boge *Rhododendron macrophyllum* Expedition, ARS Journal, Portland, Vol 40, No 2, Spring 1986.

10. Author's personal observations.

11. *Menzies Journal*, op cit, page 18.

12. Mitchell, Alan, *Trees of Great Britain & Northern Europe*, Collins, London, 1982, pages 60 to 62.

13. Stewart, Hilary, *Cedar*, Douglas and McIntyre, Vancouver/Toronto, 1984.

14. Clallum names for some trees Menzies found. Some of the other Menzies discoveries in this narrow inlet, like the Pacific madrone, the Clallam called kokweltsh while they called the wild crabapple, *Malus fusca*, kukh-whetsh and its fruit, ka-akhw. See also note 6, chapter 2. For the role of *Thuja plicata* in the culture of the North American indigenous peoples of the Northwest coast see Stewart, Hilary, *Cedar*, op cit.

15. Garden Clubs of America, Janet Poor, editor, *Plants that Merit Attention, Vol. 1, Trees*, Timber Press, Portland, Oregon, 1984. Mitchell Alan, op cit, page 79.

16. *Menzies Journal*, op cit, page 49.

17. Klinaj K., Nuzdorfer, F., *Biogeoclimatic Units Of Central & Southern Vancouver Island*, Ministry of Forests, Victoria, 1979, & McMinn, R., *The Nature of British Columbia Forests*, British Columbia Heritage Record #1, Victoria, 1976.

18. *Menzies Journal*, op cit, Pages 28, 71 & 112.

CHAPTER 10

1. *Menzies Journal*, op cit, pages 42 & 51.

2. Twaites, R. G., Editor, *Original Journals of the Lewis & Clark Expedition*, Dodd, Mead, New York, 1905.

3. Clark, Lewis J. op cit, pages 20 & 21.

4. *Menzies Journal*, Appendix, Plants Collected by A. Menzies on the North-West Coast of America, op cit, page 136.

5. Preston, Isobella, *Garden Lilies,* Orange Judd Publishing Company Inc., New York, 1935.

6. Ewan, Joseph, *Rocky Mountain Naturalists*, University of Denver Press, Denver, Colorado, 1950, page 61.

7. Rockwell, F.F. et al, *The Complete Book of Lilies*, Doubleday, New York, 1961.

8. Clark, op cit, pages 26-27.

9. 12th World Orchid Conference lecture session: *Dendrobium in New Guinea and the South Pacific Islands.* P.J. Cribb, Curator, Eric Young Orchid Foundation Gardens, on Jersey, the Channel Islands, 12th WOC, Toyko, Japan, 1987.

10. Calder and Taylor, op cit.

11. Clarke, Lewis J., op cit, page 400-401.

Greg Foster's drawing for his
replica of one of *Discovery's* boats.

APPENDIX A

A Chronology of events relating to coastal and botanical discovery in the Pacific Northwest.

1767 - San Blas the Spanish Port on the Pacific serves the Northwest coast until 1800

1786 - English trader John Meares lands at Friendly Cove on the island of Nootka and builds a small hut.

1788 - Archibald Menzies with Capt Collnet visits and names Banks Island after sir Joseph Banks founder of Kew Gardens and collects his namesake the shrub *Menziesii ferruginea*.

1789 - Menzies visits Santa Cruz and Santiago on his return to England collecting the coast redwood in California.

1790 - Spanish occupy Nootka's Friendly Cove

1792 - Archibald Menzies Surgeon-Botanist with Vancouver in the ships' boats of *Discovery* and *Chatham* botanize along:
   - Discovery Bay, Hood Canal and Puget sound in May collecting Pacific madrone, rhododendron and dogwood.
   - Birch Bay, Whidbey and San Juan islands in June, collecting the trees Douglas fir, western red cedar and juniper.
   - Desolation Sound and Menzies Bay during July, collecting western hemlock, penstemon and salmonberry.
   - Rivers Inlet and South Bentinck Arm in August collecting shore pine and saskatoon berry and his namesake false azalea.
   - Nootka Island and Tahsis Inlet during September collecting yellow cedar, salal and Oregon grape.
   - San Francisco Bay and Monterey during October collecting California Liveoak.

1792 - Galiano and Valdes sail from San Blas in *Sutil* and *Mexicana* for the Northwest Coast
   - Peter Puget charts Puget Sound in May
   - Vancouver charts Burrard Inlet in June
   - Galiano and Valdes chart the Fraser River Estuary in Georgia Strait, missed by Vancouver.
   - William Broughton, master of *Chatham*, charts the both shores of the Columbia River to the Willamette River
   - November, Discovery and Chatham provision at Monterey then sail from San Diego to winter in the Sandwich, (Hawaiian) Islands.

1793 - Alexander Mackenzie treks overland to South Bentinck Arm and into Dean Channel and sees the Pacific Ocean.

1805 - Lewis and Clark reach the Pacific via the Snake and Columbia Rivers.

1808 - Simon Fraser reaches the Strait of Georgia at Musqueam via the Fraser River

APPENDIX B

A list of Hawaiian Plants discovered by Archibald Menzies and bearing his epithet, collected on his three visits with the Vancouver Expedition in *Discovery* and *Chatham*, 1792, 1794 & 1796 as recorded on page 5 of the Introduction in: Menzies, Archibald, *Hawaii Nei 128 Years Ago*, Edited by W.F. Wilson, Honolulu, January 1920. Nomenclature changes in accordance with Wagner, Herbst and Sohmer, *Manual Of The Flowering Plants Of Hawaii*, Bishop Museum, Honolulu, 1990.

Abutil(l)on menziesii Seem. *Abutilon menziesii*, Menzies abutilon is a hairy shrub with coarsely serrate heart-shaped leaves about 2.5 to 8 cm long. The attractive flowers are dark red and only 20-25 mm across. Usually they occur singly on long drooping pedicels and hang like christmas ornaments on a silvery green tree. Menzies found it on the "Sandwich Islands", specific location not noted. The botanist Wilhelm Hillebrand found it on the Waianea side of the Kohala Mountains while Lydgate, his associate, collected a light pink form on Lanai. It is also found on Kona, Hawaii, Lanai and Ewa and Oahu. Menzies abutilon or flowering maple is endangered in the wild.

Astelia menziesiana Sm., now *Astelia menziesii*. The genus *Astelia* in the Liliaceae was first named by Joseph Banks, (Menzies' patron), and Daniel Solander, when, with Captain Cook in *Endeavour* they discovered species in both Australia and New Zealand.

Bonania menziesii Gray.= *Bonamia menziesii* a liana not in ornamental horticulture.

Breweria menziesii Benth and Hook = *Bonamia menziesii* A.Gray, see above.

Camplyotheca menziesii Hbd. = *Bidens menziesii* (A. Gray) Sherff, a shrub to 4m tall.
A number of these beggar ticks or bur marigolds, closely allied to cosmos and coreopsis are used in ornamental horticulture, while *Bidens pinnatifida* is a pantropic weed.

Cibotium menziesii Hook. The hapu iii or Hawaiian tree fern, now renamed *C. chamissoi*. The largest growing of the tree ferns.

Coprosma menziesii Gray and Waw. Now *C. montana* var. menziesii. Most coprosmas that are in cultivation for ornamental use are found in southern California and originate from New Zealand.

Cyrtandra menziesii Hook and Arn. a shrub to 5m tall in the African violet, gesneriad family. There are 350 species in the Malay Peninsula and the Pacific Islands. None of the *Cyrtandras* are listed as ornamental.

Geranium cuneatum var. *menziesii* Gray. Not in cultivation and possibly endangered.

Kadua menziesiana Ch and Schl.= *Hedyotis coriacea* Sm. A small shrub in Rubiaceae probably now extinct. H. caerula is the bluets or quaker ladies, native in eastern North America. All of the North American hedyotis were once classified as houstonia.

Lycopodium menziesii Hook and Grev. Menzies club-moss

Selaginella menziesii Spring. Moss-like branching plants grown for ornamental foliage.

Pandanus menziesii Gaud. Now *Pandanus tectorius* S.Parkinson ex Z. A screw pine, a small tree less than 10m in height. Said to have originated in Tahiti; possible that it was brought to Hawaii in *Endeavour* with Captain Cook.

Pleiosmilax menziesii Seem. = *Smilax melastomiflora* Sm. A tuberous rooted liana
The tubers of S. officinale furnishes the Jamaican sarsaparilla used as a drug for rheumatism and gout.

Raillardia menziesii Gray. = *Dubautia menziesii* (A. Gray) D.Keck. The Hawaiian naenae. A tree in the daisy or compositae family. A genus of trees and shrubs with clusters of small yellow daisy flowers found only on the Hawaiian Islands. Menzies probably collected this shrub or small tree to twenty feet, on his climb up Mauna Kea in 1794; although Joseph Rock collected it near the summit of Mt. Haleakala between 7000 and 10000 feet in the first decade of this century.

Scaevola menziesiana Cham. = *S. gaudichaudii* Hook & Arnett. The lobelia shrub; although most come from Australia the genus is pantropic. One species used for hedges in Florida.

Scheidea menziesii Hook. Scheidea is a small sprawling sub shrub in the Caryophllaceae or pink family, (carnations). An obscure genus not in cultivation.

Vicia menziesii Spring. The Hawaiian wild broadbean or Hawaiian vetch is a perennial vine that is endangered in the wild. With dark pink flowers it is pictured on one of four US postage stamps showing endangered species of plants that were issued in the 1970s.

The suffix, *iana*, to Menzies epithet is one given in compliment, while the suffix, *ii*, denotes either the person who was the first discoverer or describer. This was codified in an obscure article, (no. 33), in the 1867 *Laws of Botanical Nomenclature* by Alphonse de Candolle. William T. Stern, writing in *Botanical Latin*, Timber Press, 1998, states that "...this might have made a useful distinction. Apparently, most of those who then and thereafter named new species paid no attention whatever to it; probably they never knew such a distinction had been proposed." (Stearn, page 294.)

BIBLIOGRAPHY OF PRIMARY AND SECONDARY SOURCES

Anderson, Bern, *Surveyor of the Sea, The Life and Voyages of Captain George Vancouver,* University of Toronto Press, Toronto, 1960.

Burke, Edmund, *A Philosophical Inquiry into the Origin of our Ideas of the Sublime and the Beautiful,* (1757)

A.B. Nordbok, *The Lore of Ships,* Crescent Books, New York, 1975.
B.C. Ministry of Agriculture *Climate of British Columbia,* Report for 1976, Victoria.

B.C. Heritage Trust/B.C. Society of Landscape Architects, *Vancouver Heritage Tree Inventory, 1982 - 83.*

Bailey, L.H., *Hortus Second,* Macmillan, New York, 1942.

Bell, Edward, *A New Vancouver Journal on the Discovery of Puget Sound, by a member of the Chatham's Crew,* edited by E.S. Meany, Seattle, 1915.

Bligh, William, *A Voyage To The South Seas,* Griffin Press, Adelaide, 1975,

Bloom, Adrian, *Conifers for Your Garden,* Floraprint Ltd, Calverton, Nottingham, 1974.

Bowditch, *American Practical Navigator,* U.S. Navy Dept. Hydrographic Service, 1943.

Bramwell, David and Zoe, *Wildflowers of the Canary Islands,* Stanley Thornes Publishers Ltd., London and Burford, 1974.

Brayshaw, Christopher T., *Catkin Bearing Plants of British Columbia,* Occasional Papers of the British Columbia Provincial Museum N0. 18, B.C. Provincial Museum, Victoria, 1976,

Bretschneider, E., M.D., *History of European Botanical Discoveries in China ,* Zentral - Antiquaritariat, Der Deutschen Demokratischen Republic, Leipzig, 1962, Reprint of the original 1898 St. Petersburg edition.

Calder, James A , & Taylor, Roy L., *Flora of the Queen Charlotte Islands,* Research Branch, Canada Department of Agriculture, Roger Duhamel Queen's Printer, Ottawa, Canada, 1968.

Cave, Henry W., Golden Tips, *A Description of Ceylon & Its Great Tea Industry,* Samson Low, Marston & Company Limited, London 1901.

Clark, Lewis J., *Wild Flowers Of The Pacific Northwest,* Gray's Publishing Limited, Sidney, B.C., 1976.

Cook, Warren, *Flood Tide of Empire, Spain and the Pacific Northwest, 1543-1819,* Yale University Press, New Haven & London 1973,

Coomber, J.B., *Wayside Orchids of Southeast Asia,* Heineman Asia, Kuala Lumpur, Malaysia, 1981.

Corner, H., *Wayside Trees of Malaysia.* Malaysian Nature Society, Kuala Lumpur, 1988. Reprint of 1940.

Cox, Peter A., *Dwarf Rhododendrons,* Macmillan, 1973.

Cox E.H.M., *Plant Hunting In China,* Collins, London, 1945.

Davidson, John, *Conifers, Junipers and Yew: Gymnosperms of British Columbia,* T. Fisher Unwin, London, 1927.

Davies, John, *Douglas of the Forests, The North American Journals of David Douglas,* University of Washington Press, Seattle, 1970.

Dressler, Robert L., *The Orchids, Natural History and Classification,* Harvard University Press, Cambridge, Mass., & London, Eng., 1981.

Durham, Bill, *Canoes of the Northwest Coast,* 1960 reprint, Shorey Publications, Seattle, Wash., n.d.,

Ewan, Joseph, *Rocky Mountain Naturalists,* University of Denver Press, Denver Colorado, 1950.

Fairchild, David, *Gardens of the Great East,* Charles Scribner's Sons, New York, 1943.

Fortune, Robert, *A Residence Among the Chinese,* John Murray, 1851,

Fox, Stephen, *John Muir And His Legacy, The American Conservation Movement,* Little, Brown and Company - Boston - Toronto, 1981.

Gallo, Fred C., *Azaleas,* Timber Press, Portland, Oregon, 1985

Garner, Joe, *Never Fly Over an Eagles Nest,* Oolichan Books, Lantzville, B.C., 1980.

George Forrest, *Scottish Rock Garden Club,* Edinburgh, 1935.

Goddard, Pliny Edward, *Indians of the Northwest Coast,* Handbook No.10, American Museum of Natural History, 1945.

Goodspeed, Harper, *Plant Hunting in the Andes,* University of California Press, 1940.

Henry, J.K., *Rubus parviflorus var fraserianus*, *Torreya*, 18:54 (1918).

Hillebrand, W.F., 1965 reprint ed., *Flora of the Hawaiian Islands*, Hafner Publishing Co., New York & London.

Hitchcock, C. Leo, Cronquist, Arthur, Owenby, Marion and Thompson, J.W., *Vascular Plants of the Pacific Northwest*, University of Washington Press, Seattle Wash., Second Printing 1971.

Hobhouse Henry, *Seeds of Change, Five Plants that Transformed Mankind*, Harper and Row, Publishers, New York, 1985.

Holttum, Prof. R. E., *Plant Life in Malaya*, Longman Group, London, 1969.

Hornibrook, Murray, *Dwarf and Slow Growing Conifers*, Country Life Ltd, London, Second edition, 1938.

Hosie, R.C., *Native Trees of Canada*, Canadian Forestry Service, Dept of Fisheries and Forestry, Queens Printers, Seventh Edition, 1969.

Hulten, Eric, *Flora of Alaska and Neighbouring Territories*, Stanford University Press, Stanford California, 1968.

Hunt, John, Dixon, and Willis, Peter, *The Genius of the Place, The English Landscape Garden 1620-1820.*, Paul Elek, London, 1975.

Islands Protection Society, *Islands At The Edge, Preserving the Queen Charlotte Islands Wilderness*, Douglas and McIntyre, Vancouver, 1984.

Jaynes, Richard A., *The Laurel Book*, Hafner Press, New York, Collier Macmillan Canada Ltd., 1975.

Jeckyll, Gertrude, *Colour in the Flower Garden*, Country Life Ltd., London, 1908.

Kalm Peter, *Travels in North America*, translated into English (from Swedish) by John Reinhold Forster, The Imprint Society, Barre, Mass., 1972.

Kimura, Bert Y., and Nagata, Kenneth M., *Hawaii's Vanishing Flora*, The Oriental Publishing Co., Honolulu, Hawaii, 1980.

Klinaj, K., and Nuzdorfer, F., *Biogeoclimatic Units Of Central and Southern Vancouver Island*, Ministry of Forests, Victoria, 1979.

Kopas, Cliff, *Bella Coola*, Tenas Tiktik Publishing, Vancouver, Second Printing 1985.

Kunkel, Gunther and Kunkel, Mary Anne, *Flora de Gran Canario, Tomo I, Arboles y Arbutos Arboroes*, Editiones del Excmo, Cabilda Insular de Gran Canaria, Las Palmas, 1974.

Lamb, Kaye, editor, *The Letters and Journals of Simon Fraser 1806 - 1808*, Macmillan and Company, Toronto, 1960.

Lyons, C.P. Lyons, *Trees Shrubs and Flowers To Know in British Columbia*.

Lyte, Charles, *Sir Joseph Banks, 18th Century Explorer, Botanist and Entrepreneur*, David and Charles, Newton Abbot, London, North Pomfort (VT) 1980.

MacDonald, George F., *Haida Monumental Art, Villages of the Queen Charlotte Islands*, U.B.C. Press, Vancouver, 1983.

MacMillan, H.F., *Tropical Planting and Gardening*, 5th Ed. MacMillan, London, 1952.

Macoun, John, *A Catalogue of Canadian Plants*, 7 Parts in Three volumes, 1883-1886.

McClintock, Elizabeth, *Trees of Golden Gate Park, 41 - The Sequoias*, Pacific Horticulture, Vol. 50, No 1, Spring 1989, Pacific Horticultural Foundation, San Francisco.

McMinn, R., *The Nature of British Columbia Forests*, British Columbia Heritage Record #1, Victoria, 1976.

Meany, Edmond S., *Vancouver's Discovery of Puget Sound*, Binfords and Mort, Publishers, Portland, Ore., 1957.

Millais J.G., *Rhododendrons and Their Various Hybrids*, Longmans Green and Co., London, 1917.

Mitchell, Alan, *Trees of Great Britain and Northern Europe*, Collins, London, 1982,

Moore, David M., *Flora of Terra del Fuego*, Anthony Nelson, England, 1983.

Mozino, Jose, Mariano, *Noticias de Nutka, an Account of Nootka Sound in 1792*, Translated and Edited by Iris Higbie Wilson, McCelland and Stewart Limited, Toronto/Montreal, 1970.

Naish, John, M.D., *Archibald Menzies: Surgeon and Botanist*, International Dendrology Society Yearbook 1988, London, pages 123-128.

National Geographic Magazine, *The World's Tallest Tree Discovered*, 1-9, July 1964.

Newcombe C.F. Md., *Botanical and Ethnological Appendix to Menzies Journal of Vancouver's Voyage*, William H Collin Printer to Kings most Excellent Majesty, Victoria, B.C., 1923.

Newcombe, C.F., Md., *Menzies Journal of Vancouver's Voyage, April To October 1792*, Archives of British Columbia, Memoir No.V, William H. Cullin, King's Printer, Victoria, B.C., 1923.

Palow, *Noticias de California*, Vol.1, Bosqui, San Francisco, 1873.

Pizzetti, Ippolita & Henry Cocker, *Flowers, A Guide For Your Garden*, Harry N. Abrams, Inc., Publishers, New York, 1975.

Preston, Isobella, *Garden Lilies*, Orange Judd Publishing Company Inc., New York, 1935.

Range Plant Handbook, Forest Service, U.S. Dept of Agriculture, U.S. Govt. Printing Office, Washington D.C., 1937,

Red Books Of Humphrey Repton, 4 vols., Basilisk Press, London, 1976.

Roberts, John E., *A Discovery Journal. Vancover's First Survey Season, 1792.* Victoria, 1999.

Rockwell, F. F., Grayson, Esther C., and Jann de Graff, *The Complete Book Of Lilies*, Doubleday and Company, Inc., Garden City, New York, 1961.

Royal Horticultural Society, *Journal Kept By David Douglas During His Travels in North America, 1823-1827*, William Wesley & Son, London, 1914.

Sargent, Charles Sprague, *Manual of the Trees of North America*, 2 vols., 1961 Dover edition of the 1922 Houghton Mifflin edition, Dover Publications Inc., New York.

Schofield, W.B., *Guide to the Common Seaweeds of British Columbia*, Handbook No.27, B.C. Provincial Museum, Victoria, B.C.

Schofield, W.B., *Some Common Mosses of British Columbia*, Handbook No. 28, B.C. Provincial Museum, Victoria B.C. 1959.

Scoggan, H.J., *Flora of Canada*, 4 volumes, National Museum of Natural Sciences, National Museum of Canada, Ottawa, 1978-80.

Scouler, John, *Journal of a Voyage to N.W. America*, The Oregon Historical Quarterly, Vol. VI, 1905.

Shadbolt, Doris, *Bill Reid*, Douglas and McIntyre Ltd., Vancouver B.C., 1986.

Sheppe, Walter, *First Man West*, University of California Press, Berkeley and Los Angeles, 1962.

Sherk, Lawerence C. D., and Buckley, Arthur R., *Ornamental Shrubs for Canada*, Research Branch, Dept. of Agriculture, Ottawa Ont., 1968.

Spanish Voyage to Vancouver and the North - West Coast of America, Being the Narrative of the Voyage Made in the Year 1792 by the Schooners Sutil and Mexicana to Explore the Strait of Fuca, Translated from the Spanish with an Introduction by Cecil Jane, The Argonaut Press, London, England, 1930,

Stevenson, J.B., Editor, *The Species of Rhododendron*, The Rhododendron Society, Second Edition, 1947.

Stewart, Hilary, *Cedar*, Douglas and McIntyre, Vancouver/Toronto, 1984.

Stroud, Dorothy, *Humphrey Repton*, Country Life Ltd., London, 1962.

, *Capability Brown*, Country Life Ltd, London, Revised Ed., 1957.

Sudsworth, George B., *Forest Trees of the Pacific Slope*, U. S. Dept of Agriculture, Forest Service, U. S. Government Printing Office Washington, D.C., 1908.

Szczawinski, Adam, *The Heather Family of British Columbia*, B.C. Museum Handbook No.19 B.C. Museum Publications, Victoria, B.C., 1962.

, *The Orchids of British Columbia*, Museum Handbook No.16, B.C. Museum Publications, Victoria, B.C., 1959,

, and Harrison, Anthony S., *Flora of the Saanich Peninsula, An Annotated List of Vascular Plants*, British Columbia Provincial Museum Occasional Paper No. 16 B.C. Museum Publications, Victoria, B.C. 1972.

Taylor Roy L. and MacBryde, Bruce, *Vascular Plants of British Columbia, A Descriptive Resource Inventory,* Technical Bulletin No. 4, The Botanical Garden, The University of British Columbia, The University of British Columbia Press, Vancouver, 1977.

Taylor, T.M.C., *The Figworts (Scrophulariacea) of British Columbia*, B.C. Museum Handbook No.33, B.C. Museum Publications, Victoria, B.C. 1970.

– , *The Lily Family of British Columbia*, B.C. Museum Handbook No.25, B.C. Museum Publications, Victoria, B.C., 1975.

– , *The Ferns and Fern Allies of British Columbia*, B.C. Museum Handbook No.12, B.C. Museum Publications, Victoria, B.C., 1971.

– , *The Rose Family of British Columbia*, B.C. Museum Handbook No. 30, B.C. Museum Publications, Victoria, B.C., 1971

– , *The Sedge Family of British Columbia*, B.C. Museum Handbook No. 43, B.C. Museum Publications, Victoria, B.C., 1983.

Trorey, Lyle, G. *Aerial Mapping and Photogrammetry*, Cambridge University Press, 1952.

Turner, Nancy, *Plants in British Columbia Indian Technology*, B.C. Museum Handbook No.38, B.C. Museum Publications, Victoria, B.C., 1979.

Turrill, W.B., O.B.E., F.R.S., *Joseph Dalton Hooker, Botanist, Explorer and Administrator*, Thomas Nelson (Printers) Ltd., London and Edinburgh, 1963.

Thwaites, R. G., editor, *Original Journals of the Lewis & Clark Expedition*, Dodd, Mead, New York, 1905.

Waaland, Robert J., *Common Seaweeds of the Pacific Coast*, J.J. Douglas, Vancouver, 1977.

Walbran, John, T., *British Columbia Coast Names, University of Washington Press*, 1976, Reprint of the 1905 original.

Wang, Chi-Wu, *Forests of China*, Maria Moors Cabot Foundation Publication Series No.5, Botanical Museum Harvard University, Boston, Mass., 1961.

Warnock, Barton H., *Wildflowers of the Big Bend Country, Texas*, Sul Ross State University, Alpine Texas, 1970.

Watkin David, *The English Vision, The Picturesque in Architecture, Landscape and Garden Design,* John Murray, London, 1982.

Watts, May Theilgaard, *Reading The Landscape* (of America), Collier Books, Macmillan, 1975.

Weatherstone, John, *The Pioneers, 1825 - 1900, The Early British Tea and Coffee Planters and Their Way of Life*, Quiller Press, London, 1986.

Wilson, Earnest H., *China Mother of Gardens*, The Strattford Company, Boston, Mass. 1929.

Wing, Robert C., and Newell Gordon, *Peter Puget*, Great Beard Publishing, Seattle, Wash., 1979.

Wood, J., *The Southern Beeches*, Year Book of the International Dendrology Society for 1989, pages 99-106, London, 1990.

Woodworth, John, *In the Steps of Alexander Mackenzie*, John Woodworth, Kelowna, B.C., second edition, 1987.

INDEX OF BOTANICAL NAMES

Page numbers in italics indicate
the illustration of the plant.

Abelia 9,
Abies grandis 46, 48, 96,
    lasiocarpa 37,
Acer circinatum 38, 46,
    glabrum 38,
    glabrum douglasii 46,
    macrophyllum 36, 38, 57, *66,*
Abutil(l)on menziesii 134,
Aconitum 124,
Agathis 31,
Aidiantum pedatum 125, *125,*
Allium acuminatum 48, 50
    cepa 81,
Alnus rubra 36, *36,* 114,
Amalanchier 60, 61,
    alnifolia 58, *61,*
    alnifolia var cucksickii 61,
    canadensis 60,
    laevis 60, 61,
    Amsinkia intermedia 96,
Andromeda 64,
    coerula 63,
    polifolia 63, 64,
Angelica archangelica 81,
Anthericum caclyculatum 65,
Apium graveolens 81,
Aqualegia 124,
Araucariacae 31, 36
Araucaria araucana *27,* 30,
    bidwillii 31,
    columnaris 31,
    cookii 31,
    cunninghamii 31,
    heterophylla 31,
Arbutus canariensis *88,*
    kiangsinensis 103,
    menziesii 24, 38, 46, 88,
    90, *90,* 103, *104,*
    peninsularis 89,
    unedo 88, *88,*
    unedo vars 88, 103,
Arctostaphylos columbiana 47, 103, *104,*
    manzanita 104,
    patula 104,
    tomentosa 37,
    viscida 104,
Arnica cordifolia 97,
    menziesii 97,
    mollis 97,
Artocarpus incisus 9, *10,*
Astelelia menziesiana 134,
Athyrium filix femina 125,

Banksia 85,
    ericifolia *14,*
    menziesii 32, *84,* 86,
Berberis aquifolium 101,
    juliana 101,
    nervosa 102,
Beta vulgaris 81,
Betula occidentalis 51, 58, *59,*
    papyifera var commutata 51, 58, *59*

Blechnum spicant 64, 125, *125,*
Brassica napus 81,
    oleracea 81, 82,
Brodiacea 115,
    congesta 40, *41,*
    cornaria *41,* 41,
    douglasii *41,* 41,
Bryum menziesii, moss 95,
Bonania menzieii 134,
Breweria menziesii, 134,

Calandrina ciliata var menziesii *96,* 97,
Calypso borealis 37,
    bulbosa 37, *37,* 38, 121,
    forma alba 37,
    subsp bulbosa 121,
    subsp occidentalis 121,
Camassia leicthtlini 116, *116,*
    quamash 51, 116, *116,*
Camplyotheca menziesii, 134,
Capsicum annum 81,
    grossum 81,
Cascara sagrada 113,
Ceonothus velutinus laevigatus 38,
Chamaecyparis lawsoniana 106, !07, *108,*
    nukatensis 106, *106,*
Chimaphila menziesii 97, *97,*
    umbellata var occidentalis 97,
Cibotium (Dicksonia) menziesii 86, *86,* 134,
Cicer ariethinum 82,
    var. *82,*
Claytonia filicaulus 38,
Compositae 97,
Compromsa menziesii 134,
Cornus canadensis 47, 112,
    florida 110, *111,*
    nuttallii 22, *47,* 110, *110,*
    nuttallii 'Creamedge' 111,
    nuttallii 'Eddieii' 111,
    nuttallii 'Goldedge' 111,
    stolonifera 47, 75, *75,* 111, 112,
    stolonifera flaviramea 112,
    suecica 75,
    unalaskensis 47, *111,*
Corylus californica 38, 46,
Crataegus brevispina 67,
    douglasii 67,
    oxycantha 67,
    oxycantha 'Pauls Scarlet' 67,
Crucifera 100,
Cupressocyparis leylandii 107,
Cupressus macrocarpa 107,
Cynara scolymus 82,
Cyrtandra menziesii 134,
Cypripedium acaule *122,*

Daucus muricatus 81,
Davidia involucrata 110,
Delphinium 98,
    menziesii var menziesii 98, *98,*
    var pyramidale 98,
Dicksonia menziesii, see Cibotium menziesii
Dodecatheon dentatum 126, *126,*
    jefferii 126, *126,*
    hendersonii 125,
    pauciflorum 125,
    pulchellum 125,
Drosera rotundifolia 65,
Echium menziesii 96,
Egeregia menziesii *75,* 95,

Empetraceae 75,
Empetrum nigrum 75, *76,*
Enkianthus 124,
Epilobium angustifolium 52,
    luteum *53,*
    munitum 52,
Epimedium 121,
Epipactis 122,
Ericaceae 58, 95, 97,
Erythronium 116, 117, 125,
    grandiflorum 116,
    hendersonii 116,
    montanum 116,
    oregonum 116, *117,*
    revolutum 116, 117, *118,*
Eucalyptus 10,
    globosus *10,*
Fatsia horrida 123,
Flora boreali-americana 19,
    Japonica 9,
Forsythia viridissima 101,
Fraxinus oregona 40, *40,* 46,
Fritillaria camschatcensis 48, *82,* 83, *114,* 115,
    imperialis 115,
    lanceolata 115,

Gaultheria fruiticosa 47,
    shallon 47, 102, *105,*
Goodyera menziesii 96,
Geranium cuneatum var. menziesii 134,
Gypsophylla 119,

Habenaria 122,
    (menziesii) orbiculata 95, 96,
    dilatata var. *leucostachys* 122,
Hellabore 124,
Hesperis menziesii *99,* 100,
Hibiscus sinensis 87,
Holodiscus discolour 47, 112, *112,*
Hookera pulchella 40,
Hordeum vulgare 81, *81,*
Hosta 124,
    baileyii (undulata) 122,
Houstonia 9,

Juncus falcatus 96,
    menziesii 96,
Juniperus scopulorum 50, *51,* 90,

Kadua menziesiana 134,
Kalmia 64,
    polifolia 64, *64,*
Kerria japonica 9,

Lactuca sativa 82,
Leguminosae 87,
Lepidium virginicum var menziesii 100,
Leucolepsis menziesii, Moss 65, *65,*
Liliaceae 115, 120,
Lilium canadense 48, 118,
    chamschatcense 48,
    columbianum 48, 118, 119, *119,*
    dauricum X maculatum 119,
    davidii 119,
    parviflorum 118,
    philadelphicum 118, *120,*
    washingtonianum 120, *121,*
    washingtonianum var minor 120,
Linneae borealis 65, *65,*
Listera convallarioides 122,

Lonicera ciliosa 47,
Lycopodium complanatum 64, *65*,
    menziesii 134,
Lysichitum 123,
    americanum 122, *123*,

Mahonia 101
    aquifolium 47, 101, *102*,
    nervosa 101, 102,
Maianthemum diliatum 120,
Malus columbiana 47,
    fusca 36, *36*, 47,
Malvaceae 87,
Menyanthes trifoliata 65,
Menziesia 9, 85, 124,
    ciliicalyx 85,
    ferruginea *19*, *26*, *72*, 75, 85,
    multiflora 85,
    multiflora var longicalyx 85,
    pentandra 85,
    pilosa 85,
    purpurea 85,
Mespilus germanica 60,
Metasequoia 30,
    glyptostoboides 29,
Minium menziesii, 95,
Montia parvifolia 38,
Myrica gale 65

Neckera douglasiana 95,
    menziesii 65, 95,
Nothofagus *32*, *33*,
    antarctica 33, 34,
    menziesii 33, *33*, *34*, 85,

Oplopanax horridum 123, *124*,
Opuntia var. 36,
Osmoronia cerasiformis 62,

Pandanus menziesii 134,
Parkinsonia aculeata *23*,
Parrya menziesii 100,
Pastinaea sativa 81,
Penstemon 69,
    davidsonia forma ALBA 69,
    davidsonia var menziesii 68, 69,
    davidsonia var davidsonia 68,
    menziesii 69,
Phacelia linearis 96,
Philadelphus cornarius 48,
    lewisii 48, *48*,
Phyllosmara menziesii 95,
Picea engmannii 91,
    glauca 11, 91, 92, 94,
        Albertina 92,
    mariana 11, *11*, 13,
    pungens 92,
    rubens 91,
    sitchensis 13, *13*, 46, 48, *92*, 96,*96*,
Pinus 96,
    banksiana 86,
    canadensis 73,
    contorta 86,
    contorta var contorta 37, 64, 78, 90,
    menziesii 96,
    monticola 63, 64, 100,
    sitchensis 96,
    strobus 63, 100,
Plathanthera menziesii 96,
Plecteitris congesta *44*,

Pleiosimilax menziesii 134,
Polygonum spurgulariaeforme 52,
Polypodiaceae 124,
Polystichum munitum 64, 124,
Populus tremuloides 42,43, *43*, 46, 51,
    var vancouveriana 43,
    trichocarpa 40, 41, *42*, 46, 42, 51,
Prunus serrulata var Amanagawa 61,
Pseudotsuga brevifolia 93, *94*,
    forrestii 93, *93*,
    gaussenii 93, *94*,
    japonica 93,
    macrocarpa 93, *93*,
    menziesii 37, 46, 48, 67, 85, 91, *91*,
    92, 94,
        glauca 93, 94,
        fletcherii 94,
        pendula 94,
        stairii 94,
        standishii 94,
    sinensis 93, *94*,
    taxifolia 92,
    wilsonii 93, *93*,
Pyrola 63,
    aphylla 63,
    dentata 63,
    picta 63, *63*,
    secunda 63, *63*,
Pyrolaceae 63,
Pyrus fusca 36, *36*

Quercus agrifolia 22, *23*,
    garryana 38, 46,

Raillardia menziesii 86, 134,
Rhamnus purshiana 38, 112, *112*, *113*,
Rhodiala rosea 75,
Rhododendron arboreum 105,
    catawbiense 105,
    dalhousiae 105,
    falconeri 105,
    griffithianum 105,
    macrophyllum 37, 47, 103, 105, *105*,
106, *106*,
    maximum 105,
    occidentale 102, *103*,
    ponticum 105,
    schlippenbachia 101,
Ribes 100,
    lacustre 75,
    laxiflorum 47, 63, *64*,
    menziesii 99, 100,
    sangineum 47, 64, 100, *100*, 101,
    speciosum 47,
Rosaceae 60,
Rosa gymnocarpa 47,
    nutkana 47,
Rubus menziesii 96,
    nootkagensis 47,
    parviflorus *21*, 47, 57, 58,
    spectabilis 40, 43, 47, *72*, *72*, 96,
    stellata *21*,
Salix scoulerii 38, 46,
Sanicula crassicaulis 96,
    menziesii 96,
Saxifraga ferruginea 52,
    var ferruginea *54*
    var macounii, *54*
Saxifrage 52,

Scaevola menziesiana 134,
Scheidea menziesii 134,
Scheuchzeriaea 43,
Sedum 75,
    ferrugineum 75,
    roseum 75,
    roseum var integrifolium 75, *76*,
Selaginella menziesii 134,
Sequoia 28,
    gigantea 28,
    sempervirens 28, *28*,
Sequoiadendron giganteum 29, *29*, 102,
Shanus albus 65,
Silene gallica 99,
    menziesii 98,
    pendula 99,
    sitchensis 96,
Solanum melongena 82,
    tuberosum 81,
Sorbus sitchensis 40,
Spiraea douglasii subsp menziesii 99,
    X vanhouttei 99,
    serrulata 47
Spurgula spergulariae *53*,
Stauntonia 9
Symphoricarpos orbiculatus 119,

Tamalpias Mt 27,
Taxodium distichum 28,
    sempervirens 27,
Taxus brevifolia 46,
Thuja 108,
Thunbergia 9,
Thuya occidentalis *12*, 14,
    plicata 46, 67, 108, *109*,
    aurea 109,
    excelsa 108,
    lobbii 109,
Triandra 115,
Triflorum frimbriatum 83, *83*,
Triglochin maritimum 40, 43,
Triteleia grandiflora 41, *41*,
Tsuga canadensis 12,
    heterophylla *12*, 12, 13, 46, 48, *73*,
Typha latifolia 51, *52*,
Typhus latifolius 51,

Urtica dioca var. lyallii 51, *51*,

Vaccinium 58, 60, 72,
    caespitosum 60, *60*,
    ovalifolium 59, *59*, 72, 75,
    ovatum 38, 47, 59,77,
    oxycoccus 75,
    oxycoccus var intermedius
    parvifolium 47, 59, 60, *72*, *72*, 75,
    scoparium 60,
    tetrogonum 47,
    uglinosum 75,
    vitis-idea 47, 59, 77,
    vitis-idea ssp minus 59,
Vancouveria hexandra 121, *122*,
    chrysantha 121,
Vicia menziesii 87, 134,
Viverra putorius 36,
Wollemia nobilis *30*, *31*,
Woodsia obtusa oregona 125,

Zygadensis gramineus 50,
    venenous 50,

GENERAL INDEX

Abel, Clarke, plant collector 9,
Acadian plants 25,
Activa, Spanish brig 79,
Addenbrooke, Mt 57,
Adelaide 31,
Admiralty Inlet, Wash 39, 115,
Agamemnon Channel 49,
Aiton, William T. King's Grdnr 84,
Alaska, Cedar 107
Albert Close, Rhdn Hybrid 105,
Alder Oregon 114,
        Pacific 114,
        Red 114,
        Succession 114
American Arborvitae 14,
American Cockspur Thorn 67,
Animals, domestic in Nootka 80,
Araucas 30,
Arbor de vitae 14,
Arborvitae 67,
        American 14,
        Western 108,
        Exelsa 108,
        Golden 109,
        Lobb's 109,
Arbutus, Pacific 85, 88, 89,
Arbutus Street, Van. B.C. 108,
Argentina 31,
Arrowgrass, Sea 40, 43,
Arrendo Toba (Tov), Antonio 58,
Artichoke 82,
Ash, Oregon 40, 41, 46,
        Sitka Mountain ash 40,
Aspen, Parkland Belt 42,
        Quaking 42,
        Trembling 42, 51,
Astoria, Oregon 30,
Astronomical Observations 48, 68,
 Attingham Park, U.K. 36,
Audubon, John James, Ornthghst 22,
Australia 15,
Avalanche Lilies 116,
Azalea, deciduous 101,
        False 26, 72, 75, 85,
        Western 102,

Baja California 89,
Baker, Mt 62,
Bald Cypress 29,
Bali 19,
Baja, California 89,
Balm of Gilead 42,
Balsam Cottonwood 42,
Balsam Poplar 42,
Banda Sea 19,
Banksia 86,
Banks Island 25,
Banks, sir Joseph 7, 8, 10, 15, 85,
Barley 80,
Barton, Benjamin Smith, Dr. Bot Prof. 22,
Basalt Point, Wash. 38,
Beacon Hill Park, 116,
Beardtongues 63, 69,
Beer, Spruce 11, 12,

Beetroot 81,
Behring Straits 9,
Bell Pepper 81,
Bella Coola, Indian Village 76,
BellflowerChinese 87,
        Hawaiian Koolaoula 86, 134,
Bellingham Hybrid Lilies 119,
Bellingham, Wash 45,
Bengal, brig 76,
Bigcone Douglas fir 93,
Bigeneric Hybrid 107
Bigleaf Maple 36, 41,
Bigtree 28, 29, 102,
Birch, Black 51,
        Western 51, 58,
Birch Bay, Wash 39, 48, 49, 51,
Black Birch 51,
        Cottonwood 40, 41,
        Currant 72,
        Haw 67,
        Poplar 41,
        Spruce 11,
Bligh, Capt., Eng Navigator 8, 16,
Blister Rust of White Pine 100,
Blue Camas 116,
Blueberry 47, 59,
Bluets 9,
Bodega Bay 107,
Bog Blueberry 75,
Bog Rosemary 63, 64,
Bongard, August H.G. 95,
Botanical Gardens
        Fairchild Tropical Grdns 19, Jardin
        des Plantes 96,
        Kew Gardens 8, 16,
        Peradeniya, Sri Lanka 31,
        Vandusen Gardens 15, Vancouver
        B.C. 49,
Botanical Taxonomists
        Acharius 19,
        Bongard 95,
        Calder 99,
        Don, David 19,
        Esper 19,
        Hooker, sir William 10,
        Hooker sir Joseph 10,
        Lambert 19,
        Lindley 96,
        Meyer 97,
        Pursh 19,
        Taylor, Roy L. 99,
        Trautvelter 97,
        Smith 19,
        Turner 19
Botanizing
        by boat 18, 19,
        Birch Bay 39,
        shipboard 19,
Botany Bay 16,
Bougainville, Capt. 10,
Boundary Bay 49,
Bounty, ship 9,
Breadfruit 9,
Brewers 13, 73,
Bridalwreath Spiraea 112,
Broadbean, Hawaiian Wild 134
Brodie, James Sottish Bot. 40,
Broughton Inlet 74,
        Island 19, 74,
        Strait 74,

        Lieut Cmdr Wm Robert 21, 48,
        Archipelago 74,
Brown William, Grdnr/Plnt Cllctr 9,
Brown, Robert Taxonomist 85,
Bunchberry 112,
Burke Channel 75,
Burrard Inlet 49,
Bute Inlet 62,

Cabbage 82,
 Cable's length 39,
Calaveras County, Calif. 28,
California 20,
        Spanish 104,
Camano Island, Wash 45,
Camas, Blue 51, 116,
        Great 116,
        Leichtlinis 116,
        poison 50,
Campion, Common Grdn 99,
        Menzies 98,
Capability Brown 35,
Cape Blanco 107,
        Good Hope 26,
        Horn 80,
        Mendocino, 107,
        Mudge 67,
        Roberts 55,
        Saint James 71,
        Scott 30, 71,
Carriere, Elie Abel, Nurseryman 95,
Carrot 81,
Cartier, Jacque, French Explorer 14.
Cascade Mountains
Cascara 112,
        Trees 113,
Cassia 23,
Cattail 51,
Cedar, Western Red 14, 67, 108, 109,
Celebes 19,
Celery 82,
Chaparral 104,
Chaps 104,
Charting 38, 44,
Chatham , Ship 21, 22, 39, 49, 55, 69,
        Point 70,
Cheng Ho, Junk 19,
Cheslakees
Chilcotin Indians 62,
Chick Pea 82,
Chile 27, 30,
Chilean Pine 27, 30,
Chives 82,
Chocolate Lily 115,
Clark, Capt William, Explorer 21,
Clark, Lewis J., Author 37, 41, 52, 53, 64, 120,
126,
Climate at Nootka 82,
Clover 83,
Clubmoss 64,
Coast Redwood 27, 29,
Collnet, Capt James 12, 20, 25,
Columbia Manzanita 103,
        River 21, 22, 103,
Columbine 119,
Commencement Bay, Puget Snd, 40,
Cook, Capt James, Eng. Nvgtr 9, 10, 79,
        Pine 31,
Cornel 112,
Cortes Island 55,

Cortez, Hernando 55,
Crabapple,Ornamental 120
        Pacific 36, 47,
        Rosybloom 120,
Cranberry, wild 75,
Crespi, Fra Juan, Spanish Priest 87,
Crowberry 75,
Crown Imperial 115,
Cryptogamic Plants 64,
Cryptomania 124,
Currant, Redflowering 47,
Cutters 40, 43, 57, 73, 82,
Cyanide 43,

Daedalus, Storeship 76,
Dalco Passage, Puget Sound, 39, 40,
Davidson, John, UBC Bot Prof 69,
Dawn Redwood 29,
Dean Channel 76,
Deception Pass, Wash 48,
Deciduous azaleas
Deerfern 124,
Delphinium
        Menzies' 98,
        Pacific Hybrids 98,
Desolation Sound 55, 67,
Devils Club 123,
Discovery, ship 15, 16, 17, 39, 49, 55, 69,
        Bay 37,
        Inlet 37,
        Passage 69,
        Reenactment Voyages '92 106,
Dog Rose 47,
Dogwood Act 109,
        Canadian 47,
        Common 47,
        Goldspot 111,
        Eastern 110,
        Hybrid 111,
        Pacific & vars 111,
        Western 109,
Don, David, Botanist
Douglas, David, Bot Explr 21, 41, 107,
Douglas Channel 26,
Douglas Fir 48, 67, 85, 91, 94,
        Bigcone 92,
        Blue 93, 94,
        Chinese Species 92,
        Christmas Trees 94,
        garden forms 94,
        Japanese 93,
        milled timbers 92,
        ornamental 94,
           Taiwan 93,
Douglas Maple 38, 46,
Douglas Spiraea 99,
Dove Tree 110,
Dropmore Manitoba 99,
Duncan's Port Safety 74,
Duncan, Capt Charles 26,
Dusky Sound, S. I. N.Z. 33,

East Redondo Island 57,
Easter Lilies 116,
Eastern Dogwood 110,
        North America
           Eddie's White Wonder
Dogwood 111,
Eddy Henry, Pioneer Nrsymn 111,

Eggplant 82,
Emerson, Ralph Waldo 37,
Endlicker, Stephan 28,
Epimidium, Vancouver's 121,
Escheverria, Sr Atanasio, Nat Hist Pntr 80,
Eucalypts 10,
Everett, Wash 45,
Fairchild, David , Hd. USBPI 19,
Fairy Slipper 121,
False Azalea 26, 72, 75, 85,
False Lily of the Valley 115, 119,
False Onion 40,
Fawn Lily 116,
Ferneries 124,
Ferns, 124, 125,
Fidalgo Islands, Wash 39, 39,
Fife Channel 72, 73,
Fir, Douglas 48, 91,
        Grand 48,
        Lowland 41,
        Menzies 95,
        True 46, 48, 96,
Fireweed 52,
Fisher Channel 75,
Fitzhugh Sound 74,
Fleas 57,
Flowering Currant 100, 101,
Flowering Maple 134,
Forest scenery 45,
Fortune, Robert, Plant Collector 7,
Foul Weather Bluff, Wash 38,
Fraser, George, Nrsymn 123,
Fraser, Simon Explr. 49,
Francis I, King of France 14.
Friendly Cove, Nootka Is 79,
Gable, Joe, Nrsrymn 105,
Galiano, Capt Dionisio Alcala 49,
Garden Hutch 17,
Garden(s), English 8,
        Great Britain 8,
        Kew 8,
        Nootka Village 81,
        Pacific Northwest 101,
        Rock & Alpine 52, 117,
        Vegetable, 81& 82
        Versailles, 68,
        Victorian & Edwardian 101,
Garry Oak 38, 46,
George, Alex. S. Banksia Auth. 86,
Georgia Strait 49, 55,
Golden Hind Mtns 71,
Gooch, Mr William, Astrnmr 76,
Gooseberries 63,
Grand Fir 46, 48, 96,
Grenville Channel 26,
Greymouth, S.I., N.Z.
Griffith, D. Dr., USDA Lily Brdr 119,
Ground orchid 121,
        habitat 121,
        pink 121,
        white 121,
Groundcovers
        Complete or Partial Shade 121,
        Fawnlilies 116,
        Lingonberry 59,
        Vancouver's Epimedium 121,
Grouse, Blue & Sooty 100,
Gulf Islands 36, 42, 116, 117,

Habitats, logged over 106,

loss of 117,
        Pink Fawn Lily 116,
        tropical island 121,
Haida Canoe 67,
Hairy Manzanita 47, 103,
Halifax N.S., English Naval Sta 25,
Halmahera 19,
Handkerchief Tree 110,
Hanson Island 72,
Harmon Point, Wash 38,
Harrison Lake 72,
Hawaii 20, 25,
        native trees 86,
Hawaiian Islands 87,
Hawaiian Vetch 87, 134,
Hayden Is., Columbia R. 22,
Hazel, Common 46,
Hazelnut 38,
Hecate Strait 26, 71,
Hedges, formal & informal 101,
Hemlock, Canada 12,
        Western 12,
Henderson's Fawn Lily 116,
Herbarium 18, 85,
        Banks' 18,
        Chicago 18,
        Chengdu 18,
        Kew 18,
Hergest, Richard, Naval Agent 76,
Highway(s) 3 Ore & 199 US, 90,
        11& 20, Wash 46,
        101 Wash 91,
        299 Cal., 90,
        Port Renfrew 106,
Hobart Tas 31,
Homfray Channel 57,
Honeysuckle 47,
Hood Canal, Wash 38,
Hooker, Mt 106,
Hooker, sir Joseph 10, 85, 105,
Hooker, sir William 10, 19, 85,
Hoop Pine 31,
Hope, John , Teacher, 25,
Housto(u)n, William, Surg-Bot 9, 20,
Howe Sound 49,
Huckleberry 47,
        Black 59,
        Evergreen 38, 59,
        Red 59,
Hudson's Bay Company (HBC) 21,
Humphrys, Henry Mr 57,
Hunter Island 75,
Hydrangeas, 101,

Ireland 30, 88,

Java 19,
Jefferson, Thomas, US Pres. 21,
Jervis Inlet 49,
Johnstone Straits 70, 71,
Johnstone, James Mastr 48, 74,
Juan De Fuca Straits 72,
Juan Fernandez Island
Juniper,Rocky Mountain 50,
        Western 50, 90,
Junk, Cheng Ho 19,

Kalm, Peter, 18th Cent Bot 64,
Kamtchadales 115,
Kauri Pine 31,

Kelp 89,
Kerr, William, Plant Collector 9,
Kew Gardens 8, 16,
King George's Sound 85,
King Island 75,
Kingcome Inlet 117,
Kinghorn Island 55,
Kinikinnik 79,
Kitimat 26,
Kitisat, Wash 38,
Knight Inlet 73,
Knotweed 52,
Knight's Island 71,
Koolaoula,, 87, 134,
Kwakiutl Canoe 67,
         Paddle 67,
         Village 67,
Labouchere Channel 72,
Lady's Slipper 37,
         Fairy 37,
         Pink 37,
         Venus 37,
Ladyfern 124,
Landscape,attractive visual aspect 45,
         Canadian 43,
         coastal forest 45,
         descriptive 35, 45,
         designer 35,
         English 45,
         forest edges 91,
         gardener 35,
         non pastoral 45,
         Nootka 81,
         panoramic 45,
         pastoral 35, 46,
         sublime 58,
         sublime & beautiful 55,
         sublime & picturesque 45, 64,
         topography & vegetation 46,
         Vancouver Island 71,
Latitude and Longtitude 67,
Laugborough Inlet 73, 76,
Launch, Spanish 82,
Launches 40, 49,
Laurel, Sticky 38,
Laurel, Swamp 64,
Lawson Cypress 107, 108,
         Upright Golden 108,
Lawson, James, Scots Agrcltrst 107,
Leichthlini's Camas 116,
Lesser Sundas 19,
Lettuce 82,
Lewis Channel 57, 70,
Lewis, Meriwether, Explr Ntrlst 21,
L'Hertier Botanist 10,
Leyland Cypress 107
Lichens 95,
Lilies, Avalanche 116,
         Bellingham Hybrids 119,
         Chocolate 115,
         Easter 116,
         Fawn 116,
         Fiesta Hybrid Grp 119,
         Harlequin Hybrids 119,
         Mt Hood 120
         Pink Fawn 117,
         Prairie 119,
         Shasta 119,
         Stenographer Series 119,
         Tiger 118,

Trumpet Type 119,
Turks Cap 118,
Lily of the Valley, False 119,
Lindley, John, Botanist 96,
Lingonberry 47, 59,
Linnaeus 64,
Linnean Society 19,
Lobb, William, Plant Coll. 28,
Longboats 39, 73, 82,
Lougborough Sound 72,
Lowland Fir 41,
Lummi, Clallum Tribe 108

Macoa 97
Madera County, Calif. 28,
Madrone Menzies 87,
         Pacific 87,
         Pacific at Baja Calif 89,
         Spanish 88,
         Strawberry 88,
Mahonias 101,
Maidenhair Fern 124,
Malaspina Straits 55, 88
         Alexandro Capt. 55,
Malcom Island
Manning Provincial Park 105,
Manzanita, Columbia, 103,
         Hairy 103,
         Whiteleaf 104,
         Woolly 104,
Maple, Bigleaf 36, 38, 46, 58,
         Douglas 38, 46,
         Oregon 36, 38, 46, 58,
         Pennsyvanian 46,
         Sugar 46,
         Sycamore 46,
         Vine 38,
Mapping 44,
Maquinna, Nootka Ind Chf 83,
         daughter 83,
         sister in law, friend of Menzies 83,
Marin County, Calif 27,
Marine Algae 89,
Mariposa County, Calif. 28,
Masson, Francis, Grdnr & Plnt Explr 8,
Matthews, John D. Plant Coll. 28,
Maweena Bay 83,
         Harbour 83,
Meadow, natural 35,
         landscape 35,
Meerkerk Grdns, Whidbey Is 119,
Medlar 60,
Menzies Abutilon 134,
         Aster 97,
         Bay 68,
         Banksia 86,
         Campion 98,
         Delphinium 98,
         Falsecyparis 107
         Onions, 115,
         Plants, Mosses, Lichens & Marine
                 Algae 77, 95,
         Island 22,
         Journal 39,
         Madrone 85, 88, 89,
         Penstemon 69,
         Pipsissewa 97,
         Point 75,
         Raspberry 47, 57, 72, 95,
         Spiraea 99,

Spruce 93, 95,
Treefern 86,
Wintergreen 63, 97,
Menzies, Archibald, Surgn-Bot 21, 25,
Mexicana 49, 55, 82,
Missouri River 21,
Moe, Ron & Julia 30,
Mockorange 48,
Moluccas 19,
Monkey Puzzle 27, 30,
Monument, Simon Fraser 49,
         Vancouver-Galiano 50,
Mosses 65, 95,
Mountain Laurel 64,
Mountainash, Sitka 40,
Moyeha Mt. 71,
Mozino, Jose Mariano, Sp Bot 80,
Mt Hood Lily 117,
Mudge, Lieut William T. F. 60,
Muir, John, Naturalist 37,
         Woods 27,

Naenae Tree 86,
Naniamo Lakes 106
Napier, New Zealand 31,
Nat Hist Mus., Chicago 18,
Nelson, David, Bot Plnt Clctr 9,
Nettle, stinging 51,
New Caledonia 31,
         France 14,
         Guinea 31,
         York State 36,
         Zealand 33,
Newcombe, Dr Charles F., Ntrlst & Editor 18, 38,
Newfoundland 11, 43,
Niger, Brig 11,
Nipple Mountain 63,
Noble, David 31,
Nodales Channel 70,
Nomenclature, Intenat Rules of 85,
Nootka 79,
         Sound 79,
Norfolk Island Pine 31,
North Bentinck Arm 76,
         Broughton Is. 73,
Noticias de Nutka 80,
Nova Scotia 25,
Nuttall, Thomas, Bot & Explr 22,

Oahu natives 76,
Oak, evergreen 23,
         Garry 38, 46,
         Live 23,
Oak Cove, Wash 47,
Observations, astronomical 48, 68,
Ocean Spray 112,
Olympic Mountain Range 38,
         Peninsula 38,
Onion 82,
         False 40,
Orcas Island, Wash 48,
Orchids, attractant scent 122,
         epiphytic 122,
         fairy 38,
         ground 121,
         lady's, 38,
         mimics 122,
         native 122,
         Pacific Northwest 121
         pink 38, 121,

pollinators 122,
symbiotic fungus 37,
terrestial 122,
tropical 122,
Venus 38,
Oregon Alder 114,
Ash 41, 46,
Grape 47, 100,
Maple 41,
Oriental Arbutus 46,
Strawberry tree 89,

Pacific Alder 114,
Coast 7,
Coast Hardwoods 113,
Crabapple 36,
Dogwood 22,
Madrone 85, 87, 89, 90,
Rhododendron 37, 47, 103,
Yew 46,
Palomar, Mt 9,
Provincial Park, Manning 106,
Parlors, Victorian 124
Parsnip 82,
Pata-patos 25,
Patagonia 33,
Patterson, C.F., Prof., Lily Brdr 116,
Pemberton Valley 72,
Pennsylvanian Maple 46,
Penstemons 63, 69,
Pepper Grass 100,
Peradeniya Gardens, Sri Lanka 31,
Pheasant's Eyes 125,
Philadelphia, Penn . 48,
Philippine Islands 21,
Pigeon, Band Tailed 22,

Pine, Jack 86,
Lodgepole 86,
Shore 64, 90,
Western White 64,
Weymouth 11,
Pink Fawn Lily 117,
Pinnace 43, 49, 57, 73, 74,
Pipsissewa, Menzies 97,
Pitcairn Island 9,
Plant(s), California Coastal 80,
collected by Nuttall 22,
Cryptogamous 64,
·Menzies 1787-88 coll. 32,
stream and waterside 123,
Plant Hardiness Zones
CA 2b, 99,
USDA/CA 2 & 3, 61,
USDA/CA 6 & 7, 110,
USDA/CA 8, 88,
Plant Hutch 15, 16, 24, 50,
flooded 20,
Plant Introduction U.S. Bureau 19,
Plean Castle, (Castle Menzies) 25,
Pocket Handkerchief Tree 110,
Point Defiance Park, Wash 59,
Point Grey 49,
Poison Camas 50,
Pollarding 112,
Pontic Rhododendron 105,
Poplar, Aspen 42,
Balsam 42,
Black 41, 42,
Tacamahac 46,

Poppy, Opium 82,
Porlock, Capt 16,
Port Discovery, Wash 38,
Gardner, Wash 47,
Hadlock, Wash 38,
Ludlow, Wash 38,
Orford Cedar 107,
Safety, Duncan's 75,
Townsend, Wash 30,
Wilson 38,
Potato(e) 81,
Preston, Isobella, Hybdzr 119,
Price, Uvedale 38,
Prickly pear cactus 36,
Prince of Wales 12,
Prince Rupert B.C. 30,
Princess Royal, Ship 12,
Princess Royal Island 12,
Protection Island, Wash 35,
Ptolemy 48,
Puberty ceremony 81,
Puget Sound 38, 39,
Puget, 2nd Lieut, Peter 43, 44,
Punta Langara 49,
Pursh, Friedrich, Botanist 19,
Puyallup River 40,

Quadra Island, B.C. 55,
Quadra, Don Bodega y 55, 79, 82,
Quaking Aspen 42, 43,
Quebec 43,
Queen Charlotte Sound 71,
Straits 74,
Qeensland, Australia 31,

Rainfall at Nootka 82,
Rainier, Mount 40, 62,
Rape 82,
Raspberry, Menzies' 47, 57,
Red Alder 114,
Cedar 108,
Spruce 91,
Flowering Currant 100, 101,
Redondo Island 62,
Redwood, Coast 28,
Dawn 29,
Repton, Humphry 35,
Republic, Wash 29,
Restoration Pt, Puget Sound, 41,
Rhododendron, 'Albert Close' 105,
Catawba 105,
Lake V.I. 106,
Pacific 37, 47, 103,
Pontic 105,
Rosebay 105,
Rice Root 84,
Richards, Capt George, 49,
Ripple Rock 70,
Rocky Mountain Juniper 50,
Royal Horticultural Society 21,

Safety Cove 75,
Salal 47, 102,
Salish 51,
Salmonberry 40, 43, 47, 95,
San Blas, Mexico 26,
San Diego 22,
Spanish Calif 22,
San Francisco 22,
Spanish Calif 22,

San Juan Islands, Wash 36, 48,
Sandwich Islands 13,
Sandwich, Earl, First Lord Admlty 10,
Santa Barbara, Spanish Calif 27,
Cruz, Spanish Calif 27,
Saskatoon Berry 58, 60,
Western Alderleaved 61,
Save the Redwoods League 27,
Scenery, forest 45,
landscapes 45,
Scouler, John, Surg-Bot 21,
Scurvy 11, 14,
Sea Arrowgrass 40, 43,
Seablush 36,
Seattle, Wash 22, 30, 45,
Sechelt Peninsula 59,
Seed Collection to Kew 84,
Sedums 75,
Semiahmoo Bay, Wash 48,
Sequoyah 28,
Seymour Narrows 68, 70,
Shasta Lily 120,
Sheffield Park, U.K. 35,
Sherinham Hall, U.K . 36,
Ship's Boats, Cutter 40, 43, 57, 73, 82,
Launch 40, 49,
Longboat 39, 73, 82,
Pinnace 43, 49, 57, 73, 74,
Spanish Launch 82,
Ships Activa 79,
Bengal 76,
Bounty 9,
Chatham 21, 39, 55, 69, 74, 79,
Cheng Ho 19,
Daedalus 76,
Discovery 15, 39, 49, 55, 69 74, 76,
79
Endeavour 25,
Mexicana 49, 55, 82,
Niger 11,
Plumper 49,
Prince of Wales 20, 25, 57, 76,
Princess Royal 20, 25,
Reliance 16,
Sea Otter 74
Sutil 49, 55, 82,
Shooting Star, Broadleaved 125,
Few-Flowered 125,
Shore Pine 64,
Sierra Nevada Mountains 19,
Silver Beech 33,
Siskiyou Mountains 116,
Sitka, Russian Alaska 95,
Spruce 13, 92,
Skagit River 46,
Skinner, Frank, Plnt Brdr 99,
Skunk 36,
Skunk Cabbage 123,
Smith, Sir J.E., Founder Linnean Soc. 18, 25,
Smith's Inlet 74,
Snake River 21,
Snake Root, Western 95,
Sonora Channel 70,
Island 70,
Snowberry 110,
South Bentlnck Arm 75,
Southern Beech 33, 85,
Spanish Banks, Vancouver 49,
Watering Party 49,
California 27,

Spiraeas 99,
Spring Beauty 38,
Spruce, Alberta 92,
          Black 11,
          Blue 92,
          Hemlock 46,
          Koster's Blue 92,
          Menzies 92,
          Norway 46,
          Red 91,
          Sitka 46, 92,
          Tideland 13
          White 11, 91,
Spruce Beer 11, 12, 39,
St Johns, Newfoundland 11,
Stanley Park Vancouver B.C. 59,
Staunton, Sir George, Plant Collector 9,
Sticky Laurel 38,
Stinging Nettle 51,
Strawberry Madrone 88,
Sublime & Picturesque Landscape 45,
Sulawesi 19,
Surgeon-Botanist(s) Naturalist(s) 7,
Sutil 49, 55, 82,
Swamp Laurel 63,
          Cypress 29,
Swanson Island 71,
Swordfern 64, 124,

Tacamahac 46,
Tacoma, Wash 30, 45,
Tahiti 9,
Tahsis excursion 83,
Tall Mahonia 47,
Taro 123,

Tasmania 9,
Temperature at Nootka 82,
Terra Del Fuego 33,
Texada Island 55,
Thomson, R.E. Ocngrphr, 68,
Thunberg, Peter, Bot. 8,
Tideland Spruce 13,
Tiger Lily 118,
Timor 19,
Toba Inlet 58, 61,
Treeferns 86,
True Fir 46, 48, 96,
Tulare County, Calif 28,
Tuolumne County, Calif 28,
Turks Cap Lily 118,
Twinberry 98,
Twinflower 65, 98,

UBC Botanical Garden 49,
Ucluelet, V.I., B.C. 123,

Valerian 36,
Valdes, Don Cayetano, Capt 49,
Valpariaso 27,
Vandusen Gardens 15,
Vetch, Hawaiian 134,
Victoria, V.I., B.C. 30,

Village Point 115,
Vine Maple 38,
Vitamin C 11, 14,

Waddington, Mt 62, 74,
Walbran, Capt John T. 26
Walpole, Horace 65,

Ward, Dr, N.B., Invntr Wrdn Case 17,
Wardian Case 16,
Washington State-Flower 106,
          Geo, US Pres 28,
Washingtonia 28,
Wellington, N.Z. 28,
Wellingtonia 28,
West Craecroft Island 71,
West Indies 20,
Western Azalea 102,
          Oregon 106,
          Red Cedar & vars 14, 67, 108, 109,
          Sword Fern 124,
Weymouth Pine 11,
Whidbey Is Wash 48, 106, 116,
          Mstr Joseph 39, 43, 48, 57, 74,
Whortleberry, Black 58, 75,
          Dwarf 47, 59,
          Red 58, 75,
Willamette River, Ore 22,
Willow Herb 52,
          Point on Quadra 1s. 57,
Wintergreen Family 63,
Woakoo natives 76,
Wollemi Pine 31,
Willow Herb 52,
          Point 57,
Wreck Beach (Point Grey) 49,
Wyeth, Nathaniel J, Capt U.S. Army 22,

Yaculta Indian Village 67,
Yellow Arum 123,
Yellow Bell 115,
Yellow Cedar 106
Yucwitte, Yucuot or Yucuat 79,

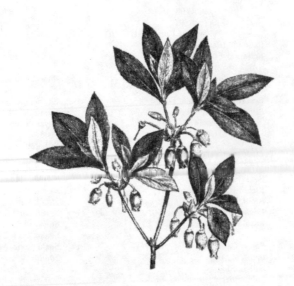